FROM CAMPUS TO

CAREER SUCCESS

FROM CAMPUS TO

CAREER SUCCESS

Elwood N. Chapman

Chaffey College, Alta Loma, California

SCIENCE RESEARCH ASSOCIATES, INC.

Chicago, Palo Alto, Toronto, Henley-on-Thames, Sydney, Paris, Stuttgart

A Subsidiary of IBM

Acquisition Editor	*Michael G. Crisp*
Project Editor	*Sara H. Boyd*
Text Designer	*Carol L. Harris*
Cover Photographer	*John Larsen*
Compositor	*Chapman's Phototypesetting*

Information for ordering this book and the author's
other books (listed on the back cover) may be obtained from:

Science Research Associates, Inc.
College Division
1540 Page Mill Road
Palo Alto, California 94304

Library of Congress Cataloging in Publication Data

Chapman, Elwood N.
  From campus to career success.

  1. College graduates—Employment.   2. Vocational
guidance.   3. Success.   I. Title.   II. Title:
Career success.
HD6277.C48   650'.14   78-9085
ISBN 0-574-20580-2

10 9 8 7 6 5 4 3 2 1

A NOTE FROM THE PUBLISHER

Career Success is the last in a series of three publications designed to help students prepare for successful career planning, preparation, and adjustment. The first volume, *College Survival* (1974), helps incoming students make the transition from the home to the academic world and starts them thinking about how to use their education to further their career goals. The second volume, *Career Search* (1976), provides a search system for students without firm career goals. This, the third volume, assumes that the student has a career direction and is preparing to make the transition from the campus to a position of significance in our society.

Each book was designed to be used independently; however, we believe a student will benefit from reading all three to help make the many complex decisions and adjustments which must be made between the time he or she leaves home, completes an education, and begins a career.

Our author, E. N. Chapman, has spent a lifetime making students aware of avenues available to them, and guiding them to make intelligent and realistic educational and career choices.

Michael G. Crisp
Vice-President and
College Publisher

CONTENTS

TO THE STUDENT

The author views the transition from campus to career success as a major passage in your life. This book is, therefore, a very personal guide designed to help you make the passage successfully. It includes suggestions on finding a good starting job (Part I), launching yourself with confidence (Part II), assessing your personal progress (Part III), using and improving your skills (Part IV), and creating your own promotion opportunities (Part V).

A primary premise of the book is that by planning beyond "just getting a job"—by learning what will be expected of you professionally—you also prepare yourself for job interviews. In other words, the last four parts of this book provide major assistance in winning a job, which is probably the immediate goal of most readers.

But whether you are now at work or still in college, you can benefit from the six special exercises and five case problems found at the end of various sections. Practice in interviewing, self-assessment, and goal setting is an important part of the learning process and one that will lead you to career success.

The profiles that follow the first 18 chapters constitute the very essence of this book. There is no adequate way to thank these guest authors for their major contribution. I can only hope they will derive personal satisfaction from knowing they have helped others who have yet to make the transition from campus to career.

Elwood N. Chapman

Part I

GETTING A GOOD ENTRY JOB

Objectives

When you have finished this section you should have

1. Constructed and committed yourself to a personalized, step-by-step, job finding system that will achieve desired results

2. Identified those behavioral changes that you wish to make in order to communicate to others the personal image you desire

3. Achieved the know-how and personal confidence to improve your interviewing skills 100 percent

First Things First

Part I will help you find the best possible starting job for yourself. If you are currently employed but dissatisfied, it will help you discover a new beginning. The remaining four parts are designed to assist you in *converting* your first job (whatever it may be) into a long-term career with either the same or another organization.

ORGANIZING YOUR SEARCH
A Job-Finding Pattern That Works

1

Now that you are ready to enter the job market, it is only natural and healthy for you to experience some anxieties. Where can you find a challenging starting job that will make use of the skills you learned on campus? Where can you find a progressive organization that wants you and will help you reach your career goals? Who will hire you at a salary that will permit you to live decently and independently, and perhaps permit you to pay off some accumulated debts? Will you, in the end, have to settle for an entry job below your expectations?

Fortunately, there are some professional people you can turn to for assistance. Your first visit could be to your college placement bureau. Next you might talk to people at your state-operated Employment Development Department; you may also wish to consider other agencies, individuals, or a private employment agency. There are also many publications, including this one, that can assist you.

But more than all such sources combined, you will have to depend upon yourself. Your career future is in your hands. You should, perhaps more than at any previous time in your life, look to yourself for answers, motivation, and decisions. Your education or training has provided experience in solving problems logically. You have learned how to define a problem, how to break it into manageable components; how to gather and to analyze information; how to consider alternative solutions; how to select the best solution, and finally, how to complete the task by taking some action. The following problem-solving skills come into play primarily as you make decisions regarding a career prior to starting your actual job search.

3

- What are my job interests?
- What skills do I have to offer?
- What kind of employer do I want to join?
- What kind of a job do I want and how would it fit into my life-style?

All of these questions and many others are a part of what may be called advance career planning. You may have already completed this planning phase. If so, you are ready for this publication. If not, Appendix I (pages 269–80) contains a career planning workbook developed by the Atlantic-Richfield Company of Los Angeles, California. It has been highly successful and has been reprinted with their permission. If you are not reasonably sure of your career goals, it is strongly suggested that you complete this exercise before continuing.

This first chapter provides a pattern around which you may wish to organize your job-hunting approach. It has been tested and found to be successful for many users. You may wish to evaluate it critically, and should it meet your needs, you could consider making a contract with yourself to use it.

STEP 1: Prepare for a lengthy, organized, successful search.

The first thing you should do is condition yourself psychologically for a systematic, lengthy job search—one that might take weeks or months. Realistically most individuals will not find a good starting job quickly. Read the following comments from two qualified graduates.

> It took me six months to find the right starting job. I had to take a night interim job that I hated to make it through the search period.

> Graduates who anticipate finding the right opportunity within a week or two usually wind up discouraged. They should be told in advance that locating and winning a decent job is a long, demanding, and complicated process.

Not only might your job search take longer than you anticipate, but unless you employ some kind of system, the search might cause you great personal frustration. The following quotations from two additional graduates provide insight.

> I just didn't stop to think that I needed a logical approach to my job-hunting efforts so I spent two months spinning my wheels. If a good placement counselor hadn't provided me with a step-by-step system, I might still be out there in the marketplace frustrating myself.

I didn't realize when I started out that I needed some form of organization to give the entire job-finding process meaning. Later I discovered that having a system to lean on was a little like having a security blanket; it kept me from getting too discouraged, and ultimately it helped me reach my goal.

If you recognize that you have a demanding challenge ahead of you and that your chances of success will be enhanced if you follow a system, you have completed the first step.

STEP 2: Choose your geographical boundaries.

In a sense, the whole world is your employment market, but most people have strong preferences about where they want to live and work because it is a major factor as far as their future life-style is concerned. For example, if working in a downtown urban area would keep you from living where you want to (perhaps in a small town or in the country), then you must come to grips with the problem *now*. You need to sit down and decide where you want to work, where you are willing to work if it is necessary in order for you to get a job, and *where you draw the line*. As a job seeker you have choices and you must exercise them. It is your decision and you need to give it serious and lengthy consideration, but it is best that it be done as step two in the process, not later. Here are three quotations from graduates who were less than honest with themselves, and as a result, had to start their job-hunting process over at considerable personal delay and cost.

I wanted a job in my chosen field so desperately that I accepted one in an isolated area where I was miserable. I didn't last six months.

I grew up in a beautiful valley with lots of friends and a large family. I didn't realize how strong the emotional ties were until I got a job in an urban area miles away. I finally gave up and went back home.

It took me five years to discover that *where* I lived was more important than how I earned my money. I wish someone had made me think this out years ago.

Sit down with a map and chart out the geographical area that meets your needs. If you have a close friend who is job hunting, work it out together. Take into consideration all factors that might influence the life-style you hope to lead. When this has been accomplished, and you know your geographical limitations, if any, you have completed this step.

STEP 3: Initiate and maintain an organizational prospect list.

Within the boundaries you have chosen, you should seek and find those organizations that are good prospects for your services; that is, *those that you feel are worth visiting for interview purposes.* Most people need a system to do this properly. Here is the way one successful applicant handled the problem.

> I used a stack of index cards to list the firms I might want to contact. Every time I would come up with an organization that appeared prom-ising, I would write the name down on a separate card and then do a little preliminary research. I would take time to see if there was any information in the campus or community libraries, the career center, or the local chamber of commerce. Then I would either talk to our place-ment counselor or someone in the community about the reputation of the company. You know, how does it treat people? What kind of future does it have? If what I discovered sounded encouraging, I would look up the telephone number and try to make arrangements for an inter-view. If not, I would tear up the card. It may sound like an oversim-plified procedure, but it worked for me.

If the card-index idea has little appeal you might consider a Pros-pect Checklist similar to the one printed here.

Prospect Checklist

Possible employer	Research indicates not worth contact	Research indicates worth contact	Results of interview
Acme Investments	X		
Central City Gov't.		X	
AJ Manufacturing		X	
Allied Distributors	X		
Rain Corporation		X	
Celter's Shops	X		
County Gov't.		X	

Such a chart can help you to screen and rate the prospects you are thinking of interviewing. It can also assist you in determining which prospect to contact first, and it gives you a place to record results of interviews.

Whether you decide to use a card-index or checklist system, you need some way to record your list of prospects as you discover them. Mary is a good example. Before she ultimately uncovered her first job opportunity, she listed a total of 37 prospects that *sounded* good at the beginning. Then, through research, she screened out those that were unsuitable for one reason or another. Eventually she contacted 16 out of the 37 for interview purposes. It took her three months using this procedure to land the job she wanted.

As you compile your list of prospective employers, and make decisions about whether or not an employer is worth interviewing, please keep the following points in mind.

1. Unless only a certain type of employer can use your special talents, a wide variety of prospects is recommended. For example, Sid, an accounting major, would be wise to look for a starting position in a private firm, a school or government agency, a hospital or any sizable organization that has an accounting department.

2. The company or agency you eventually decide upon is *most* important; it could, in fact, be as important as the entry job you are offered. Jane, as an example, decided that her first priority was finding a company with good personnel policies, a good benefit package, and a rapid growth rate. Her second priority was the nature of the starting job itself.

3. Take into consideration your financial needs, both immediate and long term.

4. Evaluate the "little fish in the big pond versus the big fish in the little pond" concept. Although large organizations often have many advantages, many people find greater rewards with small firms.

Many college placement bureaus invite organizations to come on campus to interview pending graduates. This, obviously, is a good place to start in your search for organizations to put on your list. You can find other prospects through the *College Placement Annual**, newspaper ads, trade journals, personal friends, teachers, business acquaintances, computer placement listings at government agencies, city and county government offices, Yellow Pages, union halls, professional magazines, professional association meetings, private employment agencies, *Dun and Bradstreet Refer-*

---

*The College Placement Council produces this publication, which is distributed by college placement offices to graduates without charge.

ence Book of Corporate Management, Moody's Industrial Manual, and *Thomas' Register of American Manufacturers.* Your campus or local librarian can help you locate these materials or recommend others.

Step 3, then, is generating and maintaining a master list of possible employers—those that your research and judgment tell you are worth visiting for interview purposes.

How many "live" prospects should a list contain at any one time?

Obviously, the moment you do not have a "fresh" prospect to contact, your entire search system is in danger of faltering. The more prospects you have on your list the better it is, because without them you cannot develop interviews. Here is the way Jack views the process.

> During my job search period I tried to generate five interviews per week. This meant that I had to continually search out new possibilities and research them. Toward the end I was listing three prospects for every interview I was eventually able to set up.

Please remember that another good source of prospects is the people you talk to when you go for interviews. For example, personnel people in one company may know of job openings in other firms. If you go about it in a sensitive manner, it is often possible to inquire about such possibilities at the end of an interview.

STEP 4: Prepare a résumé for mailing or hand delivery.

A résumé is a one- or two-page summary of your education and experience. It is designed to give a potential employer a quick "profile" of you to give him or her the kind of information needed to make a decision about whether or not to pursue an in-depth interview. Note the résumé at the right. You can easily find others in your placement bureau or campus library. You should feel free to use them as models but it is very important that you give yours an original, creative touch.

The big advantage of a well-done résumé is that it can be mailed to prospects who, if they react well and have openings, may invite you to interview. This gives you wide market coverage with only a minor expenditure of time and money.

Here are some tips to follow in the preparation of your resumé:

1. Unless you have years of job experience, limit your résumé to one page.
2. Present your material in blocks for easy reading. Include:
   Career goals

```
                            RESUME

John E. Smith                      Home phone (714) 222-2346
210 W. Sixth Street                Message phone (714) 666-6907
Ontario, California  91762


CAREER OBJECTIVE

     To work in a city recreation facility, preferably in a program
     for handicapped children.  Plan to study for master's degree at
     night in order to qualify eventually for administrative position.

EDUCATION

California State Polytechnic University, Pomona.
Bachelor of Arts degree in Behavioral Sciences, June 1978.

     Specialized in the study of the effects of family and community
     relationships on child development.  Related courses include Child
     Psychology, the Family as a Societal Institution, Juvenile
     Delinquency, Child Welfare Service, the Socially and Culturally
     Handicapped Child, and the Developmentally Disabled Child.

Citrus Community College, West Covina, California.
Associate of Arts degree, June 1976.

WORK EXPERIENCE

     Camp counselor, Camp St. Michael, June 1978 to September 1978.
     Group counselor for ages 10-14.  Taught swimming, crafts.

     Student clerk, Cal Poly Pomona, April 1977 to June 1978.
     Behavioral Science Department, 10 hours per week.

     Waiter, Stickney's Restaurant, June 1975 to September 1976.
     Worked evenings and weekends earning college expenses.

VOLUNTEER EXPERIENCE

     Crafts teacher, 1976.  Four hours per week at a state institution.
     Worked with emotionally disturbed children.

     Teachers aide, 1975-1978.  Nine hours a week at inner-city school.

COLLEGE ACTIVITIES

     Varsity football and baseball, two years.
     Member Behavioral Science Club.
     Student government in Junior College.

PERSONAL DATA

     Play guitar and piano.  Enjoy all sports and outdoor activities.

REFERENCES AVAILABLE ON REQUEST
```

A Sample Résumé

Education
Work experience
Personal data
School and community activities and honors

3. Between each block provide ample white space to avoid a crowded appearance.
4. Good résumés usually have points of greatest strength at the top.
5. Have your résumé reproduced professionally; do not use carbon copies or washed-out photocopies.

You will want to send a special letter to each prospective employer with your résumé enclosed. If possible, it should be addressed to an individual within the organization and not to the organization itself. This letter of transmittal or application should include:

1. A mention of the specific position or positions you are applying for and the way you learned about the opening or openings. If you are applying for a management training position, for example, make this clear.
2. A short reference to the enclosed résumé and a summary of its highlights.
3. A request for an interview (in the last paragraph).

A copy of a standard letter of transmittal is printed on the facing page.

In addition to the standard one- or two-page résumé, some individuals prepare more sophisticated portfolios that include birth certificates, college transcripts, and other official papers. Such portfolios are most appropriate for individuals who are applying for positions so far away that an interview would be extremely expensive or for art majors who wish to show some of their designs or illustrations in applying for a job with an advertising agency.

As you make your plans to prepare and use a résumé, please keep in mind the following:

1. A résumé should be well designed, original, and letter-perfect, or it shouldn't be used at all.
2. Résumés should be mailed *only* to prospects that have been previously researched as good possibilities.
3. A résumé is an "interview getter" and "backup tool" for most applicants. One should not expect more from such a device than it can realistically produce.
4. Résumés should be taken along during an interview in case the employer either did not receive one or misplaced it.

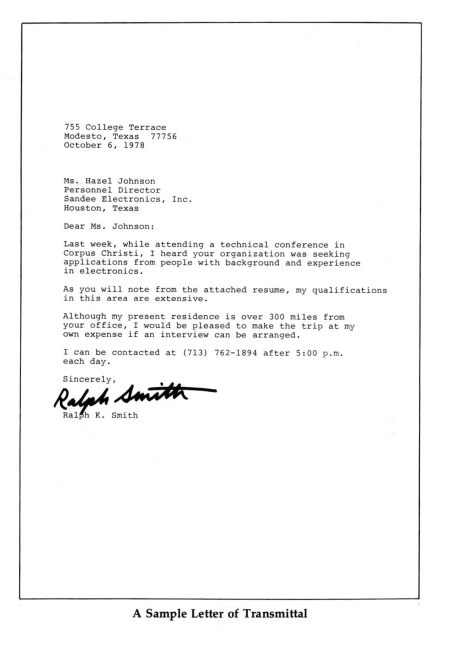

755 College Terrace
Modesto, Texas 77756
October 6, 1978

Ms. Hazel Johnson
Personnel Director
Sandee Electronics, Inc.
Houston, Texas

Dear Ms. Johnson:

Last week, while attending a technical conference in
Corpus Christi, I heard your organization was seeking
applications from people with background and experience
in electronics.

As you will note from the attached resume, my qualifications
in this area are extensive.

Although my present residence is over 300 miles from
your office, I would be pleased to make the trip at my
own expense if an interview can be arranged.

I can be contacted at (713) 762-1894 after 5:00 p.m.
each day.

Sincerely,

Ralph K. Smith

A Sample Letter of Transmittal

Here are three quotations from applicants who have used résumés:

> I feel I got better than average response from mailing out résumés because I was selective and used some creative artwork to get attention.

> I got more than ten excellent interviews from mailing out my résumés; one was in Texas, where they sent me a round-trip ticket and paid all expenses.

> It is easy to become overdependent upon a résumé. I sent out a large number to good prospects and then sat around waiting for something to happen. I got some replies but no interviews.

You may wish to get some personal assistance on the preparation of both your résumé and letter of transmittal. It is sometimes a good idea to type up what you feel is a perfect example and then take it to others for suggestions. If you decide to be innovative and do something special, make sure it is in good taste and that you don't overdo it. Above all, you want to be highly professional.

STEP 5: Select a job-hunting wardrobe.

There are three primary reasons why you should give careful consideration to what you wear during the interview process.

1. Your wardrobe should project an image of yourself appropriate to the particular company and the position you are applying for. A cocktail dress is not appropriate when applying for the job of secretary; a leather jacket is not appropriate for a management-trainee position. Here is the way one personnel director reacts.

> As a professional personnel officer, I can tell a little about whether or not applicants really want to come to work for us by the manner in which they dress. If they have taken time to project the best possible image, they are serious; if not, you get the feeling they don't care that much.

2. Some psychologists believe that you have more confidence in yourself when you know you look your best. They claim that how you look to others is important, but how you look to yourself may be even more important. Read what a department store stylist has to say on the subject.

> When I have spent some time putting myself together, I articulate and communicate much better because I just feel better about myself. I want to feel relaxed, poised, and confident; this seems to happen when I know I am wearing the right things.

3. There is usually a large parade of applicants each day in a

typical personnel office. The ones who make it through the pre-liminary stages must transmit a positive image. Here is a statement from an employment interviewer.

> We attempt to be objective in evaluating applicants. We seriously follow the fair employment practices rules. But we are in a consumer business and the way people look has to do with our profit picture. We don't hire people because they own expensive clothing, but we do appreciate people who make the effort to look their best.

Ralph, like many college graduates did not possess a good, con-servative, job-hunting wardrobe.

> I had to go out and spend more than $200.00 on a job-hunting outfit. Was it worth it? I have to think it was a good investment because I got a good job—one I could be enthusiastic about. When you come to grips with this image problem, you have taken an important step as far as putting your job-hunting act together.

STEP 6: When possible, arrange interviews by telephone.

Once you have done a little preliminary research regarding a pros-pect, the easiest way to set up an interview is to use the telephone. The following quotation from a successful job hunter tells the story.

> I had no idea how simple it was to arrange an employment interview with a key personnel officer or executive until I tried it a few times. Usually all you need to do is give your name, state when you completed your education or training, and ask to be placed on the interview sched-ule. If you wish to talk to the top person in charge, you can usually get the name from the telephone switchboard operator if you go about in in a nice way.

There is nothing wrong with showing up at the personnel office of a large company or presenting yourself unannounced to any organization as a possible employee. Sometimes you hit it just right, and there is no waiting involved; most of the time, however, you might be forced to "sit it out" waiting for the right person. In addition, most people feel it is more professional to set up advance appointments; they claim you often receive better treatment. A personnel officer for a retail store made this statement.

> I have no objection to a telephone call requesting an interview appoint-ment; in fact, I rather like it because it demonstrates advance thinking and planning. I am sure that time is just as important to the applicant as it is to me.

Most individuals searching the job market feel that they can do justice to only two or three interviews per day. An interview may take longer than the standard 30 minutes, and you would not want to excuse yourself for another interview—or be late for it. A good pattern is one in the morning and one in the afternoon, so you should be careful not to overschedule yourself.

STEP 7: Prepare for each interview.

Most experts agree that advance thinking and planning pays good dividends when it comes to employment interviews. Here is how one successful applicant views it.

> In doing my research on an organization before an interview I try to discover something about their history, product line or services, earning record, personnel policies, formal training programs, job openings, and organizational structure. The more you know the better, but a little information seems to go a long way during the interview process.

Most professional actors subscribe to the premise that their best performances come when they are nervous and therefore "psyched up." They claim that stress makes them try harder and reach for their peak performance. It would appear that the same process will help you live up to your full potential during the interview period.

One reason for the recommendation of advance preparation is that you never know how many people are applying for a single job opening. Another reason is that sometimes you can anticipate the kind of individual they want to hire and adjust to their needs. Here is the approach one person claims is successful.

> When I am going out for an interview, I keep thinking that the employer wants to hire someone to help solve a problem. I try to figure out what this problem might be, and then I present myself as an individual who is willing to learn and work hard to contribute to the solution. After all, I guess an employer without problems wouldn't need to hire anybody.

STEP 8: Follow these tips during the interview process.

Although the interview itself is so critical that it will receive special attention in Chapter 3, some simple tips are provided here to get you started. Many more can be found in various publications in your career center or library.

1. Sit up straight in a relaxed manner.
2. Keep eye contact with the interviewer.
3. Use her or his name but don't overdo it.

    4. Refrain from smoking.
    5. Demonstrate an eagerness to learn.
    6. Enjoy any humor that develops.
    7. Don't overstay the interview period.
    8. Ask questions openly and freely.

It is most important to understand that the employment interview is a two-way process; the employer wants to learn as much as possible about you; in turn, you wish to learn as much as possible about the job opportunity and the long-term possibilities with the employer.

STEP 9: Be prepared for decision making.

During the normal interview process, one of the following will almost always occur.

    1. You may decide it is not the job or the company you desire, so you may back away with a thank-you.
    2. The employer may decide you do not have the qualities the company seeks so he or she thanks you for your interest and you depart.
    3. They want you and make you an offer but you hesitate because you want to think it over.
    4. They show a definite interest in you but may wish to schedule a follow-up meeting with other executives involved.
    5. They make you a firm offer and you accept on the spot.
    6. They say they will call you, but don't.

One of the main reasons going through a sizable number of interviews is valuable is that you can compare one job opportunity and organization with another, and thereby understand the job market potential better. It can often be a mistake to accept an offer too quickly as this recent graduate points out.

> The reason so many graduates accept the first thing that comes along is that they are afraid nothing else as good will show up down the road. This shows inexperience. If one organization likes you, others may like you better and provide a better opportunity.

Accepting a job opportunity is a crucial and important decision on your part. Because of recent legislation increasing the rights of employees, it is even more important for the employer to make a sound decision. Good decisions usually require time to weigh the advantages and disadvantages; good decisions require that all facts be introduced and evaluated. This is why you should not hesitate to ask for thinking time if you need it. All you need to say is, "How much time do I have to think it through so that I can make the right decision for both of us?" Under no circumstances should you permit an employer to push you into accepting an employment contract until you have weighed all the facts involved.

How do you handle the situation where one firm has made you an offer and another (perhaps one you like better) is still making up their mind? The same approach as above is recommended. Simply ask for "thinking time" to avoid a wrong decision.

STEP 10: Stick with your job-hunting system until it produces.

Once you have accepted a search pattern and made a contract with yourself to use it, do not desert it prematurely. It is impossible to predict the condition of a specific job market in advance. There may be such a high demand for your specialty that your system will work quickly; on the other hand, you may have to stick with it for months. If the latter happens and you become discouraged, you may wish to revise the system but you should not throw it away. It may be the best thing—even the only thing—you have going for you. If the applicant is qualified, a system will eventually produce.

As you conclude this first chapter, it should be restated that searching for and finding the right career opportunity in a difficult labor market can be one of life's most interesting challenges. As you start the process, the following quotation from a perceptive career counselor should be most reinforcing.

> Many graduates show more personal growth during their postcollege job-hunting days than at any other period in their lives. When they come back to see me they often say that they are glad they had to go through it, although they also seem to feel good that it is over.

In going about your own personal search, using your own adaptation of the ten-step system proposed in this chapter, please keep the following points in mind.

1. *Your job-hunting expenses are tax-deductible.* You should keep track of all transportation, parking, and other expenses (not meals unless you stay overnight) because you can deduct them from your income as soon as you have one.

2. *An interim job can turn into a career opportunity.* Some graduates find it necessary to hold down a part-time or interim job of some kind to support them during their career search periods. Surpris-

ingly, now and then one of these jobs becomes so interesting and challenging that the individual converts it into a full-time career. An example follows.

> I had to settle for a job as a bartender in a franchise restaurant while looking for a career in city management. Well, I became so involved in the possibilities of food and restaurant management that I stuck with it. I wouldn't change now even if I had the opportunity.

3. *Your attitude toward the search process you use will have an influence on its effect.* No matter how you organize your search system, it will not work for you unless you believe it will. A high level of expectancy is necessary if you are to be successful.

4. *In working with private employment agencies, please follow these rules.*

- Make sure the agency is licensed by the Bureau of Employment Agencies in the state where you reside.
- Know the fee schedule in advance; some agencies require a deposit before you go out on an interview; others require nothing until you are employed.
- Remember that you do not have to pay unless you *accept* a job.
- Sometimes employers pay all the agency fee, sometimes you do; sometimes the fee is split between the two of you. Make sure you find out in advance.

The ten-step system found in this chapter is presented in the box below for review purposes. Why not cover the box with a sheet of paper and see if you can write out all ten steps without peeking?

Ten-Step Search System

1. Prepare for a lengthy organized, successful search.
2. Choose your geographical boundaries.
3. Initiate and maintain an organizational prospect list.
4. Prepare a résumé for mailing or hand delivery.
5. Select a job-hunting wardrobe.
6. Where possible, arrange interviews by telephone.
7. Prepare for each interview.
8. Follow these tips during the interview process.
9. Be prepared for decision-making.
10. Stick with your job-hunting system until it produces.

Discussion Questions

1. Why might a person decide not to pursue a job-search system similar to the one outlined in this chapter? List several reasons.
2. Which of the ten steps would be the most important to accept and complete? Why?
3. Assume you were asked to reduce the ten-step system to seven steps. Which three would you eliminate? Why?
4. Assume you were asked to increase the ten-step system to twelve steps. What two additional steps would you recommend? Why?
5. In a graduating class of 100 students, how many do you think would seriously employ such a system? Defend your answer.

**Career
Profile**

*Nancy L. DeDiemar
Research Associate
SysteMetrics, Inc.*

EMPLOYMENT OPPORTUNITY New research and consulting firm seeks right person. If you are bright, eager, and willing to work; can type, do bookkeeping, set up office systems, photocopy, file, answer phones, do errands, and manage an office single-handedly; want to work part-time; and don't mind occasionally getting your paycheck late—call us. We have a deal for you.

The unconventional ad above is fictitious. I wrote it because it summarizes my unconventional transition from college to career. I am a research analyst for a consulting company working in the health care field. With other staff members, I study various aspects of medical care—services provided by doctors and hospitals, costs, quality of care, alternate ways of providing care, and so on. Though I've worked for this consulting company for almost three years, I've only been a member of the technical staff for one year; before that I was the office person described in the ad above. The deal offered was the chance to progress from administrative to technical staff by training on the job.

I was lucky to have been offered that chance. In today's employment market, it's rare. On the other hand, I got the chance because I was qualified for it. I had a college degree, office and administrative skills from previous jobs, and a background in the medical field. I convinced my prospective employer that I had something unique and valuable to offer.

I also was prepared to offer a personal commitment to the job. I am married and have children. Before I accepted the job, I considered its effect on my family. I knew it would be significant. I would no longer be in a position to volunteer my time to support my family's activities. I wouldn't have time available to take the first graders to the fire station, be a Girl Scout leader, prepare gourmet meals on weekdays, or do housework. Those activities would have to be done by others, primarily family members, which would mean an increase in their work. I had to be prepared for the changes that the shift in workload would bring in two ways: by learning how to stop doing things I had always done, and by gracefully relinquishing my position as "boss" of the home-centered activities. That required the support of my family, and a personal confidence that my decision to take a demanding job was the right one for me.

I have had some problems making the transition to a career position. Though I am intelligent, learn quickly, and can work independently, I frequently found myself with more work than time to do it in. My on-the-job training meant that I would be taught new skills, and be given the chance to use them, but would also be required to finish all my routine work. Since the regular workload was constantly increasing, I frequently had to work late and come in on Saturdays. Those times were lonely and difficult—the office was deserted, and my family was unhappy with my absence from home. During these times I drew strength from my personal commitment that I was working for me—because I wanted to work, not because I needed the money, or wanted to seem important to my friends. Luckily I had chosen a job well-suited to my natural abilities and academic training, and so the lack of time was really the biggest hurdle to overcome. I expect it always will be.

In the consulting business, people sell themselves as well as their work. Part of my professional advancement is tied to my personal style: appearance, method of communicating with others, self-confidence, and similar intangible qualities. Especially because I am a woman in business, my appearance can be a critical factor. That is not to say that a woman must be beautiful to succeed or that looks are more important than intelligence and capability. They're not. What is true is that it helps to look and act the part. To be accepted as a capable consultant, I first must be so; if I also look and act that way, acceptance of me will proceed quickly.

Though I have successfully made the transition from college to career, I am not through undergoing changes. I never expect to be. My continued professional growth will come from applying the techniques I learned while making the first transition: determining the level of personal commitment to a job that fits me; being willing to sacrifice personal time to learn new skills; and having confidence and pride in my abilities and accomplishments.

SENDING SIGNALS

Communicating a Good Image of Yourself

2

Even the most qualified applicant can lose a job opportunity by projecting a negative image to the interviewer. The "first impression" is a human relations phenomenon from which there is no escape. If the employer perceives you as a confident, flexible individual with a good learning attitude and a desire to work well with others and live up to your potential, you have an advantage. If you are perceived as overstructured, somewhat critical of others, and interested only in using an entry job as a stepping stone, you will be at a disadvantage.

The results of the survey shown in the box on the next page help to answer the question, "Why didn't I get the job?" Please notice how frequently applicants are rejected because of the personal image they transmit.

No matter how capable you may be, how well your qualifications fit the job opening, or how highly you have developed your skills, you are still faced with the problem of creating a favorable impression in the mind of the interviewer. It is the primary challenge of the interview process.

What can you do so that the interviewer or employer will interpret you fairly and in the best possible light?

Recognize that the signals you send build the image interviewers receive. As you approach employers for the first time, you will transmit many little signs (signals) that will be interpreted quickly. If interviewers receive signs they are looking for (those that fit the kind of employee they seek), chances are good that they will start constructing a positive image of you. On the other hand, if they receive signs that do not fit the mold of the applicant they want

---

Why Didn't I Get the Job?

What are the reasons why you as an applicant sometimes receive only a thundering silence from prospective employers after your interview has been completed? A placement director at Northwestern University recently made an interesting survey of 405 well-known firms to find these reasons.

1. Poor personality and manner: lack of poise; poor presentation of self; lack of self-confidence; timid; hesitant approach; arrogance, conceit.
2. Lack of goals and ambitions, does not show interest, uncertain, and indecisive about the job in question.
3. Lack of enthusiasm and interest, no evidence of initiative.
4. Poor personal appearance and careless dress.
5. Unrealistic salary demands, more interest in salary than opportunity, unrealistic about promotion to top jobs.
6. Poor scholastic record wihtout reasonable explanation for low grades.
7. Inability to express yourself well, poor speech habits.
8. Lack of maturity, no leadership potential.
9. Lack of preparation for the interview—failure to get information about the company and therefore unable to ask intelligent questions.
10. Lack of interest in the company and the type of job they have to offer.
11. Lack of extracurricular activities without good reason.
12. Attitude of "What can you do for me," etc.
13. Objection to travel; unwilling to relocate to branch offices or plants.
14. Immediate or prolonged military obligation.
15. No vacation jobs or other work experience; did not help finance own education.

Note: The material in the box above is reprinted by permission of T/M Associates, 500 S. Main Street, Orange, California.

to hire, they may start constructing a negative image of you *as far as filling the job slot is concerned.* A prospective employer will project you into starting and advanced roles within the organization. Since that is the basic purpose of an interview, it is essential to send those signals that will cause the employer to interpret you in a positive way as a future employee.

Send enough positive signals. If interviewers do not receive enough positive signals from you, they may pass you off as lacking in self-confidence. Here is the way Dolores views her first efforts.

> The most difficult thing I had to learn during the interview process was that I was not sending out enough positive signals. I am, in my personal life, a very quiet, inside person. I had to force myself to communicate some enthusiasm for the job in question. I had to push myself to transmit that I had growth possibilities. I had to convince the employer that I was a warm, friendly person who could get along well with other employees.

Obviously, Dolores had to be careful to communicate through signals that were natural and sincere. Plastic ones can quickly be recognized and rejected. In sending more signals you must be careful that they are not contrived.

It is important to recognize that interviewers normally receive your nonverbal signals first. Here is a partial list of nonverbal signals that we send to others.

Smile	Hand gestures
Nod of head	Way of walking
Posture	Eye contact
Facial expression	Way of sitting

These signals come under the classification of "body language." When you walk into an employment office, the employees (and other applicants) will receive many "vibes" or signals from your body movements and mannerisms. As you walk into the office of the interviewer, you will transmit many signals *before* you have a chance to say anything. If you have a good, relaxed posture, an engaging smile, and excellent eye contact, and if you seat yourself properly, you will probably send out good nonverbal signals. However, if you slouch, fail to smile (perhaps you are too nervous), avoid direct eye contact, and fall into the chair with little grace, chances are you will send out negative vibrations.

It may not be fair or even wise for people to put so much emphasis on such signals, but it is *human* for people to react psychologically to whatever they see in others. The intriguing part is that many such reactions take place in a few seconds. That is why some placement directors feel that nonverbal signals are more important than verbal ones—they are received first and consequently can have greater psychological impact.

Verbal communication is also important. Nonverbal signs are often more effective when they are followed by verbal signals, such as "good morning," "hello," and other greetings. It is the combination of words and gestures that communicates warmth, sincerity, and personal strength. After a number of unsuccessful interviews, John made this discovery.

> I knew from the start that the first words I used were important, but I had to learn that good eye contact should come first. When I had learned to hold back on my verbal signals until eye contact was accomplished, I found that my interviews got off to a much better start. This gave me more personal confidence and eventually helped me land an excellent position.

The tone of a greeting can be more important than the words. Voice volume, diction, and the degree of personalization (perhaps using the employer's name) also are important.

Your attitude also transmits signals. The following is a quotation from the human relations primer *Your Attitude Is Showing.**

> First impressions are important because they often have a lasting quality. People you meet for the first time appear to have little radar sets tuned in to your attitude. If your attitude is positive, they receive a friendly, warm signal, and they are attracted to you; if your attitude is negative, they receive an unfriendly signal, and they try to avoid you.

Beyond or perhaps beneath other forms of communication is the attitude you transmit to others. It is possible for an employer to receive a positive signal from you even though you make no physical movement and you say nothing. Your mental outlook can be transmitted. For example, if you had to wait an hour to see the interviewer you could easily transmit the irritation you felt inside. Although we do many things in an attempt to hide our attitudes, most of the time they are showing.

Although different employers might be interested in different attitudes from prospective employees, most would be interested in your attitudes toward work, accepting responsibility, learning, helping others, long-term career possibilities, accepting advice,

---

*Written by Elwood N. Chapman, and published by Science Research Associates, Inc., Chicago, 1977 (3rd ed.), p. 19.

procedures, and controls. *You can transmit all of these through your attitude without saying a word.*

Some of these signals could be transmitted in the way you react to questions before you start to answer them. Others could be communicated in the questions you ask. Unfortunately, we are not always aware that this subtle form of signal-sending is taking place. As you evaluate and decide on the signals you intend to send during the interview period, please keep in mind that they should all be in harmony with your self-concept. This is another way of saying that you should be comfortable with the signals you send—they should reflect the way you see yourself so that others will interpret you the way you want them to.

Accept the possibility of misinterpretation. It would be unrealistic for you to expect that all of your signals will be correctly received. Some are bound to misfire because of timing, the prejudice and mental attitude of the receiver, or other factors. This does not mean, however, that you should be too restrictive and cautious about the number you send. The fewer signals you send, the greater the possibility you will be misinterpreted.

You can send too many signals. When you walk into the private office of the employment interviewer, you will want to send out positive signals in the right amount. Good eye contact, a friendly greeting, good posture, and a positive attitude of expectancy should be sufficient. Candice had to learn this simple point the hard way.

> During my first interviews I sent out so many signals I was overbearing. I guess I was trying too hard. I had to learn that a few strong signals are better than a barrage. It took me a while to achieve the right balance and tempo. When I finally managed to do this, my interviews were much more comfortable and successful. I guess I had to find my own inner strength and dignity under pressure before I could control my signals effectively.

Your signals can be too strong or too subdued. Quiet signals, in good taste, are the most effective, but they must be strong enough to be received. Sandy had so much anxiety during her first interviews that her voice was hardly audible and, as a result, she communicated a lack of self-confidence; Harry, on the other hand, was so loud (his voice almost always increased in pitch when he was under pressure) that it was irritating to the interviewer. Jill's hand and body gestures were so dramatic that they attracted too much attention; Rick was so uptight that he forgot to send enough signals, and as a result he appeared stiff and unapproachable.

Both Don and Martha had been out of work so long that they

desperately wanted to have successful interviews. Don's attitude signals toward wanting the job were so strong that they communicated the possibility of emotional instability; Martha, on the other hand, was so fearful of failure that her attitude signals were much too weak to be received; as a result, the interviewer mistakingly interpreted that the job really wasn't important to her.

Obviously, from the above examples, the intensity of signals is important. They need to be sent with confidence. They need to be clear and precise. They should not, however, be so strong that they backfire.

We send signals through our grooming. Although this subject was mentioned in Chapter 1, it deserves additional attention, as the following quotation from a junior executive testifies.

> Since I entered the business world, I have been amazed how much we communicate with what we wear and how we groom ourselves. If you *look* like an executive, you will probably become one; if you *look* like a job-winner you will probably get a job. I really don't understand the psychology of it, but apparently looking like you can handle a job is necessary before they will give it to you. The best way to get a job is to observe the dress standards of the organization ahead of time, and show, before you are hired, that you can meet them.

A company president who receives important clients is obviously interested in the appearance of the receptionist or secretary. The small boutique owner is concerned with the appearance of salespeople who influence customer decisions. A telephone company official cannot help being concerned with the appearance of repair people who enter the homes of clients. What you are wearing at the time of the interview can have a significant influence on the employer's attempt to project you into a job somewhere in the organization. Here is what one executive has to say.

> We seek only minimum standards that permit maximum individualization by our employees. We do, however, want them to look good to themselves because there may be a correlation between a good personal image and productivity; also, we want them to look good to their fellow employees (not a distraction) because this, too, facilitates better human relations, which has a direct bearing on productivity. Then, because we are a service business and depend upon attracting and holding clients, we want and need our employees to send out good grooming signals. We seek only limited conformity, but we do appreciate our people living up to their personal standards, which usually are very high.
>
> I have come to the conclusion that grooming is primarily a matter of personal pride. People want and need group acceptance and that is one

way to get it. There are, of course, a few people who seem to fight any degree of conformity. Their convictions must be very deep and should be recognized because they often eliminate many career opportunities for themselves—opportunities that might help them reach their true potential.

What are the minimum acceptable standards for most organizations? Because of changing fashions, a list of standards could quickly become outdated. For guidance about current standards, discuss the matter openly with a placement official on campus before going out on the interviewing "circuit." Keep in mind that your grooming decisions will depend, in part, on the kind of organization you intend to join—a fashion-oriented department store naturally has higher dress standards than a factory—and the emphasis put on appearance by the people who already work for the organization. People within organizations often generate their own grooming standards with little, if any, influence from management.

Evaluate the following quotation, which comes from an individual who works for a large business organization at the headquarters building in an urban area.

I buy the idea that grooming is vital to the communication of a good image, but I don't go along with the idea that a college graduate needs specific suggestions on grooming. It is too demeaning, and besides, conformity happens automatically. Let me explain. When you join an organization, you are immediately put in a pressure cooker. On one side you get the heat to join the group and gain acceptance; on the other side you quickly discover that to gain such acceptance you must meet their grooming standards.

You see, as a human being, you need people to *accept* you. You have got to *belong*. You have to get in the main stream or you are left on the sidelines, rejected. This need is more powerful than you can imagine. Now, a new employee might be able to resist this pressure to join the group if he or she had enough identity outside the organization. But when you leave college, you have yet to find an identity in the community, so you have to settle for an organizational identity or you have nothing at all. So what happens? You watch others and notice how they dress and then you go in hock to match. There is no choice. You go along because you've got to meet their standards or you have nothing. This all happens automatically, so the beginner does not need any little tips or suggestions.

Despite the comments above, a few suggestions are made on the following pages. Only by reading them will you be able to determine whether they are valuable for you as an individual.

A small, well-chosen wardrobe can be effective. Most individuals graduate from college with small budgets and few clothes suitable for the interview period. But the employer sees only what you are wearing for the interview, so a single job-hunting outfit is all that is necessary.

Little details in appearance make the difference. Stylists, those individuals who specialize in helping others build a "look," claim that little things are more than 60 percent of a good visual profile. They mention the following:

1. Neat, polished shoes
2. Limited but appropriate jewelry
3. Restraint in facial cosmetics
4. Well-fitting, co-ordinated outfits
5. Trim, clean nails

The style and length of your hair is important. Perhaps no other feature has had more "image" impact in recent years than hair stylings. Here is how one young executive working for a government agency views the matter.

> My wife was the one who talked me into getting my hair styled. I was a little reluctant at first, but now I think it was a good investment. I am in a highly competitive business and it is important to look the part. I think some guys would be smart to spend less on their clothes and more on their hair.

The image you have of yourself and the amount of personal confidence you possess could be related. When you ask young employees what their biggest problem was when they first got started, they often reply "lack of personal confidence." This factor is critical during the interview process. The following comment by a graduate who took six months to get a job illustrates the possible correlation.

> When I first started my interviews, I was not pleased with the reactions I received. I knew I was qualified. My grades were very high. My work experience was excellent. What was wrong? I finally admitted that I had underestimated the whole grooming thing. I could tell from the way people viewed me that I was out of phase. What did I do? I went to a fashion boutique and got some good advice along with a new outfit. Result? I discovered, after a few more interviews, that both my appearance and personal confidence had improved. I guess I had a very poor image of myself and it showed.

Your weight and physical fitness are involved. It is more difficult for those who are over- or underweight to project a good image during the interview process. Those who are overweight often seem to move more slowly; those who are underweight may communicate that they are not strong enough to do the job. Both individuals may be very sensitive about the subject and, as a result, may lack self-confidence. Here is a revealing statement from a graduate.

> I know it sounds ridiculous, but all of my interviews were duds until I lost 30 pounds. I don't feel that my problem was the weight itself, although those who are overweight must take much more care in the selection of clothes. But by not looking my best, I gave them an easy excuse to pass me over. After I lost the weight and improved my wardrobe, my personal confidence jumped 100 percent; it was then that I got a fair shake.

The kind of visual image you transmit—the signals you send—is, without question, your own personal business. Nobody, not even your best friend, is likely to introduce the subject. You must make your own decisions.

If you are perfectly satisfied with the image you project, this chapter has been a light review, with no pressure intended. If, on the other hand, you would like to make improvements before you enter the job market, there are many things you can do.

1. Consult fashion counselors or stylists in good stores.
2. Talk to your barber or hair stylist.
3. Check out some fashion magazines from your local library.
4. Talk to a close friend.
5. Enroll in a good charm school.
6. Consider training as a model to gain poise.

Mostly, of course, self-improvement is a do-it-yourself project. Great self-discipline is often involved. It is, however, an endeavor that can be most rewarding. And after you have achieved your goals, you will have the satisfaction of knowing that you will not remain unemployed because of the image (and signals) you are transmitting.

This knowledge in itself could provide a new burst of personal confidence.

Discussion Questions

1. Which classification of signals—verbal or nonverbal—do you feel has the greatest impact on the average employment interviewer during the first 30 seconds? Justify your choice.
2. What specific suggestions might you make to applicants who

admit they do not have the personal confidence to initiate positive signals during the starting stage of the interview?

3. Name five negative nonverbal signals that should be avoided during an interview. What can be done to make sure negative signals are not transmitted?

4. If an applicant admits a negative attitude toward business in general, and especially big business, should he or she apply for a job only with a nonbusiness organization? Give the reasons for your answer.

5. What precautions, if any, can an applicant take to prevent the transmission of admitted negative attitudes during the interview process?

6. Do you defend or oppose the premise that there is a positive correlation between grooming and personal self-confidence? Explain your answer.

Frederick C. Chisholm
Asst. Manager, Asst. Vice-President, Loans
Culver City Branch, Bank of America NT&SA

**Career
Profile**

"Sometimes it seems like a three-ring circus—but with some very important differences. I'm in all three rings, not in the stands, and there are no clowns because it's a very serious business.

"That doesn't mean it's not fun—and challenging. The point is that to be a good banker, particularly in a branch, you have to be able to fill a number of different roles.

"One minute I'll be dealing with a financial officer of one of the major movie studios. The next, I'm helping a customer solve a personal financial problem, say, his or her retirement plans. Next, when the manager is gone, I'm making sure that the 60 people in the branch function smoothly to do the best job we can for our clients and the bank as well. And then, I'll be counseling someone on the staff about his or her career, helping them with a complex loan package, judging their performance, or talking over a personal problem with them.

"And in a way, comparatively speaking, all of these situations are of equal importance. That's one of the most crucial perspectives to maintain. All of the advice you give, the decisions you make, may have a critical bearing on the lives of the people with whom you are dealing."

Fred Chisholm, assistant manager and assistant vice-president for loans at Bank of America's Culver City branch in Culver City, California, had no idea that banking could be this varied and interesting when he joined the bank approximately seven years ago.

He had just graduated from California State University at Los Angeles, having completed the four-year course in three and one-half years.

"I wanted a career in business, but there were a lot of options as to which kind of business. I walked into the bank almost casually, just to check out the job opportunities. And, wham! Things started happening."

He was chosen for one of the bank's advanced management training programs, finished that with flying colors, spent some time as a lending officer, and very shortly was promoted to manager of one of the bank's smaller branches.

"That training program was a crash course, a mini-college degree in itself. We learned the facets of bank operations, and then moved into consumer and commercial lending. It was a nice balance of the theoretical and the practical.

"Working with the bank's credit review team gave me exposure to all types of loans—large and small, good and not so good. I was working with seasoned bankers who shared their knowledge so I was able to see it all, or at least a big portion—the ratios, liquidity positions, quality of receivables. You learn to read a financial statement like a doctor's chart or medical history—you're soon able to spot a company's strengths and weaknesses in a very short time.

"But banking is more than a balance sheet. As manager of a branch, even a small one, you immediately become aware of the human factor, on both sides of the counter. You have to be empathetic—able to walk a mile in your customer's shoes to see it from his or her point of view. And you get to know people—after all, character is one of the criteria of granting a loan.

"The same thing applies to supervision. You learn the career goals of your staff members and help them achieve them. Often this means pointing out weak areas as well as strengths. It's a tough but extremely rewarding job."

Following his stint as manager Chisholm advanced to commercial lending officer at a larger branch, then moved up to regional leasing officer with leasing responsibilities for a geographical area as large as some states. A short time later he was promoted to his current position.

"So far, it's been stimulating and very gratifying, and I expect it to continue to be that way. I had the opportunity very early to be working alongside—and learning from—some sharp, experienced bankers; managing a branch of my own; and becoming involved in commercial lending dealing with large companies and large amounts of funds.

"Trying to distill the essence of my experiences up to this point is difficult because they have been so varied, but here are a few observations:

"Know your organization. Learn all about it that you can, even those aspects that may not be in your immediate line of work. Read or listen to the speeches of senior executives. Learn the history of the organization and keep up with current publications, internal and external. Become familiar with where your company has been and where it's going.

"Always feel that you and your co-workers are equal. It may sound a bit corny, but it's simply a matter of respect for each individual. And, after all, you are all part of a team effort and everyone's contribution is important no matter what their position may be.

"Be concerned with your career, but don't be obsessively concerned with power or status. Approach each assignment with the view that it can be valuable to you even if it's not the one you want at the time. Give it the same energy and attention that you would if it were a so-called plum. You will learn more, and it's also a good lesson in self-discipline.

"Develop the ability to accept criticism constructively and, in turn, constructively criticize when it's needed. The whole point of such counseling is to learn to do a better job yourself, and to help others do the same thing.

"Finally, treat people the way you would want to be treated. The reciprocity and mutual respect is good for you on and off the job."

THE INTERVIEW STAGE
Turning It in Your Favor

3

The purpose of an employment interview is to help both the employer and the candidate make a decision. Does the organization want you? Do you want the organization? Employers usually decide whether they want you on the basis of: (1) your résumé; (2) the application form you submit (carefully completed with all questions answered); (3) the image you transmit; and (4) the way you answer the interviewer's questions. You usually decide whether or not you want to accept the offer (if any) by comparing what you have learned about the job with your own expectations.

The interview dialogue is by far the most important part of the entire employment procedure—for both parties. Other steps should be considered a preliminary build-up to this critical phase.

How can you communicate your true potential in 30 minutes? How can you learn to answer questions from the interviewer in just the right way? How can you develop the confidence and skill to say what you want to say? How can you "come across" verbally the way you want to?

As you prepare for the final stage in the interview process, you should have definite targets in mind. Here are three general goals you might wish to consider.

Communicate your qualifications. More than all other factors combined, the decision as to whether you will be hired is based upon your qualifications to do a specific job. You should understand, however, that it is one thing to be the best qualified person; it is something else to *transmit* it. The responsibility to communicate your qualifications lies with you. Although the application form and résumé (in front of the interviewer) take you part way, you need to augment and support what you have presented on paper by doing an excellent job of answering questions. If your answers are better than your competitors', you may receive the opportunity even though others are equally qualified. What the interviewer receives from you verbally is what he or she uses in making the final decision. You do not want to overstate your qualifications, but to understate them may be conceding the job to a competitor.

Communicate a positive learning attitude. Although your education, skills, and experience are vital, what you learn after employment is equally important. Applicants are often employed more for their potential (what they can learn) than for what they already know. Usually there is more to learn about a new job than the applicant has been able to learn in the classroom or from previous experience. Your attitude toward learning—your willingness to put yourself in the role of apprentice—can be critical as far as some openings are concerned. In these situations interviewers will appreciate comments such as, "I would appreciate the opportunity to learn," or "I will try to do everything possible to reach my full potential within your organization."

Communicate a long-term interest. The expense of employment and training is only one reason why both large and small organizations favor those who are looking for long-term careers within the framework of one firm. You will not, however, be expected to make an unrealistic commitment during the interview period. Until you are employed, there is no assurance that either you or your employer will be satisfied with your work; the risk is on both sides. The attitude to communicate is that *if* it turns out to be the right organization, you will be most receptive to a long-term career. One way to transmit this attitude is to talk about growth opportunities during the interview.

The following quotation from an employer illustrates the sensitivity of this subject:

> Applicants give themselves away quickly on this matter. All you have to do is listen and watch their faces. You can almost hear them say that they prefer something else but are willing to give you a chance. Like all employers, I realize the risk of losing a good employee is always present, but I like to start out thinking that we have a chance of satisfying an individual to the point she or he will want to stay. Frankly, the easiest decision I make is passing over an applicant who doesn't anticipate staying on even under the best of conditions.

Checking your attitude toward pending interviews will help you prepare for them. Is it positive or negative? Will you welcome or fear them? If you view interviews as unwanted but necessary confrontations, chances for others to put you down, one-sided test periods that are dehumanizing, or just experiences you dread and only tolerate in order to get a job, you will only create problems for yourself; if, on the other hand, you view them as opportunities to learn, to test your ability to communicate on a one-to-one basis, to explore, and to improve your self-confidence, you will have a rewarding experience and achieve results.

Although it is natural to be nervous and concerned about the process (you *do* want a job), you must convince yourself that you are in front of the employer on an equal basis. There are no real advantages either way. The employer has the right to evaluate you; you have the right to evaluate the employer. Neither party is on trial; you are simply exploring the possibilities of employment. As you engage in the process, you may be more at ease if you realize that most interviews fall into four phases.

1. *Getting acquainted.* Most (but not all) interviewers or employers will make it easy for you. Those who help you relax and feel comfortable want to dissipate any elements of threat or discomfort when you enter. They want to be gracious and understanding because they want you to present your best "case." A few may want to "test" you a little to see how much confidence you possess. There is nothing personal about it. This approach is simply their pattern. After a few moments their manner will change, and you will feel as comfortable with them as with others.

2. *Candidate's background.* To discover more about your background, most interviewers will initiate a question-asking period to supplement your résumé. You may be asked questions regarding your family, education, work experience, and community activities. When you send out a résumé, you hope for an in-depth interview; this is the phase in which it takes place.

3. *Matching candidate with job.* The interviewer will want to try to match you with the job that is available. In fact, this is her or his primary task. An employment interviewer is paid to come up with the best qualified applicant in terms of skills, human relations, and long-term employment possibilities. Understanding this may help you interpret some of the questions asked.

4. *Conclusion.* You may be asked to return for a further interview with a department manager, supervisor, or an executive of the organization; you may be told that a decision will be forthcoming

in a few days; you may be told that you do not qualify for the position in question; you may be offered a job on the spot. The options are many, but the interview itself must be terminated eventually. As you leave, it is vital for you to know where you stand. Will you be notified? When? How? Should you call back? Do not hesitate to ask such questions.

Is there anything you can learn in advance about employment interviewers' personalities or their styles? Generally speaking, you can expect a person in this role to use one of two styles: directive or nondirective.

Directive. The interviewers who use this approach control the interview. They may even follow a specific pattern that they feel helps them make the best decision. You will quickly recognize this style because it is structured and precise. You will do less talking under this style; you will be asked more specific questions. There will probably be few periods of silence. Directive interviews are often shorter. It might be desirable for you to intervene toward the end of the interview to make a positive statement or two about your qualifications and interest. Under no circumstances should you permit the directive style to intimidate you.

Nondirective. The nondirective approach is more relaxed. You will normally talk more. There will be fewer questions. The interviewer will sit back and wait for you to communicate. You are left to "sell yourself" with little direction. The individual using this style may also be following a set pattern.

Under the nondirective style it is easier for you to talk yourself out of a job. You may be given so much freedom to communicate that you get carried away.

Which style is best for the applicant? Most people would support the nondirective approach because the applicant will probably relax more and do a better job of self-presentation. One advantage of the direct approach, however, is that it focuses your attention more on specific details of interest to the interviewer.

Ideally, the employment process should benefit both parties. The employer should feel that he or she has found the top applicant in the labor market. You should feel that you have found the ideal starting job with the best organization within your geographical boundaries, in terms of your current job values, growth potential, benefits, and educational opportunities. Obviously, some compromise may be necessary on both sides, *but the less compromise, the better.*

It is, of course, almost impossible for you to anticipate just what kind of person you will meet and what will transpire during an interview. Each interview will be a new and separate experience. Each one will teach you something; each will include a surprise; each will help in preparing you to make a better presentation the next time around. Generally speaking, however, you can expect the following treatment from those who interview you.

They will treat you in a friendly, professional way. You will be received with dignity, respect, courtesy, and warmth. Interviewers will not employ special stress or psychological techniques to trip you up or reveal hidden characteristics about you. They will—with few exceptions—honor the best standards of human relations in dealing with you. Even if you are not chosen, they want you to have a good image of the organization they represent. Some small employers, under the stress of operational problems, may not be able to give you the time and consideration that you would prefer. You should be sensitive enough to take their schedules into consideration.

They will listen to you. Some employers, like applicants, are better at listening than others, but you can anticipate a good level of two-way communications. At the beginning you may be expected to answer questions; later, you may be given the opportunity to ask questions. Because the employer *needs* to know as much about you as possible, you should speak up with confidence and without hesitation. It is important that you also demonstrate your listening skills. After all, the success of an interview is 50 percent your responsibility.

They will normally give you about 30 minutes. Although many employment interviews are much shorter, especially among small employers who are pressed for time, if you *anticipate* a 30-minute period, you will do a better job of advance planning. Do not try to extend the length of the interview—when you receive a signal to leave, you should do so with little delay—but to make *maximum use* of the time. Advance planning enables you to condense information so that you can communicate what is needed without rambling into trivia. Thirty minutes is not a long time, and you want to avoid employment-interview remorse, which occurs when you look back and realize that you said some things that were not necessary and neglected to say some that were.

They will expect you to be slightly assertive but not aggressive. Depending upon your own personality and the "touch" you have developed with other people, it is important that you show alert, positive interest in all phases of the interview. It is a mistake to be submissive; on the other hand, if you become aggressive you may shut the door quickly. Admittedly, it is a delicate balance that you alone control, and each interview will vary in this respect. Angelo required time to achieve this balance.

> As I benefited from one interview after another, I discovered that I came closer and closer to the balance I desired. My confidence grew to the point I could be openly assertive and positive without being obnoxious. For example, I was reluctant and inept about talking salary at the beginning; at the end I became rather good at it.

They will welcome some humor along the way. Forced humor from either side can quickly backfire, but usually some unexpected things take place that can be enjoyed by both parties. The applicant who can sense such moments and capitalize on them usually "comes across" much better than those who are too stiff and inflexible.

If you do a good job with the interview but are not the top candidate, they will find it difficult to turn you down. A good signal that you have presented yourself well may come at the end when the employer gives you a compliment—even though you are not hired: "If we had two openings instead of one, you would have a job." "Please keep in touch because we are sincere in wanting you in the organization." "I wish you had been in contact with us earlier when our needs were greater." Although such compliments are designed to "let you down easy," they are usually sincere. An employment officer for a large company recently made this comment.

> Most applicants do not realize that the interviewer can also become involved in the relationship. I sometimes become so impressed with a candidate that I go out of my way to set up contacts with organizations that have more openings. It is very difficult to make a decision when you have one job and many qualified people. Most of us agonize more than the applicant suspects.

This comment leads to a very important question: How will you handle being turned down? Will you be so disappointed that you will interpret it as a form of personal rejection? Or will you be strong enough (and objective enough) to see an employment rejection for what it is and bounce back?

"Rejection shock" is a very real thing, and the ability to bounce back is a key to ultimate success. *It is important to realize that being turned down does not mean you are inferior.* It could, in fact, mean any of the following:

- You are underqualified for the job at this stage.
- You are overqualified.
- Another applicant is better qualified.
- Another applicant is equally qualified but meets the cultural or minority standards (quotas) that the organization must achieve.
- Your timing is off; a week earlier the position was open and you would have been hired.

The following quotation from a graduate who learned to live with "turn downs" may be helpful:

> I was rejected more times than I want to talk about. Each time I lived through an emotionally disturbing "down" period. I finally decided it was immature of me to indulge myself in self-pity just because I was a square peg and the employer had a round hole. I decided that sooner or later my qualifications would meet a real need, and sooner or later I would put it all together during the interview.
>
> Strange thing about it all, my opportunity came when I least expected it. The truth is that I had my job-finding act together all along—I just needed to find the right organization at the right time. That is the way the job market operates sometimes. The temptation to give up is always there but you can't let it happen.

The key to success in most interviews is the skill you demonstrate in answering questions. This skill is crucial because:

1. Data to support and expand on information provided in the application and the résumé are obtained this way.
2. The ability of the applicant to communicate verbally is evaluated.
3. Insights into attitudes are detected.

To give you a major assist in preparing to answer questions more skillfully, the following questions are presented with "model" answers. The more time you spend evaluating these anwers—and adapting them to your own values and feelings—the better. Use them for comparison purposes only. They are intended to lead you to the best possible answer *you* can make when the time comes. They will also give you some idea of the kinds of questions you can expect.

Why did you apply for a job with this organization?

"I did some research and discovered that your firm has an excellent reputation in terms of steady growth over the years. I like the idea of security along with the possibilities of high personal growth. I also discovered that you have high human relations standards, and this appeals to me."

What do you feel you will be able to contribute to our organization?

"In addition to my immediate skills, I hope to work toward a supervisory role. From there, I would hope to move into upper management positions. I feel I have a high potential to learn and that eventually I could provide some sound leadership."

What specific skills do you bring with you?

"As an accounting major, I believe that I have most of the necessary skills to be of immediate value to you in this area. I also have experience with computers, including programming experience. I am an excellent typist. I also feel that I have developed good human-relations skills."

Can you be more specific about your human-relations skills?

"I believe there is a correlation between human relations and productivity; I therefore want to be the kind of person with whom others will want to work, so that I can contribute to their productivity as well as my own. I think, with more experience, I could excel at solving human relations problems. I have been told by a few people that I am better than average at building and maintaining relationships with others. I want to improve in this area."

Do you consider yourself a creative person?

"I am not a creative person in an artistic sense, but I feel I am an idea person. I think I can eventually come up with ideas that will contribute to corporate profits."

What are your long-term goals or personal targets?

"My long-term goal is upper management. I decided on accounting as a major because I enjoy statistical data, and I thought it would lead me to management; my personal targets are family oriented."

What do you consider your greatest weakness?

"It may be my impatience with others. Most people do not drive themselves as hard as I do, so I need to develop more tolerance of the pace others take."

What salary would you expect or require?

"From what I have learned so far about the job market, I should be able to start somewhere in the range of $850.00 per month. I want to take into consideration future salary increases, the total organizational benefit package, and the possibility of profit-sharing or a stock option plan. If you decide to make me an offer, where do you see me starting?"

As you know, our organization operates in all 50 states and in many foreign countries. What is your attitude toward geographical transfers?

"My wife and I have talked about this and have decided we want to be flexible. Although we have strong emotional ties to this area, we would be willing to move if moving would help me reach my long-term goals. My wife is a registered nurse, so finding employment in other states or foreign countries should not be hard for her. Nevertheless, her career future is equally important. We hope the company would provide for the expenses involved. What *is* your policy on relocation?"

Are there any questions you would like to ask me at this point?

"Yes, I have prepared a list that I would like to go over. Could you tell me more about the kinds of in-service training available? Later I would like to know more about such things as promotion policies, employee evaluation programs, and so forth."

As you evaluate the so-called model answers above, you may wish to consider the following suggestions:

1. Keep your answers short and to the point.
2. Answer clearly and without hesitation.
3. If necessary, request the opportunity to ask questions yourself.

4. Ask the employer to re-state the question if it is not clear.
5. Mock interviews are very helpful in improving the skills needed in answering questions (see Exercises for Part I, page 62).

Panel or group interviews are becoming more and more popular, especially in educational institutions where faculty and student involvement is desired in the selection of a new teacher or administrator. Should more than one individual be involved in interviewing you, keep the following points in mind.

1. Direct your answer primarily to the person who asked it.
2. Occasionally, especially when a general question is asked, rotate your eye contact among all interviewers.
3. If one interviewer shows hostility toward you, do not over-react in the hope of gaining sympathy and support from the others.
4. Be sure you answer the question asked and do not get carried away on a side issue.
5. Humorous situations are more apt to develop in a group environment, so be sure to take advantage of them.
6. Do not hesitate to ask questions of either an individual or the panel as a whole.

Knowing what to expect and how to respond helps to relieve the stress that accompanies job hunting. But it may be best for you and your future that anxiety not be eliminated entirely from the interviews that lie ahead. Why? Because the interview process is an important learning experience that cannot be duplicated in any other aspect of life. In fact, if it is necessary for you to go through a large number (instead of only a few) interviews, you may come out ahead for the following reasons:

1. The experience will aid you when you do appraisal interviews later in your career.
2. Interviews improve your ability to communicate.
3. Interviews develop your leadership ability.

The following quotation was volunteered by one of the individuals who provided a profile for this book.

I had no idea that it would be necessary for me to go through more than 30 interviews to land the job I really wanted. It took much more time and it was far more expensive than I had anticipated. It also took more out of me. Now that I can look back on it, however, I can see it was a definite "growing up" experience for me. I now have far more confidence in myself than before. I am sure that I will benefit from the experience in many ways in the future. I am glad it is over, at least temporarily, but I wouldn't trade it for anything.

Postscript

Let's be positive and assume all of your efforts have paid off, and you have just received word that you have been accepted by the employer of your choice. When this happens (and it will), are there any procedures you should follow or precautions you should take?

First, accept the contract with enthusiasm; but before you walk away or hang up the telephone to rejoice, please: (1) determine exactly when, where, and to whom you should report to work; (2) ask for a copy of any literature that describes the organization or its work procedures so that you can be as well informed as possible *before* you report; (3) make sure you understand clearly all of the terms of your employment contract, including compensation arrangements, employee benefits, withholding provisions, and other financial details; (4) ask about such things as orientation and on-the-job training, any special benefits you are entitled to, forms that need to be completed, where you should park, the possible need for safety equipment, uniform or dress requirements, where to "clock in" if required, union relationships (if involved), regulations regarding overtime, breaks, legal responsibilities to clients, and other local "ground rules."

Next you should take time to notify any employers who are still giving you consideration that you have made a decision. A few "thank you" notes might be in order here.

Your next responsibility is to get your personal affairs in shape. Do you need to move closer to your work station? Does your automobile need repairs? Do you need to spend time on your "working wardrobe"? Are there any doctor or dentist appointments you should make and keep?

And, finally, you should try to arrange for a short, relaxing vacation so that you will show up for the "first day on the job" refreshed and ready.

Discussion Questions

1. What are some of the psychological factors that cause some people to fear interviews? Be as specific as possible.
2. How would you help a person move from dreading an interview to looking forward to one? What specific suggestions would you make?
3. How would you endeavor to help a close friend recover from rejection shock?
4. How would you change the model answers presented in the chapter to adapt them for your own use? Explain these changes.
5. Prepare three additional questions with model answers. Why should they be added to the list?
6. Do you agree or disagree that the best way to prepare in advance for interviews is to go through mock situations? Defend your position.

Richard B. Kirkland
Vice-President
Wheeler Freightways

**Career
Profile**

Do you want to know how I became vice-president of a two-million-dollar company?

In 1970 I was 24 years old and newly discharged from the Navy. I was on the street, with everyone else, with one year of college to my credit.

Let's see. I was better off than the guy with no college, but I was at a great disadvantage compared to the guy with a degree, as I soon found out. Then there's the guy who's been working for a while, who has experience. Wow, what do I know?

I had a big problem. I was married. I had two kids and no money coming in. First things first: I needed money, so I went looking for a job. I found one in three days. I took my military experience to Raytheon. The Raytheon Company manufactures the radar I worked on in the Navy. Obvious choice for a job? Right.

I started with Raytheon as a bench technician. After three months I found out that my performance was making the other workers' work look inferior. That's bad. I went to the service manager and asked if I could get into the field engineering group. He was glad to get rid of me, to keep peace with the other employees. During my two months with the field engineering group, I was given an oscilloscope that was considered a dog. It was a new unit, but it didn't have the prestigious name of Tektronix on the face plate. The name on the front was Cossor. I learned to like this unit, and soon convinced my fellow workers that my oscilloscope was better than the Tektronix unit the others had been used to. As a matter of fact, I felt so strongly about it that I wrote a memo to my boss. It just so happened that the unit was on loan for evaluation, and my boss had been avoiding making a report on it. So, since I felt so strongly about it, I was assigned the task of writing the report.

Because it was my first report assignment I wanted to do it right. I decided to prepare it in such detail that it ended up a booklet. I called it "Proposal and Market Survey."

After I submitted it to my boss, I forgot about it. Two weeks later I was told by the boss to report to corporate headquarters, to the executive director of International Engineering. I just knew I was going on the carpet.

In that visit, I found out that the report I wrote was on a product manufactured in England by a subsidiary of Raytheon, and they wanted to market it in the United States.

Next step. Who would be the liaison between Cossor in England and Raytheon in the United States? Who? Me.

I had never sold anything in my life; as a matter of fact I didn't like salesmen. Obviously, I didn't want them to know that, so I volunteered my services.

The first thing I was told was that I no longer worked for the service company. I was to set up a company for Raytheon to market this new product in the United States. That meant find a building, rent space, hire a secretary, set up a budget, and prepare a five-year plan. (I'd never done that before, either.)

Well, I did it. Three years and two million dollars later I sold the operation for Raytheon to a distributor. I became the distributor's national sales manager. Six months later, he decided that he wanted out of the test-equipment business. This meant I was out of a job.

Next step. Move back to Massachusetts (my home state) where a job as a service technician was waiting with the service company of Raytheon, or stay in California and find something else?

I decided against moving. I wasn't prepared to start over again.

I went back on the street again. This time, though I thought my titles and experience with Raytheon would get me a marketing job, I was wrong. I now faced another problem: company politics.

I found out that in order to be appointed to a position of importance in a large company you have to have credentials, i.e., a degree. I was told that "it (not having a degree) wouldn't look good in a press release."

Next step. Back to basics. I needed money to support my family. Since my standard of living was high, I needed a lot of money, and since my pride was involved, I wasn't going to let the electronics industry take advantage of my situation.

I had heard that truck drivers make lots of money. So, with the help of a neighbor, I got a company to teach me how to drive in return for my time as a swamper. (In other words, I didn't get paid.)

After three months as a driver of one of those 18-wheelers, I thought to myself, I've got management experience. I could run this company. So I walked into the office of the owner and told him that I wanted his job.

This is the kind of guy everyone should meet at least once. He's one of those "I did it all myself" types. One thing, though, he's a fair person. He gave me the chance.

I started in the office as dispatcher trainee, and in January I became vice-president.

Now, what have you learned? Maybe I can tell you what's in my head.

First, forget about the idea that anyone can do exactly what I did. Think about this instead.

I'm a successful businessman in your mind. You are looking for someone to take you by the hand and show you how to be successful. Sorry, it won't happen. You've got to do it yourself.

If you're looking for advice, you can get that free, but bear in mind that advice is just an opinion with someone else's viewpoint attached. With that in mind, here's mine:

1. Stay in school for as long as you can, as long as you are learning something. If you're just sliding through, that piece of sheepskin you end up with won't do you any good.

2. Think about what you want to do. Then go do it. Don't worry about what someone else did or is going to do.

3. The one who gets the job is the one who bought it. The price is you. You have to sell yourself to the employer. Want proof? Think about all of your fellow classmates. Put them in a room with an employer who has one opening. Who gets the job? If you don't think it's YOU, you're going to have a terrible time trying to use that diploma.

4. "Minimum qualifications" are words used in newspapers as eliminators. The person screening is lazy. The same is true with résumés; they are worthless, without the person with them. Never mail a résumé to a prospective employer: send a personal letter, and bring your résumé with you and hand it to him personally.

That piece of paper isn't going to get the job. You are!

REVIEW
Questions
and Answers

4

What questions about job-hunting problems would you ask the author if you had the opportunity? This chapter presents some typical questions. You are invited to challenge the answers.

What is the exact definition of an entry job?

An entry job is a first or beginning position—one that applicants are employed *into directly,* depending upon their educational qualifications and experience. Some organizations have a sizable number of entry jobs. Frequently the entry job is one with minimum qualifications and pay, but it offers the new employee the opportunity to move on to something better. For example, an entry job in the food services business for a high school dropout might be that of a dishwasher or dining room attendant. For a high school graduate, it could be a waiter or waitress. For a college graduate (two or four years), it could be a management training program. One entry job in a banking institution is that of teller. In a supermarket it might be a checker assistant; or in a large office it might be a mail clerk. In many professional classifications (registered nurse, teacher, medical doctor) the individual must be fully qualified and licensed *before* entry is possible.

How often is it necessary for graduates to take entry jobs below their qualifications?

The answer depends, in part, on the state of the job market. When the market is tight, graduates frequently accept jobs below their qualifications. The author, for example, knows a Ph.D. from a major university who accepted an entry job with the title of clerk in order to get inside a particular organization with the hope of working up. In some organizations, however, tradition plays a more important role than the condition of the labor market. For example, if you wanted to become a professional sales representative in a wholesale drug organization, you might have to serve an apprenticeship period in a warehouse to learn the merchandise. If you wanted to be a retail buyer, you might have to start out as a salesperson or department manager. If you wanted to become a computer analyst, you might have to start out as an operator. There is nothing degrading about taking a job below your potential as long as there are opportunities for upward mobility within the organization.

Is it wrong to accept a very low-level entry job while you continue to look for a better one in another organization?

No. You might start with almost any job as long as you produce at an acceptable level, learn what you can, and keep your mind open to the possibility that the job could develop into something better. But do not make frequent moves from one low-level (low-paying) entry job to another over a long period of time.

Should I accept a good entry job with an organization if I have serious doubts about long-term employment?

You should consider many factors: (1) your qualifications; (2) how long you have been searching; (3) market conditions; (4) your present financial position; and (5) your need for experience. Generally speaking, if you sense you can do better within a month or so, hold off. However, if you have exhausted the possibilities in your geographical area and you desperately need experience, accept the opportunity with the attitude that you will do your best and keep an open mind regarding any future opportunities that might develop within the organization.

Should I seek interviews for the sole purpose of improving my technique?

No. You can improve your technique more from mock interviews through evaluations from the individual you select to play the role of the employer. Do not risk the possibility of hurting relationships with personnel people who might be able to assist you later on.

What, if anything, should I do if, after an interview, I feel I did not fully express my desire for the job in question?

Generally speaking, you will not receive a second chance from an interviewer; however, you might try calling back about any matter upon which you failed to express yourself adequately. The oversight should, however, be of sufficient importance to justify the call.

When, if ever, should I use the influence of a friend or relative to get an interview?

Any time it will help, providing that you tell the interviewer that you wish to be accepted or rejected 100 percent on your own qualifications and potential.

Do applicants eventually develop a "style" as far as presenting themselves is concerned?

Yes, and the sooner such a style is developed the better. This is the purpose of mock interviews. When you have developed a relaxed style that communicates your personality and potential honestly and clearly, and permits you to adjust quickly to the interviewer, you will enjoy successful interviews and a meaningful entry job will not be far away. Most people would agree that just the right amount of friendliness, warmth, and empathy for others should be woven into your style.

I had the opportunity to observe two mock interviews in class and watch one on tape, but I have not been personally involved. Should I now do one on my own?

By all means! In fact, more than one is recommended. Your time will not be well spent, however, unless you and the person chosen to portray the employer take the process seriously. Remember, as much time should be spent on the evaluation as on the interview itself. Here are three tips: (1) Choose an interviewer older and more experienced than yourself. (2) Provide the interviewer with 10 difficult questions to ask you. (3) Do not stop for laughter or other interruptions, but continue the process until you have been hypothetically accepted or rejected. (See Exercises for Part I for more data on mock interviews.)

How does an individual handle pressures that develop when a job is not found within a reasonable period of time?

Some observers claim that the longer a search extends, the less employable the individual becomes. Obviously, if pressures retard progress, the way they are handled is important to success. Each individual must cope with both internal and external pressures in his or her own way. The following activities seem to help some people: (1) a disciplined exercise program; (2) frequent consultation with a counselor or placement director; (3) talking things over daily with an understanding friend or spouse; (4) planning diversions from the job-hunting routine; and (5) involvement in sports. Some pressure may be healthy and desirable for those individuals who do not live up to their job-hunting potential until they are pressured into taking more active steps.

What can I do to ward off the possibility I will become so discouraged looking for an entry job that I will quit looking altogether?

A few people do seem to give up and sit on the sidelines for long periods of time. Here are some ways to resist discouragement.

1. Re-read portions of this book.
2. Keep talking to placement people, personnel directors, friends, and relatives who build up your job-hunting confidence.
3. Discipline yourself by setting a goal of five interviews or more per week.
4. Take an interim job of any kind to keep yourself busy while hunting; it is easier for most people to find a job when they are employed because their attitude stays more positive.
5. Take a short break from job hunting to regain your perspective—perhaps an inexpensive mini-vacation.
6. Analyze the possibility that you may be trying to open the wrong career doors. In short, you are restricting your search to a narrow segment of the job market. It may be more realistic to reach out in a new direction. If you are *determined and flexible,* you will eventually open a good career door.

Was this book written primarily for business majors who wish to get into management?

The book was written for *all* majors. Some business orientation is natural, however, because about 70 percent of all entry jobs are found in the business sector of our society. The book should help anyone who is making the transition from *any* campus or position of unemployment to *any* kind of job or organization.

I have a credential to teach but there are no jobs. What is worse, I am afraid I have a negative attitude toward business careers. Any suggestions?

Yes. Investigate the possibility of becoming a training specialist in a government agency. Most large organizations need people with teaching ability to train others, often in formal classroom situations. Large business organizations employ many training directors. I know a training director for a large banking organization who, like you, prepared for a teaching career. At this point, however, she would not trade the business environment for the campus. You, too, might eventually like a business career more than you think.

I sometimes find it almost impossible to motivate myself into generating interviews. Any suggestions that will help?

Placement directors make suggestions to clients regarding "motivators"; for example, you might consider the "personal reward" idea. Give yourself a very personal reward *after* you have accomplished a certain goal. If you want to take a skiing trip with friends, say to yourself, "I will take the trip *only* after I have set up five promising interviews." In short, you establish a reachable goal, then postpone the reward through self-discipline until you have reached your objective. If the rewards are motivating and realistic, this approach works well for many individuals.

Another possibility is to ask someone to "jog" you into action. Perhaps someone who is close to you would be happy to help if he or she *received an honest invitation.* For example, you might call a close friend and say, "Sylvia, I am fresh out of motivation to fight the job market, and I don't have a single interview in sight. How about giving me a boost if I pick up the tab? I thought we might see a movie and have a few beers, and you could try to get my attitude back in shape for me. Any chance for tonight or tomorrow?" Many individuals find this approach difficult to initiate because they have too much pride to admit they have lost motivation.

Under what circumstances can job-hunting pressures be detrimental?

Pressures to land a job can build up until they cause anxieties that destroy the natural "tone" of a good two-way interview. After searching without success for a long time, the individual may, without knowing it, anticipate failure and therefore communicate a less enthusiastic attitude; the worst possible result is that the applicant may anticipate failure to the point that searching activities are restricted.

My spouse has a very good starting job with an excellent future, yet I can't seem to come up with an equally good opportunity in the same geographical area. What is our solution?

First, ask yourselves this question: Have we *fully* explored the market, or do we have some biases that need to be eliminated? Next, explore the possibility of extending your geographical area. Sometimes two people can commute in opposite directions; some couples seem to be able to live apart during the week. Perhaps retraining for a different career is worth consideration. Most people would agree that this common, difficult problem should be worked out cooperatively and that neither spouse should hide behind the success of the other.

I have a good friend who has been searching for a special job for more than six months without success. I claim that she is "hooked" on this one career possibility to the point she will not consider others for which she is equally qualified. How can I convince her she is going up the same blind alley time after time?

It is extremely disappointing to set your sights and prepare for one career, then be forced to accept another. Many of us are not sufficiently flexible to accept such a switch at the beginning. You might suggest that your friend accept a second choice while she continues to search for an opening in her first choice; you might try to point out the advantages of a second choice over a first. I know a young lady who had always picutred herself as a secretary in a consumer-oriented business like a bank, where physical conditions were very clean and comfortable and dress standards were high. Only after repeated failure and some strong counseling did she agree to apply for a job in a local factory, where working conditions were much the opposite. Later, after having adjusted to the unfamiliar work environment, she discovered she was very happy with her choice.

Those who operate private employment agencies claim their primary counseling role is to persuade applicants to widen their job sights. "We keep getting qualified applicants with tunnel vision who have literally locked themselves into a few career slots where the supply greatly exceeds the demand. These people do not always sense how welcome they would be in other areas. My job is to convince them that they can comfortably and profitably fit into round, square, and odd-shaped career slots. They may resist the change at the beginning, but later they come around and thank me for forcing them to be more flexible."

Some authors state that it is both possible and advisable to classify interviewers into "types" so that the applicant can quickly identify a certain type and respond accordingly. Do you agree?

No. It might be good fun to categorize interviewers into contrived types such as the "intimidator" or the "say-nothing" individual, but it serves no useful purpose when the applicant faces the interviewer for the first time. In fact, too much time spent trying to analyze the person on the other side of the desk could result in awkward communications. The author believes that each interviewer-applicant relationship should develop on an independent, give-and-take basis without prejudging. Obviously, the applicant must react, interpret, adjust, and make sensitive decisions based upon the personality and approach of the interviewer, but to study possible types in advance can increase anxiety and accomplish very little.

Every time I sit down to do some self-assessing I become confused and despondent. How can I overcome this problem?

Since it is never easy to be objective about oneself, the feelings you encounter are more common than you might suspect. Perhaps you have a negative self-image, and you have been unsuccessful in changing it. When you start to fill out the assessment form, you lose your objectivity and attempt to probe too deeply into your own "psyche." Simply stay with the form on a step-by-step basis as you evaluate one characteristic after another. In this way you can discover weaknesses and make improvements without the confusion and discouragement that can result from too much introspection.

What should I do if I catch myself making excuses to my friends and family about my failure to get a job?

It is only natural to rationalize a temporary inability to get the right job. We do many things to protect our egos. Excuses could, however, be a warning that you are beginning to be dishonest with yourself and backing away from job-hunting realities. You may be turning negative about your future, temporarily indulging yourself, or hiding from something you are fully capable of handling but are afraid to face at this juncture. What action should you take? Perhaps it is time for a complete reassessment of your entire job-seeking approach. The form on page 63 should assist you in seeing yourself more objectively, especially if you are willing to discuss each factor openly with someone in whom you have confidence. Reassessment may improve your attitude so that you can make a fresh start that will bring results and eliminate the need for excuses.

Our placement director claims that applicants fail to find suitable starting jobs primarily because they are unorganized in their approach. Do you agree?

Yes. Frequently graduates search more by mood than by method. When their mood or confidence level is high, they schedule and attend interviews and make good presentations. When they are discouraged, rather than employ self-discipline, they sit on the sidelines for days or weeks at a time. The temptation to permit temporary discouragement to precipitate self-pity is always there, but obviously, the odds favor the individuals who organize their time, control their moods, and stick to a predetermined search plan. The reader need not adhere to the ten-step job-finding plan presented in this book; but most individuals need some form of organization.

How many "live" prospects should a full-time job hunter have at any given time?

Although all it takes for success is one prospect that eventually comes through, the old adage "the more irons you have in the fire the better" still makes sense. After a 30-day search a minimum of three good prospects would seem to be both desirable and realistic for most graduates. In other words, unless you have three job possibilities that could develop, you should reevaluate your approach. Either you have viewed the market incorrectly, or your search system is letting you down, or you are just not working at it. For some individuals, the more "live" prospects they have, the more motivated they are to search for something even better. Here is the way a successful applicant views the matter. "During my search I tried to keep up to five prospects alive at all times. At one point I was up to eight. Somehow it gave me confidence to know that on any given day a number of employers might call me. When you start relying on one or two possibilities to jell, fear is apt to set in and your enthusiasm to continue searching is destroyed. Incidentally, the position I finally took developed at the end of my search, not at the start. The development of good prospects should not stop until a final choice has been made."

What do you feel is the most serious mistake job applicants make?

Placement directors and professional interviewers indicate a very common mistake is to stop the search process prematurely because prospects for a given job appear promising. The danger of anticipating success too quickly can often be traced to inexperience. For example, Ray had what he expressed as "three super interviews" for jobs that met his needs. He was positive one would come through—so positive that he relaxed and waited for some form of communication. Result? When nothing developed, he had to overcome his disappointment, gear himself up again, and start the search process from scratch. It is estimated that 50 percent of all applicants prolong their search by waiting around for job offers that, under the harsh light of reality, were long-shots from the very beginning. The experienced applicant does not abandon the search process until a firm job offer has been accepted enthusiastically.

Do you feel that understanding more about the total transition from campus to an important career position will help a graduate get a starting job sooner?

Definitely! A major premise of this book is that if you make a sincere effort to see the entire process as a passage—perhaps the most important one in your life—you will develop more ability to articulate your goals during interviews. You will know more about protocol and procedures inside organizations. You should also be more perceptive in selecting the best job and organization for yourself. Too often in the past, applicants have devoted 95 percent of their efforts to getting a starting job—any job—instead of viewing the interview as a natural and vital phase to a total career achievement program. This short-sightedness can cause unnecessary anxiety and mistakes on the part of the applicant.

What influence are affirmative action programs having on the job-finding scene?

Affirmative action programs are being conducted both on-campus and inside organizations. Those on campus are having a substantial influence on job-hunting skills and attitudes. Those inside organizations are having considerable impact upon promotion-seeking patterns.

The major influence such programs are having on the interview process is that applicants are becoming more skillful and *assertive*. They tend to have more personal confidence and to obtain more information to benefit themselves than in the past. If you have not taken part in an affirmative action program, you may want to do something on your own to improve your chances.

In searching for and finding your first position you should also keep in mind that some organizations are still trying to balance their "minority mix." This means you could have an advantage in some organizations and be at a disadvantage in others. Whether you introduce either of these subjects during the interview process is your decision but at least you should be aware of the implications they produce.

When should one try to negotiate on the matter of salary?

This is an area where many factors, including job-market conditions, the kind of organization involved, and personal confidence come into play. If you are fresh from campus with little job experience you might decide to set a salary range (say from $750.00 to $900.00 per month) and, based upon other job advantages important to you (say location) accept a salary point within that range without introducing the bargaining process. On the other hand, you might decide to negotiate for the highest possible point within the range you set for yourself. This would be most appropriate if your career specialty is in high demand and low supply.

How can you tell if the interviewer might be receptive? You might consider introducing the subject by asking the question: "Is the beginning salary for this position negotiable?" If the interviewer replies that the salary point is fixed and firm, at least you have asked; if negotiation within a range is acceptable you should pursue the matter advancing your formal education, experiences, and leadership qualifications in the hope of justifying a point near or at the top of the range.

Any experience you gain in salary negotiations during the interview process will stand you in good stead later on in your career when you may seek a raise in your present position, when you bargain for a higher salary when offered a promotion, or when you negotiate with an organization who may be trying to attract you away from your present employer.

Discussion Questions

1. Out of a class of 30 (all of whom will soon enter the job market on a full-time basis) 24 students have expressed a desire to do mock interviews on videotape. What, if anything, should the instructor do to convince the remaining six to do the same? Defend your view.
2. There are many sources of pressure—financial, family, internal—that can surface when an applicant encounters failure in finding a job quickly. What, if anything, can an applicant do to forestall such pressures?
3. The chapter mentions two ways applicants can "jog" or motivate themselves into seeking more interviews. Which of the two could you be more enthusiastic about? If neither, what substitute would you propose?
4. Some job-seekers seem to impose unrealistic limitations upon themselves as far as geographical boundaries and career choices are concerned. Should such individuals be counseled into being more flexible, or should they be left to make the discovery themselves? Defend your stand.
5. Juanita's goal is to achieve three good interviews per week; Juan wants to achieve five. In terms of your own plans, which goal would you support? Why?
6. Doug and Sheri both agree that a job-seeker needs an organized approach. Doug claims it is better to accept one already developed; Sheri claims it is better to develop your own. Whom would you support?

**Career
Profile**

Judy Kulis
Director of Marketing, Asst. General Manager
La Mesa (California) Shopping Center

The most difficult thing I had to face upon graduating from college was how to deal with the "real world!" College was basically a very controlled environment for me. There were relatively few decisions to make—what school to go to, what subject to major in, and to a certain extent, what classes to take. Achievement was pretty well judged by what kind of grades a person got. It really didn't dawn on me until the middle of my senior year that I would really have to go out and sell myself in order to find a job. For some reason, I felt that just by graduating from college I'd get all kinds of job offers. Well, when I graduated, things just didn't work that way. Looking back, I must have been pretty naive, but that shows one important point: college doesn't teach you how to deal with real-world situations. How to go about finding a career position and what career to choose are very important steps in anyone's life, steps that college didn't prepare me for.

I think it's very important to carefully analyze one's goals and expectations regarding a career. Forget the "pie in the sky" dreams. You have to develop a feasible course of action to reach your goals and expectations. It took me a couple of years in the business world to figure that out, and I think I would have been much further along in my own career had I carefully looked at what I wanted and how to get it.

I graduated from college with a degree in marketing and thought at the time I'd like a career in retailing. I accepted the first job offered to me, which was probably my biggest job-seeking mistake. I worked in fashion coordination for a high-fashion department store and quickly realized after a few months it wasn't the job for me. At this point I knew I wanted a position that would be less hampered by corporate dictates, something in which I would have the opportunity to express my own creativity. But I didn't have to wait for long. I more or less fell into a position in the industry I am now involved in.

The department store where I was working was in a large shopping center. It just happened that the general manager of the shopping center was interviewing people in my employer's office for the position of promotion director for the shopping center. I'd seen a number of people interview for the job, and when my employer asked me if I would like to interview for the position, well, I jumped at the chance, interviewed, and got the job. I'd never considered this type of work, but it sounded challenging, so I accepted.

I was responsible for developing the advertising, promotion, and marketing research program for a major regional shopping center. It certainly was a great opportunity, and I've been involved with the shopping center industry ever since.

Two years ago I joined a large shopping center development and management company and have advanced from the position of marketing director to assistant manager to operations manager of a super regional shopping center. The company is young, aggressive, and the fastest growing in the industry, and the advancement potential is great.

Through working for different companies in the industry, I have advanced and widened my responsibilities to include all phases of shopping center marketing and property management.

My advancement has not been without its sacrifices, particularly where my personal life is concerned. My business often requires long hours and working weekends. Because I am married, there has also been the problem of coordinating two careers. This has led to living in six places in three years and living apart for as long as seven months. I've also driven as far as sixty miles to work.

I feel though, that most of the sacrifices have been worthwhile because I enjoy my work and the future seems bright. After working almost five years, I feel I've gone through my "career growing pains" and am at a position where I'm comfortable and confident in the business world. I've realized, too, that it takes more than doing just a good job these days to get ahead. Initiative, creativity, a certain amount of aggressiveness, and especially good human relations are what it takes in today's business world.

Exercises for Part I

Mock Interview

Many placement officers feel that the best possible way to prepare for employment interviews is to go through "dry runs" with a friend, instructor, or fellow student acting as the professional interviewer. Such mock interviews can be put on either audio or video tape. Most college campuses are equipped with both. Obviously, video tape has many advantages. Facing the camera, under proper direction, and then viewing results is an excellent way to increase self-confidence. It permits the identification and elimination of mistakes and facilitates evaluations by others.

How does one prepare for such an experience?

1. Make advance arrangements with the media center on your campus; you may need a requisition from your instructor or placement director.
2. Ask a fellow student or friend (or perhaps your instructor) to play the role of interviewer. Another student who is job hunting would benefit from exchanging roles with you.
3. Physical arrangements for video taping should resemble a business office. For example, you may wish to position the interviewer behind a desk so that you can develop your "approaching" skills.
4. Provide some difficult questions for the interviewer to ask you, but give this person the freedom to ask questions that you are not expecting.
5. Define the job you are applying for in advance. It is also helpful to identify an organization.
6. Try to plan for a minimum of 15 minutes before the camera because a shorter interview is not realistic.

The real value of this approach comes from the analysis of the interaction that takes place between you, the interviewer, and any others present. An evaluation form is presented here.

Interview Evaluation Form

Rate yourself on a scale of 1 to 5 for each question. Ask the interviewer and others who viewed the mock interview to rate you also. Use these ratings as the basis for an evaluation discussion.

1. Nonverbal greeting signals were perfect.　　1　2　3　4　5　　Nonverbal greeting signals were terrible.

2. Eye contact during interview was superior.　　1　2　3　4　5　　Eye contact during interview was zero.

3. Voice was outstanding.　　1　2　3　4　5　　Voice needs much improvement.

4. Applicant answered questions superbly.　　1　2　3　4　5　　Applicant answered questions poorly.

5. Applicant showed complete confidence.　　1　2　3　4　5　　Applicant showed complete lack of confidence.

6. Applicant was properly assertive.　　1　2　3　4　5　　Applicant was far too aggressive.

7. Applicant was courteous.　　1　2　3　4　5　　Applicant was far too submissive.

8. It was obvious that applicant was fully qualified.　　1　2　3　4　5　　It was obvious that applicant was not qualified.

9. Applicant needs no more mock interviews.　　1　2　3　4　5　　Applicant needs many more mock interviews.

10. Overall rating is outstanding.　　1　2　3　4　5　　Overall rating is extremely weak.

Case Study: Conflict

Tom and Janet were heatedly discussing the whole concept of sending signals, following a classroom confrontation between some students and the professor.

Said Tom, "I reject the whole idea of trying to influence others by making an effort to send positive signals. It's dishonest and hypocritical. Look—you are what you are, and the signals just flow out. When you try to control your signals, it doesn't work because you fake it and people know. Besides, I don't see why I should act differently in the working environment. I should be able to walk from my personal world into the work world without making any changes. I shouldn't have to play two roles just to please others and make a living. I think people should accept me the way I am because it's the real me, not some crazy role I cook up just to build relationships and impress others. When I get my degree, I'm going to find an employer who likes me the way I am and doesn't want me to conform to such things as dress regulations."

"You misinterpret the whole concept, Tom," Janet replied. "The signals you send should reflect the real you, not a fake you. But you should be aware of sending them, and try to send the best possible signals, because you can't be effective in the world of work unless you work closely with others. In short, you send good signals to build good working relationships so that you can make your maximum contribution to productivity. Now I admit that a person plays two roles in life in a sense. Personally, I'm ready and willing to adjust to a work environment so that I can be 100 percent free in my personal life. I need to make good impressions because what people think of me on the job will influence my future. I don't choose my co-workers or the customers; but I can choose my personal friends. If you don't make a deliberate effort to send favorable signals, you will do nothing but hurt your future. Frankly, I just don't think you're being realistic."

Would you defend Tom or Janet? Can you suggest a compromise?

Part II

LAUNCHING YOURSELF WITH CONFIDENCE

Objectives

When you have finished this section you should have

1. Internalized, selected, and accepted some of the basic challenges involved in making a successful passage from campus to a rewarding career position

2. Adequately prepared yourself to adjust to the major psychological changes that your new work environment will demand

3. Decided upon the business protocol standards that you intend to live up to and the "manners" you intend to integrate into your behavior

4. Chosen the extent to which you intend to keep your business and personal worlds separated

5. Developed your best possible pattern regarding the approach you will take in reaching productivity norms and how far you might go beyond them

Career Countdown

Whatever your entry job turns out to be, it should be considered a launching pad to help you reach your long-term career goals. Part II is designed to help you "count down" some vital factors that will give you a mistake-free lift-off.

PERSPECTIVE
The Challenge Is There

5

It's happened! You have won yourself a starting job that shows promise. Probably you have been through many interviews and some anxious moments. Although it is natural to have some doubts about the decision you made ("Would I have found something better if I had tried harder and waited longer?"), we will assume that you have a positive attitude toward your new opportunity and that you intend to make the most of it. Even if the position is not what you anticipated—it could be your third or fourth career choice—you are serious about using it as a launching pad for a successful long-term career.

Let's make another assumption. We will take it for granted that you have an open mind toward the organization you have joined. Your transition into the world of work should be a positive experience, one that reinforces your self-concept and provides a base upon which you can build an exciting career. Obviously, your attitude toward the kind of organization you join (government, education, medical, business) will have something to do with your success. The *size* of the organization is also important. If you have a deep-seated negative attitude toward all large organizations, you will be at a disadvantage if you join one. The following comment was made by a business executive.

> An individual who joined us recently had a real complex about business. He thought that American business organizations were 100 percent responsible for the pollution of the environment. He thought that being a corporate giant was automatically bad, and his attitude toward the free-enterprise system was very militant. We wondered why he had wanted to join us in the first place. Then, after he had been with us for

a few months, we were pleased to see his attitude changing. Apparently he discovered that neither the company nor the system was as bad as he had thought.

Sure, everyone in business, government, and education admits that their organizations need to be improved. The perfect organization in or out of the business sector has yet to be developed. We need to make many improvements in the years ahead, and that is why we like to hire people who want to be agents of change. Without change, we won't survive. But we also hope these people will accept a position on our payroll without too many preconceived ideas and, sooner or later, listen to both sides of the story. Later on they are, of course, free to leave us; we always hope, however, that they will stay and be satisfied to improve our organization from the inside. I feel strongly that anyone who has a negative attitude toward the kind of organization they join starts out with a psychological disadvantage.

What will your new job and organization be like? What growth opportunities will you discover? How will you be treated by fellow workers and management? How will you feel 90 days from now?

Although each individual goes through a different transition, here are some positive factors you should anticipate.

Your ability to contribute will be respected. You were employed on the basis of your special skills, your attitude, and your long-range potential. You won out over others because you have more or better skills or the potential to learn them quickly. You were not employed by accident—you were hired because you have something going for you, so have faith in your own abilities. It will not take you long to earn the respect even of those who may be skeptical at the beginning.

Your employers have confidence in you. You were employed because you can make it. Interviewers and employers get to know the kind of individual who is most apt to succeed in their type of organization. Even if no testing instruments are used, they sense the traits and characteristics required, the temperament and attitudes needed, the physical stamina or dexterity demanded. They selected you because you are an excellent risk and they intend to provide the support necessary to help you succeed. Here are the comments of a personnel director for a large financial organization.

In most organizations probationary periods are not as important as they used to be because we are far more selective in whom we employ in the first place. If we hire somebody, there is only one chance in 20 that he or she won't make it. If employees falter a little, we step in and provide additional training to help them survive.

Your organization wants you to experience personal growth. It is the policy of most employers to provide incentives for a continuous growth pattern. They encourage employees to continue their education in their off-hours in order to prepare for the job ahead of them. They know that an individual who does not continue to grow can become stale and less productive. The illustration shows the pattern an individual might follow over a 20-year period inside the framework of a large organization.

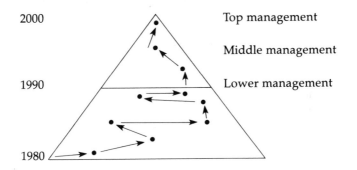

It is not uncommon for an individual to occupy twenty or more positions inside the same organization during a career period. The more upward mobility provided the better. The basic idea is to set up lines of progress that offer employees the opportunity to reach their potential so they will not be tempted to leave. Here is the way the administrator of a large hospital views the policy.

> We do everything possible to keep our capable people moving upward. It takes training on our part and patience on their part because we sometimes have more people who are ready to move up than we have positions open. But sooner or later, everyone who is deserving will get a chance. Organizations are much better today at identification of promotable people; getting lost inside an organization is not as prevalent as it was in the past. Only through the upward movement of people can an organization achieve high productivity, especially at the executive level. There is always a shortage of capable leadership. Even so, organizational loyalty is not what it was, so we anticipate a larger percentage of our good people will find better opportunities elsewhere.

You are a valuable asset. In the long run you can be a more important asset than the capital your organization possesses. The influx of new, motivated people of all ages constitutes the life-blood of an organization; that is why most agencies—both public and private—still send representatives to campuses to interview graduates, even when they have few openings. They want to get their share of the best graduates from each class to protect the quality of their leadership many years later. Money, machinery, and computers are important, but not nearly as valuable as people who know how to put them to work effectively. A civil service recruiter supports the premise with this statement: "We need strong, capable, and assertive people as much as or more than the private sector, but we are not always as good at communicating this need."

Short orientation programs can make your transition easier. You will be fortunate if the organization you join has a special one- or two-day training program for new employees. Orientation is (1) the easiest way to learn about retirement plans, profit-sharing, safety rules, regulations, and procedures; (2) the best way to gain a historical perspective of the organization; and (3) an ideal way to meet others who are going through the same transition.

Lengthy formal training programs provide advantages. Some organizations have formal training programs lasting from one week to many months. Under these programs the new employee usually attends classes and moves from one training job to another under close supervision until a final assignment is made. These programs, which come in many variations, usually have the following advantages: (1) a chance to meet executives, who often conduct classes that are part of the program; (2) the opportunity to learn the background of the operation; and (3) the privilege of making many important human contacts before receiving a starting assignment.

How do you compensate if the organization you join does not provide either an orientation or formal training program? You must do your own research. You must ask more questions, do more independent reading, and learn all you can from the position they assign you the first day.

Many other positive elements may present themselves to you. For example, a few sensitive people may provide you with assistance far beyond your expectations; your own desire to succeed may be stronger than you suspect, and this desire will help you make many otherwise difficult adjustments. If the feeling of "belonging" reaches you quickly, you will be caught up in a positive atmosphere of activity (especially during your break periods) that will dissipate any fears or misgivings you had at the start.

Now that we have discussed some positive factors, let's be realistic and look at some negative aspects that could reach out and touch you.

A few co-workers may be critical of you at the beginning. The moment you join a new organization you belong *legally;* that is, you are entitled to certain benefits and privileges. But co-workers might not treat you the same way you were treated by the interviewer. You may have to earn acceptance from a few of your fellow-workers. Some "old timers" have watched so many new employees come and go that they have little faith in new people sent to the department by personnel. If you are given more opportunities and treated better (including financial benefits) than new employees were some years ago, jealousy may cause them to set up psychological barriers. These workers will not accept you until you have demonstrated that you can carry your full share of the work load. Meanwhile, you can overcome this negative response by the way you treat these individuals. You can gain acceptance by your behavior, the way you assume responsibilities, and the way you communicate.

The conservative nature of an organization can be discouraging. It is possible that the organization you join may be more restrictive than you had anticipated. If so, you might adopt the attitude of this recent college graduate.

> I started to get negative right away when I discovered the advanced age of many executives and the conservative policies that came to the surface; then it occurred to me that maybe what I thought were disadvantages were advantages. For example, as I analyzed the age of the executives, I knew some were close to retirement and this could cause a chain reaction that would open up many positions. As far as the conservative procedures were concerned, it was obvious that changes had to come, and perhaps I could make my mark by helping to bring about change.

You may have to start out working under a demanding leader. Some supervisors are rather permissive in the way they operate their departments; others are strict disciplinarians. If you draw the latter, try to remember that you can learn a great deal from such a person and that adapting to her or his style can be a good challenge for you. Many supervisors who are very demanding of their people are the first to "go to bat" for them to obtain promotions and better learning assignments.

It is possible that nobody will take time to tell you how you are doing. You might find yourself in the same position as Helen who re-entered the labor market at the age of 39.

I received so little attention the first month on the job that I felt I was
not liked and not doing too well. Was I out of phase because of my age?
Was I failing to communicate? Neither of these things was happening.
I was doing great (I found out later), but nobody bothered to tell me.
Not even my supervisor. I guess many of us expect too much reinforcement. In many starting jobs if you don't hear much from others, you
are probably doing better than you think.

*The negative attitudes of fellow employees can lead you down the wrong
path.* Every organization—governmental, educational, or private—
seems to generate a group of people who have negative attitudes.
A few become bitter and vindictive. You will want to build good
working relationships with these individuals, but you will not
want their negative attitudes to influence you. You should make
up your own mind whether you like the organization you join. If
you eventually become negative and leave, the decision should be
your own. Do not permit those who have already become disen-
chanted (but still hang on) to persuade you.

*Frequent organizational changes (and rumors of changes) can shake you
up a little.* Some organizations, usually business or governmental,
change so often and so fast that the newcomer finds it difficult to
cope. This is the way a recent graduate explained his feelings toward the dynamic corporation he joined.

For some crazy reason, I had built a model business organization in my
mind; a company that functioned smoothly with few human problems
and great efficiency. Wow! Was I wrong! Unpredictable, disturbing, and
stupid things can happen. For a while I couldn't see how the firm could
break even, let alone make a profit. Things were far more disruptive
and unpredictable than I had expected. I had to learn that business
organizations must change with the economic winds or disappear.
Sometimes this means drastic personnel changes that come as a surprise; sometimes it means reassignments and new work responsibilities. All of these things came as a shock to me. I guess I had grown
accustomed to the stability and predictability of educational life.

All organizations have both positive and negative internal factors.
Many of these you will not discover until after you have been
"inside" for a number of days or weeks. No matter what you run
into, however, you will find some challenges that will test you.

*CHALLENGE 1: You can learn to live enthusiastically inside any orga-
nization if you want to.*

All organizations have restrictions, rules, protocol, procedures,
politics, and other factors that the newcomer must adjust to in

order to survive. In addition to this, *almost all organizations have less than perfect communication.* Result? Some new employees give up and look elsewhere. These individuals fail to accept the fact that every organization—government, educational, business—demands some conformity and adjustment. Such demands result from the nature of an organization and the very structure that holds it together. The only escape is to operate a business of your own. On the other hand, there is a certain fascination to every organization that presents a challenge. How did it get this way? How can it be improved? What are its strengths? How can I fit into it without becoming frustrated and negative? How can I use my sense of humor to good advantage?

CHALLENGE 2: You can prepare for a leadership role.

Not everyone should seek a management position; not everyone can be happy as a supervisor, but the opportunity and challenge is there if you wish to accept it. Contrary to popular opinion, most supervisors are happier than the people they supervise. Ask yourself the following five questions. If you give affirmative answers to four, you should give serious consideration to accepting the challenge. (1) Do you consider yourself a highly ambitious person? (2) Could you assume the responsibility of decision-making? (3) Would recognition from others be more important to you than taking pride in doing a detailed job well? (4) Would you be happier with more responsibility? (5) Do you desire the freedom to do your own planning rather than being told what to do?

CHALLENGE 3: You can accept the learning opportunities that surround you.

Your new job will offer you a multitude of learning possibilities concerning organizational structure, personnel policies, accounting procedures, product line (if any), leadership styles, and human relation involvements, in addition to skills you need to learn to achieve top job performance. The following comment from a city manager is appropriate.

> It took me 12 years to get a city of my own. I started out as the assistant to an assistant in a rather small city, but I was never bored because the learning opportunities were always there. I think many people underestimate the challenge of learning, or they permit periods of discouragement to turn them off. I cannot conceive of a job inside any organization that does not provide learning possibilities if the individual *wants* to find them.

As you conclude this chapter, the following data from a recent research project should be reinforcing to you. Despite frequent comments to the contrary, the CPC Foundation* reports that most employees are happy in their jobs. For example, in the monograph *Job Satisfaction—After College,* Ann Stouffer Bisconti and Lewis C. Solmon report findings that 54 percent of accountants, 69 percent of administrators, and 56 percent of allied health workers are very happy. Less than 10 percent of people in these classifications are not happy at all.

But whether you are happy or not, your first job should provide the experience you need to win a promotion—*even if the promotion is in another organization or career area.*

Discussion Questions

Six controversial opinions are quoted below. You are asked to agree or disagree with each one and then defend your decision.

1. "I honestly feel that every graduate should work for a minimum of five organizations before making a permanent choice. How else can you tell the good from the bad and eliminate the possibility of spending a lifetime with the wrong outfit?"
2. "The need to be accepted by fellow-employees is so great when you first start to work that there is no way to be selective; it is better to have a friend who hates the organization than no friend at all."
3. "There is a very dangerous trend among young people to select 90 percent of their friends from the place where they work."
4. "Once you start to become negative about an organization, there is no stopping or reversing it; you might as well resign."
5. "Unless you are a true specialist with definite skills, the only chance you have to succeed in a big organization is to prepare for management."
6. "Learning stops the moment one starts to become negative in an organization."

*P.O. Box 2263, Bethlehem, Pa.

Career
Profile

Tom Garcia
Area Personnel Manager
General Telephone of California

I consider myself a "late bloomer," since I didn't receive my degree until I was 33 years young, an age that might make some of you consider me part of the over-the-hill gang. Going to school at night, being married, and raising four children can make things pretty challenging. It seemed as though I had been going to school for as long as I can remember. There were many times when I would ask myself what I was doing among all those young people.

When I finally did finish my first two years, and considered myself to be a real academician—what a surprise I had in store. Armed with my Associate of Arts degree, I contacted some of those companies that I knew were out there just waiting for me to walk through their doors. "Sorry, but for the type of job you're looking for, you need a higher degree." So back I went.

At this point, I had plenty of time to consider what field I wanted to pursue. Finally the day arrived, June 1971, and there I was, marching in this procession about to receive what I had at one time thought to be impossible—that little piece of magic called a diploma, my Bachelor of Science degree in business administration with an option in labor relations.

One of the most difficult transitions in stepping from campus to the corporate world is learning to adjust and relate to a new environment. In my world, topics such as business, economics, and finance were subjects that other people talked about. My friends and acquaintances were the "good ole hard-working type." College and business were nice, but—.

Armed now with some stronger ammo, and convinced of my worth and ability, I was determined to convince the recruiters as well. I went through the regular series of on-campus interviews until I landed the one job that I felt was the right one. But there were a million thoughts going through my mind. How will it be? Will I be able to do what is expected? Will they like me? Will I like them?

A lot can be said for luck and being at the right place at the right time, but keep in mind that "luck is the residue of design and desire." Believe me, I had the desire. There were too many people behind me for me to fail. Without my wife's constant encouragement and support, I wonder if I would have accomplished all that I did.

I started my career with General Telephone of California as an employment representative in Santa Monica. Six years and various interesting positions in personnel later, I am area personnel manager of one of the more modern and progressive firms in the nation. It is a position where many of the things I read about in school have become realities, but the challenge never stops: there is always something new to learn and new ideas to implement.

If I had the opportunity to construct a class for graduating seniors about the adjustments and transitions that have to be made from the classroom to the office, it would deal with flexibility, adaptability, and corporate politics—a fact of life!

When going after that first job, know your priorities. Keep in mind the job climate, the labor market availability for your specific profession. You are now a commodity, and the more marketable you are the greater the demand will be. Your home state is not the center of the world. How willing are you to relocate? Texas, Arizona, Ohio, or —? Never undersell yourself; take an inventory of your abilities; know what you are worth, but be sure you can deliver!

The climb through the organizational hierarchy can be a great learning experience. Each step of the way offers an opportunity to learn, not only from the job but also from the people—new philosophies, interests, goals, and each time a little more about the ins and outs of the organization.

Don't allow yourself to judge individuals by their credentials or their lack of them, but rather on what each one has to offer. Learn to listen and listen well! I call it "picking brains." Being in personnel, I find myself interviewing almost everyone with whom I come in contact. Ask yourself, "What can I learn from this person?" I feel that this attitude has played a major part in my success thus far.

Never allow yourself to become complacent. Learning should never stop. I am currently back again working on still another piece of paper, my Masters Degree. When I graduated from Cal State University at Los Angeles, I thought this is it, I've had it! But, as I moved along my career path, values changed as well as priorities. I began to miss that learning experience, plus I didn't want to lose sight of the upcoming competition.

I am also teaching part-time at a community college. If anyone had told me when I was in high school that someday I'd be teaching, I would have told them that they were crazy. I was one of those that kept my fingers crossed in class in hope the teacher would not call on me, and I'd always be sure to be looking the other way when it came to volunteers. Remember? But being in the business world has instilled the confidence I once lacked.

Your job can have quite a significant impact on your personal life. Because a job can become very demanding at times, try to remember to keep everything in its proper perspective and balance.

Always remember: that step from campus to the office is what you make it. Set your goals realistically. Think positively; don't underestimate yourself. Learn to LISTEN, and always ask yourself, "What can I learn from this person?" *¡Buena suerte en el futuro!*

COPING

Adjusting Psychologically to Your New Environment

6

Moving from one environment to another can be an exciting but sometimes sobering experience. Many adjustments are required in moving from one organization to another, from a military role to a civilian job, from home responsibilities to a work assignment, and especially from a campus to a beginning career position. For many individuals, even those who have had many previous work experiences, some behaviorial and attitudinal changes are necessary for a successful transition.

The purpose of this chapter is to introduce you to a few situations that may require an unexpected psychological adjustment on your part. The discussion is based upon a number of interviews with people who have gone through the transition. It is hoped that the advance knowledge they provide will help you cope more gracefully and with a more perceptive sense of balance and humor. Their advice can prevent you from making some unnecessary mistakes.

Commitment remorse. A few days after you start your new job you may suddenly say to yourself, "What am I doing here? Why did I accept this job? Am I doing the right thing? Why have I made a commitment to do this?" If this happens to you, you will be suffering from a mild case of "commitment remorse." It usually comes after an individual fully realizes the magnitude of the change that has taken place. Certain events can happen to intensify the feeling. (1) You can receive an offer for another job you would have preferred in the first place. (2) Your first task can seem too easy, unimportant, and demeaning. (3) Your first supervisor may seem indifferent about your progress. Jane's reaction is typical.

I suffered a sudden case of remorse about the third day on my new job. There was nothing really wrong—just the terrible realization that my life had changed drastically. The fun years on campus were over. My career choice would be severely tested; and I had to prove to myself that I was a full-fledged adult whether I liked it or not. It was just a temporary thing with me. I felt much better about everything the following week.

Suppose, however, that after a long search you accept, through desperation, a run-of-the-mill job. Then a few weeks or months later, the chance of a lifetime occurs—you are offered the job that you really wanted in the first place. What should you do? You should accept the new opportunity and do your best to explain the situation to your first employer. No employment condition is legally binding unless a contract for a specified period of time has been signed (for example, in professional sports). You should, of course, provide ample notice and follow protocol in your resignation procedure. Chances are the organization that is losing you will understand. After all, they do not want you to remain with a feeling that your personal loyalty to them is denying you the opportunity you really want. Such a feeling would not be conducive to a positive attitude and high productivity.

Adjusting to negative comments. It is only natural that you should show up your first day at work with unusually high expectations because the person who hired you encouraged you to feel positive about the job. Negative comments from co-workers are seldom anticipated.

"It beats me why a nice person like you would join an overrated outfit like this."

"Things must sure be tough outside for you to accept a position with this organization."

"I hope you had your eyes open when you made the decision to be one of us."

Such comments should be interpreted as harmless teasing and testing and not taken seriously. It is not important what others think of the organization—it is only important what *you* think.

Rejection experiences. There is always the possibility that a fellow employee or a supervisor will openly refuse to communicate with you at the start. Such people do not want a personal relationship with you at this point, and they may reject you rudely. There are many reasons for this unexpected and uncalled-for behavior: (1)

The individual wanted someone else to receive the job you won. (2) The employee is frustrated about something else and is simply taking it out on you because you are new and available. (3) A prejudice of some kind exists. Whatever the cause, do not over-react and permit such an experience to destroy your confidence in your ability to cope. Just keep doing your job and stay ready to receive a signal whenever this person is ready to communicate. The more you stay calm and refuse to be intimidated, the sooner the individual will loosen up and be receptive.

Financial adjustments. Some unexpected, job-related problems (often financial) can cause a new employee to feel discouraged. For example, commuting may be more expensive than you first anticipated. The cost of parking may be an unpleasant surprise. Clothing demands may be higher than you expected. Salary deductions may add up to more than you originally figured. All of these possibilities, and others, can put you in the same position as Roger.

> All of a sudden, I knew my financial planning was not realistic; everything, including my apartment, was more expensive than I had figured. Although my starting salary was good, I soon discovered it wasn't going to stretch as far as I thought. It really got to me for a few days, and I guess my negative attitude was showing around the office. The realization caused me to do three things: (1) Restrict my immediate spending. (2) Revise my budget. (3) Motivate myself to get a promotion as soon as possible so my income would be higher.

Adjusting to high-discipline environments. Because of special circumstances, some organizations must maintain a high level of discipline, thereby creating an atmosphere that may be unfamiliar to, or uncomfortable for, some new employees. For example, a telephone company must require a high level of discipline to make sure all lines are open, during peak periods as well as slow periods, and that quality standards of service are maintained. Certain manufacturing firms, where safety is a key problem, must take unusual precautions that are restrictive. In the airline business, keeping time schedules puts an extra demand on employees. Such situations often force supervisors to draw very tight discipline lines. Perhaps the comment made by Steven will demonstrate the problem.

> I grew up in a rather free and open family. Very few controls were imposed. My college years were also rather permissive. You can imagine, then, what it was like to be thrown into a work situation where my

supervisor was standing over me all the time. The supervisor wasn't at fault; it was just the nature of the job. How did I cope? Frankly, I didn't think I could at first, and then I discovered my personal pride was at stake. I couldn't let my friends think I was a quitter, so I forced myself to adjust.

I don't think I was much fun to be around for a while, but I found that there are compensations. For example, you enjoy your break periods more. Then there is a better rapport among those who work with you. I think tight discipline has a tendency to pull people closer together. Maybe it is just that you learn to respect each other more. At any rate I made the adjustment and I now feel good about it.

Handling embarrassment caused by stupid mistakes. Few things can be more embarrassing than to fail at something you have been trained to do well. For example, can you imagine the chagrin of an English major who misspells an easy word in a written communication to management? Or an engineer who makes a mistake in arithmetic? All of these things, and more, can happen. Unless you can see a little humor in your own mistakes, you might get off to a rocky start with some people. Sam's error was combining business and romance.

I was accepted on a management training program for a chain of restaurants. My first assignment was operating a cash register. I permitted a waitress to check me out on it, but I was more interested in her than in what she was telling me. Result? I made so many dumb mistakes that I had to be retrained in front of everyone by the one person I was trying to impress—the manager.

Coping with skill deficiencies. What would happen if you drew a first assignment that required a skill you did not have or one you had failed to maintain? Your best procedure would be: (1) Face the problem quickly by asking someone on the job for help. (2) Cancel any plans you might have that night and spend some time on homework. (3) If necessary, pay an expert for some tutoring. Often the worst thing to do is to hide your lack of skill from others. Admitting that you need help can turn out to be an "ice breaker" with fellow employees. It is important to learn the skill so that you can demonstrate to others, including those who may have helped you, that you can achieve a high level of performance. To strengthen relationships with those who have "bailed you out," wait for an opportunity to do something of importance for them so they will fully understand how much you appreciated their help when you needed it the most.

Physical fatigue. You may be given a starting assignment that strains muscles you have not used for a long time or one that requires more energy than you have expended in a single day for months. Result? You may suffer from pure physical fatigue bordering on exhaustion. What to do? Your only answer may be to curtail your off-duty activities until you have built enough stamina. Tony's comments are appropriate.

> The best thing I can say about my starting job is that it got me back into physical shape. Of course, I almost lost the job in the process, and there were many sarcastic remarks about the physical stamina of college graduates. But I survived. My suggestion to all job seekers is to work out for five hours for every interview you have, just in case your first job is physically demanding.

Emotional strain. A new job places unusual demands upon the emotional structure of an individual. Some of the pressure, such as dwelling on unwarranted fears, can be self-imposed. Some unavoidable stress results from attempting to build good relationships with others, adjusting to the unexpected, and making the extra effort to start off on the right foot. Betty has this suggestion to make.

> After I had spent more than six months getting a job, you can imagine the emotional state I was in the day I reported. Being nervous caused me to try too hard and, what with the extra strain of coping with things and events that no one had told me about, I almost became a basket case. My advice? Find an off-the-job friend (as I did) who will help you relax by enjoying some physical exercise, prevent you from taking unnecessary stimulants, and let you "blow off some steam" away from work. The important thing is to get over the first impact without showing any indication on the job that you don't have full control of your emotions.

Mental fatigue. Your new job may put some unusual demands upon your mind as well as your body and emotional fibers. For example, chances are good you will be bombarded by all kinds of data, information, procedures, and names of individuals during your first few days. You may experience the kind of mental fatigue that occurs during final examination periods on campus. Antidote? Give your mind as much rest as possible after your workday is over.

The shock of drawing a difficult supervisor. Your chances of drawing an understanding supervisor are excellent, but if you should receive a very demanding one, your transition during the first weeks will be more complicated and difficult. In fact, your relationship with your supervisor could be your number-one problem. How should you handle it? Here are a few suggestions: (1) Concentrate on work performance in the effort to win her or his respect and understanding. (2) Work on building good horizontal relationships with fellow employees in the hope that the supervisor will appreciate your cooperative attitude and demand less of you. (3) Give the supervisor time to build a relationship with you; not all people believe that it is wise to build work relationships quickly. (4) Refuse to let anxiety intimidate you into making mistakes or reacting in a manner that shows loss of self-confidence. (5) Resist the temptation to challenge the supervisor unless, later on, you have clear evidence of prejudice or mistreatment. If it is necessary for you to go through an extremely difficult adjustment with your supervisor, many of your co-workers will be most sympathetic and supportive, and the better you handle the situation, the more respect they will have for you.

Discovering some politics you didn't anticipate. Within a few days or weeks you may realize that you have joined an organization full of internal politics. For those with high human relations standards, and little work experience, such a discovery can be most upsetting. It shouldn't be. Some degree of politics—people maneuvering for positions—can be found in *all* kinds of organizations: educational institutions, religious affiliations, government bureaus, military installations, and profit-making organizations. As an individual you can do very little to change the behavior of your fellow workers. If the level of politics is beyond your ability to cope, you should seek another work environment; otherwise, some adjustment on your part is in order. Do not abandon your own personal standards, but try to create and maintain strong, two-way human relationships with all people on an equal basis. If, in doing this, you live up to your personal standards, you are not playing politics but demonstrating good human-relations standards. You should anticipate, however, that others may interpret your efforts as politics. For a deep look into organizational behavior, read *The Ropes to Skip and the Ropes to Know.**

Recently, the author had the opportunity to ask a number of

*R. Richard Ritti and G. Ray Funkhouser; published by Grid, Inc., Columbus, Ohio, 1977.

young employees, most of whom were graduated several years ago, the following question: "What has happened to you during your transition period that you did not anticipate?" Here are the answers.

"I had never thought of myself as a leader, yet after I left school I found myself thrown into leadership roles. It has taken me seven years to accept my abilities, to feel comfortable as a leader, and to enjoy my position."

"I didn't think I had the potential. I wasn't fully aware of my capabilities as a leader."

"One month after I was hired, I was assistant manager, and I had to learn fast."

"All of the things that were expected of me from the very start were not anticipated."

"My job looked easier from the outside."

"I wasn't prepared well enough in the art of communication."

"I didn't expect I would have to become the breadwinner because of a divorce."

"Realization that *pride* was not the most important thing in life. Calling for *help* when I needed it wasn't something to be ashamed of."

"I didn't expect to be in management so fast. I thought I would be allowed a couple of years to learn the ropes."

"After not working for so many years, I never thought that I could adapt to holding down such a responsible job with so many demands on my time and physical energies."

"The relationships you build at work are not as long-lasting as I thought they might be."

"Not knowing what my next step might be within the company."

"The nature of the 'real' world outside the protected environment of the academic world."

"The responsibility of being a supervisor."

"Being on my own financially and emotionally."

"I expected to get a lot farther a lot sooner."

"The importance of maintaining a good image within the corporation."

"The pressure that exists and how to handle it."

"Having authority over people who are my own age."

"People not taking me seriously as a young married woman wanting a career."

"Having to be so aggressive."

"Learning to make it on such low starting pay."

You cannot anticipate your future fully when you start your career. The 18 profiles presented in this book clearly show that each individual must make his or her own special adjustments and develop a customized pattern.

Your transition into your new work environment will "test" you psychologically—in some ways you have never been tested before. During this period, you will need to rely upon your previous experiences, your self-confidence, and the support of others. By giving you a "preview," this chapter should help launch you in a manner both pleasing to yourself and to the organizational people who have faith in you. As you proceed through your transition, remember the following.

Adjusting to a new organization is an integral part of your longer journey to self-fulfillment. Experiences that require a difficult adjustment now may seem rather trivial later on when you have gained a long-term perspective. It is then you will discover that each experience can have lasting value, for example, by helping you to know yourself better, or by making you more flexible and more tolerant.

The great majority of people make their major contributions inside an organizational structure. You may feel resentment or even self-pity because you have to adjust to an organizational structure in order to work in our society. But more than 90 percent of all people who join the labor market are faced with the same transition problem. Only a few people can make their major contributions (or meet their personal goals) on an independent basis. Often these people achieve independence only after they have had the experiences of working for an organization.

This may not be your last organizational transition. By being objective now, you can learn to make your adjustment more quickly if a transition to a different organization seems advisable later. In other words, try not to become so personally enmeshed in the transition process that you fail to learn what you should from the experience.

Discussion Questions

Listed below are opposing statements from two different students (A and B) on the same topic. Defend the one of your choice.

1. Student A: I am going to play it safe and refuse to get involved in any politics I find in the organization I join.

   Student B: I am ambitious to move into positions of leadership, so I am going to participate in the human relations involvements that are always found in an organization—but I will do this on my terms and not lower myself to standards of those who play dirty politics.

2. Student A: I believe that at least 70 percent of the emotional fatigue a person encounters the first week on a new job is self-imposed and based upon fear of failure.

   Student B: I believe that at least 70 percent of the emotional fatigue a person encounters the first week on a new job comes from adjusting psychologically to difficult experiences that cannot be anticipated.

3. Student A: I have already made the adjustment to a few organizations, so I don't expect anything new.

   Student B: Despite the fact that I have been through some previous organizational transitions, I anticipate some surprises and difficult adjustments. I must not be smug about my previous successes.

4. Student A: Rejection by an individual in your personal life is not as hard on you as rejection at work, where career aspects are threatened.

   Student B: I am not going to be too concerned with any rejections from co-workers and supervisors; these forced relationships will have little impact on my long-term career. Such relationships can be treated lightly compared to personal relationships, which can devastate you.

5. Student A: I have accepted a job with a rather small organization that operates in a non-pressure, government-sponsored atmosphere because I don't feel I am psychologically mature enough to tackle a bigger organization at this time.

Student B: I have not had much experience and my self-confidence level is low, but I have decided to move right into a high-pressure organization because I think the demands of such an adjustment will help me mature faster and, in the long run, enhance my career.

6. Student A: I believe that the typical transition into a large organization should take about two weeks. By then you are either on your way or in trouble.

   Student B: Most transitions to large organizations take about 90 days. Up to that point you are still reacting to new experiences, adjusting to the general environment, and getting your act together.

**Career
Profile**

*Kae R. Hammond
Account Supervisor
J. Walter Thompson Company*

Probably the most impressive thought I can offer as I recall my
"beginnings" is that you don't get to the top overnight. Though this
might sound rather trite, believe me it can be tough swallowing
some of the groundwork necessary to be a real professional. I'm
afraid too many of us thought that a college degree was a guarantee
to success and rather expected to be hailed as the "educated
answer" as we entered the job market.

I would also add that at no time should you ever assume you
know enough, or worse yet, know it all. You don't.

I experienced a whirlwind job opportunity immediately after
stepping off the graduating podium. I landed a corporate publicist
position representing both NBC and Walt Disney. I was 21 years
old, had never really traveled to speak of, never lived away from
home, etc.—the real naive young girl story. My job was to handle
promotions and publicity around the country for an arena production the two giants had created and were jointly producing.

Well, I saw the world, at least most of North America, and I
learned a tremendous amount—mostly through hard experience.
Without exception, the single most difficult thing for me to deal with
in my transitory period was that college had not prepared me for
the real everyday, professional business world and that my knowledge of most things was still painfully limited.

Through the generous personal time of several professionals I met in my travels I gained a wealth of knowledge that has helped me many times since my "Disney days."

I feel that I give a good interview. But, because of my unusual first job experiences listed on my résumé, employers have often placed me in positions where I haven't always had solid experience. Because of that, one of my handicaps has been in not knowing all the things I wish I did. However, I have a lot of personal confidence and can think rather quickly on my feet. For this reason, I have been able to underplay my weaknesses by excelling in other areas. As a public relations specialist, I have served as a corporate spokesperson for several major national companies, appearing on television and radio. As I mentioned in the beginning, admitting your inabilities and weaknesses is not pleasant or easy, but I have had to do that several times. And when you are considered "outstanding" you don't like to have to backtrack and learn little things that most people assume (again) you know. But to succeed, you must.

In all of my job experiences, I have been basically on my own with little supervision. I have learned by doing rather than observing, which can be a disadvantage when pressed to excess.

After nearly two years of full-time travel, my tour came to an end with NBC and Disney. Unfortunately, even with all my current information about national media, I couldn't land the right kind of job I had in mind. So I formed my own public relations company with an associate, and we developed programs and campaigns for various companies. Though it was an extreme pleasure to be independently employed, it wasn't a gold mine. I later accepted a position with the California Avocado Advisory Board, who moved me to Kansas City and introduced me to the world of marketing development.

Although I wasn't enamored with all the job had to offer, I knew it was an opportunity to learn fast and run. That's just what I did! I found the produce industry difficult and negative since 99 percent of this industry seemed to me to be unreceptive to women.

Presently, I am an account supervisor in public relations with J. Walter Thompson in Chicago. I have been with the firm one year. The growth potential is really limitless when you are moving around the professional areas within a large agency as I am.

As you can see, I have been somewhat of a jumping jack these past six years. It can prove fatal to do this for too long a time, but in my case, I have been fortunate; I have learned in each situation something that has been needed for the next position.

When do you consider a job change? Well, it, of course, depends on each person's situation; however, if you feel you will not gain further useful experience or you have grown beyond your position demands, or if you find yourself in a nonlearning situation, that's a good time to re-evaluate your drives, needs, and goals, and then probably move along.

I can truthfully say I didn't encounter many people problems in terms of employee relations. I did experience a great deal of loneliness while I lived in Kansas City. It was a strange city and I averaged three weeks a month on the road, so making new friendships was almost impossible.

My personal life has swung with the tide. However, it would be less than honest of me to say that it was not affected by my position in the business world. Many men who have not yet reached their own success levels find it nearly impossible to cope with a genuine professional woman in their age bracket. I, therefore, saw older men socially. The benefits of this arrangement were that they knew through experience much of what I would face and gave me priceless lessons on how to combat or avoid the pitfalls.

I am now engaged to a mid-thirties professional in the publishing industry. My life will change rather drastically with marriage. I have lived alone for several years now and handled my life as it revolved around my career. There will soon be two careers to consider; so when an offer from warmer San Francisco came recently, I couldn't as easily consider it—we live in Chicago and two don't move as quickly as one.

I have achieved a level of success that is satisfying to me; I wouldn't say no to further advancement, but after nearly seven years (non-stop) of hard work, I have found someone that offers me a fulfillment that my work doesn't. I didn't think for many years that I would ever want to give enough of myself to handle the all-consuming job of wife *and* motherhood; it's amazing how time can mellow a person. Having more than tasted what goes on in the "outside" world, I can feel satisfied to devote myself to a more domestic life. However, I will always have my hand in the business world somewhere, since I seem to thrive on the stimulation gained in contact with the business environment.

It is most appropriate to label my college to present level transition a passage—one I wouldn't have passed up.

PROTOCOL
Developing Good Business Manners

7

For our purposes the word *protocol* means those courtesies, manners, and procedures considered proper in dealing with people within the typical organization. Protocol describes the acceptable but unwritten ways co-workers and executives expect you to act in certain situations. Rather than the word *protocol,* some people prefer to use the expression *business etiquette.* As you read this chapter, you may wish to develop your own code of personal behavior for the business world.

Protocol normally does not include such matters as how to complete an expense account, when to call in ill, or length of coffee breaks, because such procedures are usually specified in employee manuals. Protocol refers to more delicate matters in which you have a choice of behavior. You can act in a courteous, sensitive manner, a way accepted (and often expected) by both management and fellow employees, or you can behave in an insensitive, offensive, discourteous way that might embarrass you or injure your relationships with others. For example, it is seldom written out but generally accepted in organizations that employees should not go over the head of their supervisor to discuss problems of importance to the department. To "go over your supervisor's head" is a business cliché that refers to discussing departmental problems with an executive who has more authority than your boss.

There are many reasons why this short-circuiting violates acceptable behavior. (1) It puts the supervisor in an embarrassing position with superiors because a manager should have control over the department and be able to solve employees' problems. (2) It demonstrates a break in communication between the supervisor and the employee, and may suggest to management that the employee does not have the maturity to face the supervisor in an effort to work out the problem at the appropriate level. The seriousness of the problem is illustrated by this comment.

> It didn't seem to be a major thing when I did it, but going over my supervisor's head turned out to be a real faux pas. She never forgave me and one thing led to another until I finally decided it would be better to resign and get a fresh start.

Often demonstrating good business etiquette or protocol is simply a matter of applying common sense. Usually when you do what you interpret to be polite, in good taste, and customary, everything works out well. When work situations are more complicated, however, the inexperienced employee may not know the proper decorum. In such cases a high level of sensitivity and skill is necessary if human relationships are to remain undamaged. The following situations are therefore presented as guides to acceptable behavior in most organizations. There are, of course, exceptions and variations.

Individual communications. It is not easy to correct people, initiate conversations, and ask questions in just the *right way.* Often we offend others by coming on too strong in both face-to-face and telephone communications. In other words, there are two different ways to say the very same thing—tactfully or tactlessly. Check the examples below to see if you agree.

Tactless	*Tactful*
"Ms. Supervisor, I've got to see you by 5 o'clock. Can I come up now?"	"Ms. Supervisor, I will be able to up production tomorrow if I can get an answer from you today. Any chance you could squeeze me into your schedule for five minutes before 5 o'clock?"
"You made a dumb spelling mistake again."	"I notice that you have trouble spelling, just like me. I'd be lost without my dictionary."
"Mr. Smith, my boss asked me to tell you to get that Baker report in immediately."	"Mr. Smith? This is Mr. Brown's secretary. Before he left for a meeting, he asked me to call and remind you of the Baker report. If it is ready, I'd be happy to drop over and pick it up."

"Speak up! I can't hear you."	"Are you having trouble hearing me? Perhaps we have a poor connection."
"Hand me that tool, Hank."	"Hank, I'm in an awkward position here. Could you do me a favor and hand me that tool?"
"I'm sick and can't make it to work today."	"Judy? This is Alice Carper. I've got the flu and I don't think I'm up to coming in today. Can you get a replacement?"

Group communication sessions. As a beginning employee, you may have the opportunity to participate in both formal and informal group meetings. Your supervisor may call a staff meeting. You may be involved in special training sessions with people from other departments whom you are meeting for the first time. You may get deeply involved in informal discussions during breaks in your department or in the employee cafeteria. How can you participate effectively without offending others? How can you make a significant contribution and, at the same time, strengthen your relationships with those present? Here are some tips experienced group-dynamic experts might suggest.

1. Show that you are a patient, attentive listener by watching the speaker.
2. Avoid whispering to the person next to you. Whispering can be considered discourteous by the person speaking and by others who are listening.
3. Don't hesitate to enter into the conversation, but avoid interrupting others in the middle of their communication. Give each speaker a chance to present an idea with clarity and continuity, and withhold comment until you have complete comprehension of the topic.
4. When you sense it is your turn to speak, try not to show dislike for the previous speaker or impatience with the comments made.
5. Make your own contribution brief and to the point. Excessive talking on your part can be counter-productive in group sessions.
6. If you should offend another (and you know it), it can be a good practice to continue the communication privately after the meeting. Sometimes an apology is in order.

7. It is not a good practice to be late to formal meetings or to leave early.

Setting up communication sessions with superiors. As an employee, new or old, you have the right to seek and receive a private, two-way session with your supervisor whenever you think the need is sufficiently serious. There are even times when you can request a three-way meeting between you, your immediate supervisor, and the next superior above.

How do you set up a private session with a supervisor? In most cases, the best way is to do it in person rather than by telephone or written request. But, in all cases, remember these suggestions.

1. Make sure your timing is right. On days when your superiors are under heavy pressure, it would be to your disadvantage to pursue such a meeting.
2. The manner in which you go about making your request is important. Research indicates that supervisors prefer something like this: "Mr. Smith, I need at least 15 minutes of your valuable time as soon as you can provide it. It's very important." This request communicates that the problem to be discussed is serious, but it does not "push" the supervisor needlessly.
3. Avoid the temptation to "barge into" a superior's office under emotional stress. If this happens, chances are you will say too much in the wrong way and seriously injure the relationship. Sometimes a good night's sleep will put your feelings in a better perspective.
4. In some departments it is customary to make such appointments through the supervisor's secretary. Other, more experienced employees can tell you whether it is preferable to consult a secretary or to speak to the supervisor directly.
5. Protocol requires that you should make a firm appointment and be there on time.
6. You should usually enter another person's private office on invitation only and remain standing until offered a seat.

When and when not to go to management with a problem. You may run into some highly volatile and sensitive problems that are difficult to solve. For example, you could have a personality conflict with a co-worker or discover a dishonest employee working next to you. When should you try to solve such matters yourself? When should you go to management? And when should you forget it?

Accepted procedure in most organizations is: (1) Solve your own human relations problems if possible, but do not hesitate to go to your supervisor (or personnel office) if you have made your very best effort and failed. You should not permit a personality conflict to decrease your productivity over an extended period of time. (2) If you observe a dishonest action, the accepted procedure is to report it confidentially to management. In exceptional cases you might confront the employee on a person-to-person basis. But unless the quality of your relationship with this individual is exceptionally good, direct confrontation is not recommended. Report only what you have actually observed, then let management take charge. Do not feel guilty about the action you have taken.

What about on-the-job problems, such as those connected with production, better ways of doing things, or wasteful practices?

You are obligated to keep communication open between yourself and your supervisor for any suggestions that might improve the department. Most criticism, however, should be constructive. To report something that will place either a co-worker or a supervisor in an awkward position with superiors requires careful consideration and indisputable facts. Except in the most unusual of circumstances, such actions are not recommended. Here are some pertinent comments from an experienced supervisor.

> I learned a long time ago that going to management with a problem requires careful planning. First, you want to make sure the problem is one you can't solve yourself. Second, you want to make sure you have all the facts. Third, you want to weigh the human relationships involved. I try to make at least three positive suggestions for each problem that is distasteful. I want my overall image to be that of a source of good solutions, not someone who is always bringing unsolvable problems to management.

Keeping your personnel department informed. Your first responsibility is to report to your immediate superior. If your organization has a personnel department, you may be expected to inform personnel of changes in address, marital status, health matters, and other factors that might influence your work schedule or alter important permanent records.

Keeping your business and personal life separated. Your private life is your own business, and you are free to live any life-style you choose without interference from your employer. Protocol suggests, however, that you keep the two worlds separated. There are three areas in which social life is often intrusive: (1) Most organizations recognize that occasionally a personal telephone call is necessary to keep your personal life in order. Such calls may even help you function better as an employee. But do not abuse the privilege by making or accepting long phone calls that make work more difficult for others, and remember that those who charge long-distance calls to the organization are being dishonest. (2) Often two people who meet at work have a personal relationship off the job. To spend your working hours developing and enjoying such a relationship, however, is not acceptable behavior. (3) Employers want their employees to relax occasionally and have some on-the-job fun. But they do not appreciate socialization that lowers efficiency and productivity standards.

Many employees prefer to choose their personal friends among those they meet outside of the work environment. Your social life will be more varied if it includes both co-workers and others. An officer of a bank made this comment.

> We have a few employees around here who use their jobs as a launching pad for social purposes. This is wrong. The individual who depends upon fellow workers exclusively for a social life is overly dependent upon the company. I think keeping the right balance between your work and personal world is a matter of good taste.

Protocol when traveling as a company representative. A company expects an employee working away from the supervision of management to behave in a manner that will reflect a positive corporate image. An employee driving a company vehicle is expected to observe all traffic laws and highway courtesies. A telephone installer is expected to show good manners in the home of a customer. A sales representative on the road is expected to be courteous to travel agents, taxi drivers, hotel clerks, and other service people. Employees should follow standard tipping practices and report them honestly on expense accounts. Company plans should be kept secret and not discussed openly in public places. The new employee, going on a trip for the first time, should ask questions in advance so that acceptable patterns will be followed.

Grievances. If you work for a nonunion organization, a grievance should be presented to your immediate supervisor first. If the grievance is not resolved in a reasonable length of time, ask the supervisor to set up a three-way meeting between you, the supervisor, and the supervisor's superior. If this request is refused, inform the supervisor that you are going to take it further—even though this step is in contradiction to the rule of not going over your supervisor's head. If you work for a unionized firm, you should follow the procedures specified in detail in your union contract.

Resignations. It is still customary in most organizations to give advance notice of resignations. A minimum of two weeks is expected. Resigning on a face-to-face basis, with your supervisor and/or personnel officer, is the most acceptable form. Resigning by telephone or letter, without face-to-face communication and advance notice, is considered unacceptable behavior. The way you handle a resignation can affect recommendations to a future employer.

Appointment protocol. When a business meeting ends, watch for a signal that you should now make your departure. The supervisor terminates the meeting. To over-stay can be interpreted as discourteous, especially if the conversation has become trivial.

Attending off-hour company functions. Although attendance at company parties is not mandatory, before you decline such invitations it might be wise to: (1) evaluate the organization's expectations regarding such functions; (2) study the human relations implications to avoid offending your co-workers or superiors. It is considered polite to let those in charge know whether or not you will attend.

Telephone etiquette. There are a few simple rules you should follow in using the telephone for business purposes:

1. When answering the phone, it is considered a professional practice to identify yourself by name and department.
2. If you must ask the caller to hold the line, you should excuse yourself and return to the phone as quickly as possible.
3. When calling others, it is better to call back or leave a message than to interrupt an important meeting.
4. Telephone communications should be terminated as soon as the purpose for making the call has been accomplished adequately.
5. It is good business practice to return telephone calls as soon as possible.
6. Sensitive communications should take place in a private office, not over the telephone.

Regarding telephone conversations within hearing distance of other employees, the following comments are appropriate.

It took me a long time—and a very pointed comment from my supervisor—to realize I was talking too loudly into the instrument. My voice was so strong that I was disturbing others. It was also obvious to others that I was talking so much that I must be "turning off" the people on the other end of the line. This realization brought home the message that business telephone conversations usually should be like business letters—short and concise.

Written communications. A written communication should not leave your desk until errors have been corrected. Good grammar and spelling are especially important if the communication may reach upper management or leave the organization. Also, be sure that your data are accurate. Larry had to learn this the hard way.

> One day I became excited about a suggestion that could save the organization a lot of money. I wrote it out quickly, did my own typing, and submitted it to management. Later I discovered my memo included some obvious errors. From this unfortunate experience I learned three things: (1) Management *does* read such suggestions. (2) People can be extremely critical of errors. (3) A written signature implies agreement with the message, even if the information is wrong.

When in doubt, it is always best to take the time to consult a dictionary or a person who is well informed. A duplicate should be retained for all correspondence. Answer all incoming correspondence as soon as possible; to delay or forget is considered by many to be an act of incompetence.

Let others know where you are. If you find it necessary to leave your work station (except for regular breaks and lunch), you should let others know where you can be reached. This courtesy is particularly important when you leave the premises on personal business. When you must leave work early, perhaps for a dental appointment, most firms will expect you to request permission from your supervisor.

Utilization of equipment. It is considered a breach of etiquette to use a piece of company equipment and leave it in poor condition. If equipment breaks while you are using it, report the breakage immediately. Also, any room or office that you use should be left the way you found it. If you borrow equipment, return it promptly.

Eavesdropping. To deliberately position oneself to overhear private conversations is an invasion of privacy and very poor taste. If you inadvertently overhear something of a private nature, good etiquette says that you should not repeat it to others.

Report all mistakes. Should you make a mistake in procedure, slightly damage company equipment, or offend a customer, it is a good policy to report this fact as soon as possible. To cover up a mistake, even a very small one, can result in serious consequences later.

Asking questions. New employees need to ask questions to avoid making mistakes or violating protocol, but to ask at the wrong time or in the wrong way offends others. It is considered taboo to ask too many questions. Here are some tips.

1. Don't interrupt a person who is in conference.
2. Don't ask a question if you can look up the answer in a manual.
3. Don't ask a contrived question in an attempt to compliment a person or to initiate communication for your own purposes.
4. Don't ask prying questions involving matters that are none of your business.
5. Ask questions in a quiet way.
6. Listen carefully as you receive the answer. To ask a question and then not listen to the answer is impolite.

Promises. Most executives and co-workers consider a promise a personal commitment that should be honored. Good business practices are violated if you fail to keep appointments, keep others waiting by showing up late, or fail to deliver something that you have promised. If you say you are going to do something, *do* it. A manager comments on the high cost of broken promises.

> When I first started my career I was free with promises but sometimes forgot to honor them. No more. I discovered that breaking a promise can damage a working relationship faster and more permanently than anything else you can do. There is just something about a broken promise that people can't forget.

Miscellaneous. Here are some other rules of good business etiquette.

1. Talking in a negative manner about a person not present is considered unprofessional.
2. Discussing a business matter in a crowded elevator is in poor taste.
3. Stealing an idea from another person and taking credit for it is unethical.
4. Smoking in someone else's office or presence is considered impolite unless you ask and receive permission.
5. Learning names, pronouncing them properly, and using them at appropriate times in the communications process is

very important. For those who find learning and using names difficult (most people), enrolling in a memory course may be helpful.

6. Using formal names in addressing others is considered polite until permission to use first names is given.
7. Demeaning advances to a member of the opposite sex is a breach of good taste.
8. "Crashing" a formal or informal business meeting, even a group having lunch together, is often considered brash. Moving ahead of others when a line is forming is impolite.
9. Asking superiors for favors that are not being granted to others is considered a breach of good human relations.
10. Speaking or laughing in a voice so loud it disturbs others is considered insensitive and poor manners.
11. Failing to contribute your full share toward coffee funds, co-worker gifts, and other expenses, including lunch or refreshments with co-workers, is damaging to human relationships.

Just as each separate culture develops its own code of behavior, so does each organization. When you join an organization, learning and adapting to the mores and customs is necessary if you are concerned about your personal image and reputation. To violate customary practices without a good reason often invites censure from those who have been adhering to the rules before your arrival.

There is usually an accepted or best way to do everything within an organization; if you are in doubt, do not hesitate to ask for guidance. Learning by making unnecessary mistakes is damaging to a career. If you unknowingly violate a standard procedure, it doesn't hurt to apologize to those who have been offended.

Chances are good you will discover some obsolete and archaic customs inside your new organization. You can become an "agent of change" if you are patient enough to follow accepted procedures and protocol.

Discussion Questions

Six vignettes appear below. Please defend or oppose the action taken by the employee in each vignette.

1. For three months Katy did everything she could to work out a good relationship with her supervisor. She carried her part

of the work load and more. She made at least five special efforts to establish communication. She built good relationships with her co-workers, but all she received from her supervisor was behavior that she interpreted as rejection. Yesterday she took the problem to her supervisor's superior. *Would you defend Katy's actions?*

2. Juan had been a participant in five sessions of a management training seminar conducted by a company official. Most sessions were dominated by a fellow trainee who was so offensive that Ralph was certain his own resentment was shared by the other 18 members. During the sixth session Juan deliberately challenged this trainee. The atmosphere became tense, but Juan thought that his action would win the support of the majority of those in the seminar even if it annoyed the company official and made an enemy out of the abrasive member. *Was Juan's strategy wise?*

3. Eloise had tried in a quiet way to set up an appointment with her supervisor for six weeks. Each time she made a request, the supervisor made an excuse. Finally, Eloise cornered the supervisor and made this statement: "Look, I've been trying to get some time with you for weeks. Now either I'm worth 30 minutes of your time, or I'm going to create some fireworks above you. I'm willing to do this even if it costs me my job." *Did Eloise do the right thing?*

4. Mel gets along beautifully with all but one of his co-workers. This individual seems to have some kind of deep-seated resentment toward Mel. The resentment or jealousy manifests itself in various forms of innuendo and "cheap shots" so subtle that only Mel knows what is going on. Yesterday Mel spent more than an hour discussing the problem with his supervisor and the personnel officer. *Was Mel's action justified?*

5. Last week Margaret's son broke his leg in a ski accident. Since that time Margaret has been calling him from work on the average of four times each day. She spends about ten minutes on each call. *Are these telephone calls defensible?*

6. Two weeks ago Maria was asked to fly to a major city in a neighboring state to consult with a client on some computer problems. Maria permitted the client to buy her a number of drinks before dinner. The discussion that followed dealt with personalities of officials in her company as well as the problem itself. *Could Maria be censured for her conduct?*

**Career
Profile**

*Theresa Lock
Travel Agent
Ontario (California) Travel Bureau*

I went to school in Hong Kong and graduated from a school that is roughly equivalent to a junior college in the United States. My goal was to major in biochemistry at an American university.

Unfortunately my plan was interrupted by my mother's poor health. Disappointed but not discouraged, I decided I would step into the job market for a while.

Like most new graduates, I didn't know what field I should enter. As I had no specific skills, I had to rely on selling my only asset—my pleasant personality. Bearing in mind that all jobs are beneficial, because they bring in not only money but also valuable experiences that can lead to better and more responsible positions, I decided to apply for any position open in the airlines. (In Hong Kong airline offices, there is a frequent turnover because most girls resign when they get married.)

My second step was to prepare an impressive résumé. I typed it neatly in an organized manner so it could be understood at a glance. I also found that letters of recommendation from teachers, parish priests, and persons of responsible position helped a great deal in introducing the applicant.

I was indeed very lucky. After several interviews and physical tests, I, along with a few others, was chosen from hundreds who applied. My first position was as a check-in clerk with a locally based airline. I was told later that the main reason I was picked was my sincerity and self-confidence during the interview.

I always liked people, so I knew that I would be very comfortable in this job. During the first month of training, I studied very hard so I could be top of my class. (Secret for future promotion!) I tried to comprehend all phases and responsibilities of this position by observing others and reading our company manual. I had always thought that airline hostesses had glamorous jobs. I then realized it took a lot to project that image. You have to be very efficient and fast and at the same time stay calm, cool, and collected trying to beat the clock. The flight must leave on time! This is the final goal of our teamwork.

I also learned that when in doubt always consult your senior. The worst thing you can do is to pretend, for eventually your ignorance will show by the mistakes you make. The best way to learn is to ask. There is a Chinese saying, "A great scholar is one who, when in doubt, is not ashamed to ask even his inferior."

As much as I loved the airlines job, I had to resign after five years of service. I got married and emigrated to the United States where my husband works.

I was very sad to leave the career that I enjoyed so much, but I was also looking forward to my new role in life and to this new country that I wanted to go to five years before.

After I was more or less accustomed to my new environment, I began to look for work. The irregular hours of airport jobs did not suit my married life; therefore, I chose a related field—travel agent. Once again, I was very lucky. After I made a few phone calls to the travel agencies listed in the Yellow Pages, one company asked me to come in for an interview the next day, and I got the job without difficulty. I'm still working for that agency.

The work of a travel agent is more complex than airline work since it covers flights, cruises, and tours. It is even more competitive than airlines since there are many agencies in the same area. The best ways to win clientele are good manners, efficiency, and empathy. I always put myself in the position of the client and work out the best possible deal for them.

This is a very challenging and interesting job. However, I do feel my limited English vocabulary is a big drawback and slows down my usually fast working pace. I am currently enrolled in an evening college to improve my writing skills. To work full time and then go to school at night for several nights a week is not too easy when I have to also take care of household chores. But with the understanding of my husband and careful planning, things usually work out.

OVERLAPPING
Impact of Life-Styles on Career Progress

8

Some executives feel that a growing number of recent graduates are not keeping their private and career worlds sufficiently separated. Here are three quotations from personnel directors confronted with what they see as a growing problem.

> I realize that employees work primarily to support their life-styles and that is the way it should be, but I hate to see their private lives overlapping into their work world to the point that they are hurting their career progress.

> Our most promising young executives often let their personal lives get so mixed up that their on-the-job productivity is seriously damaged. You'd be amazed how often we have had to pass up promising prospects for a promotion because they can't come up with a proper mix between their two worlds.

> What our employees do with their private lives is none of our business. We are only concerned with their work behavior. The vast majority have learned to keep the two areas separated like professionals; a growing number, however, seem unable to do this, or they don't want to. I hope they realize what it is doing to their careers.

What causes this injurious overlapping? What are the tolerance levels of organizations regarding this problem? What can you do to keep the problems of your personal life from damaging your career?

Many things that happen to people make it difficult for them to keep their two worlds separated. Here are a few.

Extended weekends. Weekend activities such as long trips, mini-vacations, and difficult hikes can cause problems two ways. First, when they are poorly planned and overextended, they can cause the employee to report for work a few hours or even a day late. Second, they can cause the employee to be so exhausted that productivity is lowered and damaging mistakes result.

Jake and Sally had an enviable life-style because Sally, as an airline employee, could arrange free trips on a stand-by basis. They took weekend trips to Hawaii, Miami, and other points of interest. The fun lasted for more than two years, but finally Jake, who had begun a brilliant career as an executive with a large investment house, was released because he had neglected too many responsibilities. Both Jake and Sally had to learn the hard way about balancing their roles in their two worlds.

Excessive commuting. In most cases people can live where they want to live and commute to their jobs without any trouble. But a few people stretch their commuting too far. Some try to drive as far as 100 miles each way. Others want to live in the mountains, where they are frequently snowed in. Still others buy a place in the country and spend more time trying to fix it up than they spend on their jobs.

Linda had always wanted to live high in the mountains where there was clear air and the scent of pine trees and where she could ski on weekends. Although her career as a teacher was forty miles away in the valley, she thought she could make it work. When she was refused tenure, it was pointed out that in one year she had called in nine times saying that roads were not passable and had been late to her classes twelve times. Many serious student complaints had been received.

Affairs and separations. Most people can have involving love affairs or go through a separation or divorce without any appreciable damage to their careers; others cannot. Although most organizations have a high tolerance level for affairs of the heart, the mental, emotional, and physical health of some people is so damaged that they cannot prevent a spillover into their career progress. An executive for a large retail chain made this comment.

> There was a time in this organization when someone would go through a divorce and we would never know about it. The personal pride the individual had in keeping his or her job performance high was so great that there was little, if any, overlapping. Today, people don't seem to have the personal discipline or pride to keep things separated. I have watched divorce really ruin promising careers for both men and women and, in my opinion, it really didn't have to happen.

Children. Many unmarried men and women are faced with the

challenge of rearing children while keeping their careers on a successful track. Some of these single parents become too absorbed in their children. They may spend 30 minutes a day talking to their children over the telephone, or talk so much about their children that they alienate co-workers and supervisors. Some worry about their children so much that poor on-the-job concentration results in unnecessary mistakes. Here is the comment of a perceptive woman personnel manager, who is rearing children alone.

> I think it all boils down to a matter of personal discipline. We have many employees at all levels who are rearing children as singles or under strained circumstances. Most do a great job because they put their small children in good preschool programs and train their school-age children to understand that trying to run their homes from work will have a negative influence on their lives if the parent's career is damaged. We honestly feel at times that we are being needlessly "used" by some parents. We are going to continue to employ singles and others with children to rear, but we are going to provide more guidance in counseling sessions so that they will have more success in keeping their two worlds more clearly separated.

Financial pressures. Those who work in personnel services departments are in an excellent position to see and evaluate the overlap of financial stress on career progress. Here are the comments from an assistant personnel officer for a transportation firm.

> Inflation puts a heavy burden on many of our new employees, especially those who have yet to move into positions of greater responsibility and financial reward. We understand this and worry about it, but we also sense that it is self-defeating for ambitious employees to permit themselves to be constantly in an emotional state over their financial problems. Some employees try to live a life-style that is beyond their means at this point in their lives. I have heard a number of them say they wish they had taken a course in financial planning when they were in college.
>
> I have also watched many highly promising careers fall apart because the employees were poor at financial planning. Some resort to "moonlighting," which can hurt progress in their primary jobs. Some damage their credit ratings to the point that we are notified. Still others permit financial worries to drag them down instead of motivating them to work harder and eventually earn more. Last month, during an exit interview with a promising employee, I gambled and made the statement that when he reached financial maturity, he would also reach career maturity. I hope he got the message.

Alchohol and drug excesses. In many firms it is acceptable to laugh off a hangover now and then. But when excessive drinking or drug use becomes a common occurrence, it has a subtle way of destroying working relationships with fellow employees and managers. Mistakes caused by excesses, especially when safety regulations are involved, are cause for termination or transfer. The president of a large corporation indicated that the problem is critical.

> Alcoholism has been a major problem with us. We have lost not only many capable people in the junior management level, but also some of our promising vice-presidents. Although many individuals are temporarily successful in keeping alcohol excesses from overlapping into their career world, eventually it shows up in lower productivity and poor decision-making. It hurts to watch a highly capable person spend 20 years reaching the top in a corporation and then blow it all through excessive drinking.

What is the tolerance level for life-style spillovers, including extended weekends, alcoholism, and other excesses? Obviously, each educational institution, government agency, or private firm has its own tolerance point beyond which some action is taken.

Organizations vary in the extent to which they will tolerate disruption resulting from an employee's life-style. The chart below shows how, in a typical organization, excesses can rise from a level of little or no damage to the level that precipitates termination.

Human-relations damage level. Career damage first becomes evident when human relationships—both horizontal and vertical—are hurt. The employee who frequently takes three-day weekends

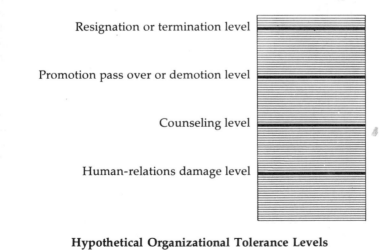

Resignation or termination level

Promotion pass over or demotion level

Counseling level

Human-relations damage level

**Hypothetical Organizational Tolerance Levels
for Life-Style Overlappings**

or arrives at work exhausted on Monday, for example, is placing an extra burden on fellow employees in the department and unnecessary demands on his or her immediate supervisor. Fellow employees and supervisors tolerate inconvenience if a co-worker has been ill, but the tolerance level drops when they suspect the cause to be a life-style overlap, rather than a legitimate illness.

Counseling level. Although it is very difficult for supervisors or personnel directors to talk about life-style "spillover" problems, action is necessary when productivity and the morale of other employees is measurably lowered. In calling individuals in for this kind of counseling, supervisors are fully aware of the possibility of invasion of privacy, so they deal *only* with on-the-job performance and hope the employee gets the overlap message. Absentee records, personal productivity figures, and previous evaluation forms are often introduced at such sessions.

Such counseling sessions (often called discipline counseling) are also documented, sometimes on forms requiring the signature of the employee, so that there can be back-up evidence in case more serious action, including termination, should take place at a later date.

A distinction should be made between voluntary life-style overlaps (such as extended weekend vacations) and unavoidable overlaps. Most organizations are both liberal and understanding when it comes to unavoidable personal problems, like the serious illness of a spouse. Most organizations will also do everything possible to assist the employee who has a serious problem. Such assistance can include a series of counseling sessions or visits to medical doctors, private counselors, or psychiatrists. Most organizations make a serious and concerted effort to save the career of an employee no matter what the cause. When life-style overlaps result from voluntary behavior, however, counseling is a warning that should be taken seriously.

Promotion passover or demotion level. Sometimes, but not always, an organization will go through a series of counseling sessions before passing the employee over for a promotion. Counseling sessions almost always precede more serious actions, such as geographical or horizontal transfers, demotions, and other serious actions. Although each case is different, and each needs to be fully documented, such actions are often justified on the basis of the measurable damage to employee morale and productivity. A surprising number of life-style spillovers reach this stage. Some observers think the number will continue to increase.

Termination level. Under present laws, termination must be for causes that can be fully documented. In most organizations, very few formal terminations take place. Many individuals, however, choose to resign when they sense that their careers have been damaged through their life-style spillovers. They wisely make the decision that a fresh start is much better than trying to live down damages that have already taken place. In many cases, moving to another organization motivates the individual to achieve a better balance between his or her two worlds; in other words, the employee doesn't make the same mistake twice. In other cases, however, the individual has so little self-discipline that the same mistake is made repeatedly.

What can you do to keep your life-style from hurting your long-term career? Here are two simple suggestions.

Take pride in keeping your worlds separated. You can live the life-style you wish without any career conflicts if you choose to do so. It will take self-discipline, but it can be done if you want it that way. What motivates those who are most successful? Personal pride! They want to be professional in their career world, and they know professionalism is impossible unless their worlds are separated. They often view co-workers who needlessly let their life-styles overlap as weak, immature people who lack high career goals.

Take any signals you receive seriously. You will need to be realistic about what you can and cannot get by with in your organization. The tolerance levels are there, and you don't want to push too hard. A few people think they can deceive their employers. For the most part, these individuals deceive themselves by ignoring the preliminary signals that would keep them from reaching the first level of human-relations damage.

Discussion Questions

1. Which of the following kinds of organizations do you feel have the highest and lowest tolerances for life-style spillovers? Justify your selections.
    a. Government bureaus
    b. Educational institutions
    c. Industrial factories with union contracts
    d. Hospitals
    e. Giant service corporations (nonindustrial)

     f.   Small business organizations

     g.   Retail store chains

     h.   Professional sports

2.   Life-style spillovers seem to be increasing. Two possible explanations are: (1) Modern life-styles are more difficult to keep separated; (2) people leading these life-styles have less self-discipline. Which do you feel is the primary cause? Explain your choice.

3.   What changes would you make in the tolerance chart presented in the chapter? Explain your answer.

4.   If you were president of a company, would you post such a chart in the employee lounge? Defend your decision.

5.   Do you know an unmarried individual who is rearing children and has mastered the spillover problem? How has the individual accomplished this goal?

6.   Do you know an individual who has gone through a difficult divorce but managed to keep it from injuring her or his career? How has the individual been able to achieve this goal?

**Career
Profile**

Lynda Nichols
Executive Secretary
First National Bank and Trust Company

I am a graduate of a community college where I received my Associate of Arts Degree as well as supplemental merit awards and honors in the Secretarial Business Division.

Most first jobs are a steppingstone to better jobs. If you can't get into your chosen field immediately, by all means do as I did. Get as much preliminary or temporary experience as possible in a position where you will be able to practice your skills. Even if your first job is in an unrelated field, just remember that all your subsequent and varied knowledge will be valuable wherever you decide to "make your home." For example, I have worked in a bank now for eleven years, but my first job experiences were in a school district. Needless to say, dealing with instructors and teaching materials in no way relates to banking. Except in both experiences I used my secretarial skills and learned helpful things about human relations and job responsibility. For instance, for a while I think I treated people like objects. I had to develop a sense of caring and compassion for the staff I worked with, as well as for people in general. People have feelings—and for the most part you deal with a new combination of people every day. I'm glad I realized that fact before I lost my job!

I really believe every job hunter should assemble a résumé, either alone or with the help of an agency. And it's important to review it yearly and keep it up to date. I believe my neatly prepared résumé showing my past work experiences and schooling made a tremendous impression on all my prospective employers. Not because it showed a long list of prior experience (wishful thinking!) but rather because they could see at a glance my background, and it also provided a real base for conversation between my prospective employer and me.

The first thing I did on my new job was to learn my duties and responsibilities. I tried to be as accurate and consistent as possible in my daily performance. Achieving these two qualities required a positive mental attitude and a great degree of concentration.

Patience is another virtue well worth mentioning. From October of 1966 to June of 1968 I worked as a teller. This, remember, was only an entry-level position to me because all the time I had dreams of becoming a secretary. Then, after graduation in 1968 I became a full-time employee and was promoted to a secretarial position. Since starting my secretarial career in 1968 I have reached different levels of success in the secretarial ranks—from new accounts clerk to my present position as executive secretary to the manager of the largest office in the system, from which I am preparing for a management position.

The road has not always been paved with gold. As you will see, there will be a number of forked roads. How will you know which one to choose? It's sometimes very difficult. Whatever you decide, try and gauge it as a means to the attainment of your goals and aspirations. For instance, I was proficient and reliable as a teller, and I probably could have remained there very comfortably. Nevertheless, I gave up the known for the unknown because the switch meant that I was on the way to fulfilling my ambitions.

Making the change from school to everyday real-life situations can be stressful. I've found that when you work with people, you have to be somewhat flexible in your actions, evaluations, and decisions, lest you group everyone into little boxes. The phenomena of change is always present. By working as I went through school, I had a chance to view and compare both life-styles simultaneously. I really learned that being a good, competent secretary involves a great deal more than typing and filing and making coffee. Often you're called upon to be a public relations person, to plan and organize internal activities, coordinate and arrange appointments and meetings—just a fantastic realm of "glamour" assignments. But there are times when the job demands all the patience, stability, calm, level-headedness, organization, and inner faith you can muster.

I feel that a change in position, or to another office, is a good morale and confidence builder in that it gives you a chance to grow in knowledge about the company as well as to develop new personal and work skills. Whenever you can, take a beneficial or a refresher course so that you will be prepared when the opportunity does come for advancement.

My husband and I took a number of night classes together until about four years ago when we became parents of twin girls. After being on maternity leave for five months, I returned to my former position. The experience of working, caring for my husband and our children, and maintaining a home brought some interesting changes and attitudes to my life. It seems that a major adjustment had to do with keeping my thoughts on my job. How tempting it was to call and ask about the children. Of course you should be a concerned parent! And it's normal to want to be sure they are being taken care of properly. Know what I discovered? I had to put my confidence in my babysitter and rely on her judgment. If there is a problem, then she lets me know by a brief, informative telephone call. If you find it difficult to rely on your babysitter, change to another helper. You're in a situation now where you must have an extension of yourself in order to accomplish all or most of the daily tasks. Your "extension" usually is a babysitter, either in your home or at someone else's, and later on possibly a nursery or preschool. I believe that having a very competent babysitter to begin with, and later on a preschool, was the secret to my success of keeping my working hours virtually free of telephone interruptions concerning my family. Any firm will be quick to tell you that they pay you for job productivity and not for personal phone conversations. Only an emergency call should take you more than two or three minutes of your employer's time.

As you enter the job market, plan your future, set high attainable goals, review them regularly, and check your progress, watch your steps as you go, and have a good laugh as often as you can, occasionally at yourself. A good sense of humor is indispensable!

PRODUCTIVITY
Reaching Standards and Beyond

9

When you join a new organization, you may have the opportunity to learn a great deal *before* you receive your first assignment. You may, for example, spend some time on a formal training program; you might receive some specialized technical training; there may be some other form of preparation. *But one day you will receive your first permanent assignment.* When this happens, your career reputation depends upon two things: (1) raising your personal productivity to acceptable standards; (2) going beyond that level to reach closer to your personal potential. The illustration below will help you understand the challenge.

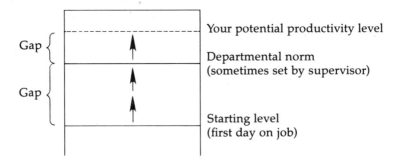

For the purposes of this chapter, productivity means the total contribution the individual is making to the department. Measuring productivity is not always easy. For example, it is relatively easy to measure the productivity of a salesperson because results are recorded primarily in dollars; on the other hand, the productivity of an airline steward is more difficult to measure because of many intangibles, such as handling difficult situations, providing services to passengers, and making other important contributions that do not show up in figures. But even if value judgments by superiors are involved, everyone, to a degree, is measured.

The term *norm* is used to designate that level where most employees in a specific job *normally* operate. In assembly-line work, where piece work is involved, norms can be set scientifically. For example, in the needle trade, the norm for a button-hole machine operator could be two per minute or 120 per hour. For a teller in a bank the norm could be 25 transactions per hour. In some departments norms are set by the employees themselves on a very unscientific, observation basis. In short, they have figured out in their own minds just about what a good day's work amounts to.

In isolated jobs where comparison between employees is impossible, norms or acceptable standards are set by management. The employee who reaches or comes close to the acceptable standard is considered to be a good, average employee. The employee who is somewhere below the standard is considered marginal. To be considered exceptional, excellent, or above average, the individual must be consistently above the norm.

The new employee must realize that in almost all cases productivity *is* measured. There is virtually no escape. It is also important to realize that the term *standard of performance* can mean different things in different organizations: (1) *average performance* (the mean of all employee productivity on identical jobs); (2) the minimum level of performance *acceptable* to management (not always clearly defined and communicated); (3) the base or *bottom line of excellence*. (In other words, excellence is required, and each employee is expected to reach that level in order to stay on the job.)

What all this means is that the employee needs to discover quickly the standards of performance expected where he or she is employed. How such standards are measured is of secondary importance.

The term *potential* means the highest level of personal productivity that it is possible for you to reach under ideal circumstances when you push yourself. Some highly ambitious people live close to their potential, but few actually reach it. There is usually a gap between performance and potential.

The first day on a new job nobody expects you to contribute as much to departmental productivity as you will at a later date. In a very simple job you might reach acceptable standards in a few days; in other assignments it might take weeks. Your first goal, however, should be to reach the norm set by co-workers or your supervisor. In other words, you want to reach that point where you are contributing as much to the total productivity of the unit as any other person. Put another way, you want to "carry your full share of the work load." There are two basic reasons why you want to reach this point as soon as possible.

You will earn the respect of your supervisor and co-workers. Although you might build excellent relationships with others by being friendly, courteous, and understanding, some people will not fully accept you until they know you are doing your full share of the work. Martha had this experience when she joined the data processing center of a large organization.

> Everything went well for the first few months. My co-workers were very considerate and polite. Yet I felt they were holding back a little until I demonstrated that I could handle the job. They seemed to have their eyes on my performance as much as on me as a new personality in the center. Then, when I was finally processing as much data as the others, relationships quickly improved. It seems they withheld a small portion of their friendship until I had passed an unspoken, unwritten performance test. At that point I relaxed and knew that I was accepted.

You will feel better about yourself. The anxiety that accompanies a first job assignment cannot be dissipated until the individual knows that existing standards have been met. Self-criticism is the outgrowth of personal pride. The experience Jerry had on his first assignment is typical.

> I already knew the norm I had to reach in my first assignment because technical skills were involved, and my training had been very specific. Could I meet the standard in a reasonable length of time? Some days at the beginning I had my doubts; but, thanks to the help of some fellow workers, I finally saw the light at the end of the tunnel. It's hard to describe the good feeling I had about myself—the way a mountain climber feels when he or she has scaled a difficult peak. There is nothing in the world more personally satisfying than accomplishing something difficult that you prepared yourself to do.

How do you go about equaling the productivity of those already working? How do you meet the standards expected of you? How soon should you be able to reach the norm? Here are some suggestions that could help to answer these questions.

A few mistakes will not impede your progress. In their rush to reach higher personal productivity levels, some ambitious employees pay the high price of making too many mistakes. Haste is unnecessary because most employers allow ample time for newcomers to reach expected levels. But if you make a mistake, remember that sometimes co-workers will identify with you if you show the right attitude. Hans made this discovery.

> I was so nervous about making a mistake that I made more than I should. Then I discovered that a few of my co-workers were willing to come to my rescue in a nice, friendly way. Later I also discovered that these individuals were my greatest supporters. I learned from them that it is important to accept help gracefully and with appreciation. Funny, but they actually like me better because I had made some mistakes.

It is often better to try and fail than to hold back. You do not want to make the mistake of barging ahead too fast on your first assignment, but you don't want to sit back on the sidelines too long, either. If you show a willingness to learn, a willingness to try, you will quickly gain the support of others, and you will "catch on" sooner than you think. Mary and Joyce were assigned to the computer section of a large insurance company after two days of orientation. Since neither had received advance training, both were assigned to a sponsor. Mary, however, was more cautious than Joyce. She kept saying, "Is it okay if I wait another day or so to try?" Joyce, on the other hand, would try anything at the drop of a suggestion. Of course, she made more mistakes than Mary, but it was obvious to all, including Mary, that Joyce had learned more by the end of the first week. This bothered Mary because she thought she actually had more ability than Joyce.

All new employees are expected to ask questions. Without formal training, you cannot expect to adjust to a new job or skill without asking questions. People expect them and you should ask them— as long as you don't ask questions that have already been answered or those that you should be able to look up yourself. Of course, there are good and bad ways to ask such questions. You do not want to show a lack of confidence or in any way demean yourself, yet you want to communicate a degree of humility so that the co-worker or supervisor will take time to give you the kind of instruction you need. You might consider asking questions in the manner illustrated below.

> "This just isn't my day. Would you mind helping me out on this problem?"
>
> "I hope everybody you train is not as slow as I am with this machine. Would you mind going over it again for me?"

"I'm a little embarrassed to ask, but frankly, I'm lost. I would really appreciate it if you could show me what I'm doing wrong."

You may ask for a report on your *progress*. After you have been on your first job assignment for a week or so, you will need the reinforcement that comes from knowing you are making good progress. You will not always be given this reassurance. You may approach your supervisor with a question like this: "Good morning, Mrs. Smith. May I have a few moments of your time? I know how busy things have been, but I'm starting my third week in your department and I'm anxious to know how I'm doing. I feel I'm making good progress, but I want to make sure I reach your standards as soon as possible."

On-the-job training is an excellent way to learn. As you move up to the productivity standard of your department and beyond, please remind yourself that there are many skills that you can learn only by actually practicing them. In other words, consider your first job assignment as a learning laboratory. When you reach a satisfactory productivity level, you want to make sure that you have learned everything possible on the way. José views the transition from the starting level to an acceptable level this way.

It's a mistake to try to beat the time schedule that management has set for you to reach their productivity standards. Why? Because you may not learn everything that you should along the way. Nobody is going to give you a big trophy for getting there a few days or weeks ahead of time. They can be very critical, however, if they discover you're still making unnecessary mistakes. My suggestion is to reach productivity on time with as much knowledge tucked away as possible.

How do you know how soon you will be expected to reach acceptable productivity standards? A good way to find out is to ask your supervisor a question like this: "Mr. Smith, I naturally want to carry my full load around here as soon as possible, but I also want to learn as much as I can en route. If you want to provide a time goal, I will do my best to reach it. If this is impossible, I would at least appreciate knowing when I *do* reach a level that is satisfactory to you. I don't mean to imply that I won't eventually go beyond your acceptable norm; I just want to make sure I pull my full weight when I should."

If you prefer not to ask a direct question, you will probably be able to make an estimate by observing what others in similar positions accomplish. If there is no job to compare with yours, asking is probably advisable. The choice is yours.

How can you tell when you have reached acceptable standards? If you prefer not to ask your supervisor, your co-workers will probably tell you through the kind of acceptance you receive from them. Otherwise, you will just have to compare the quantity and quality of the work you are doing in the best way possible.

What should you do after you have reached the productivity norm? Should you be satisfied to stay at that level or try to move closer to your potential? Must you demonstrate better-than-average performance to get the attention of management for promotion purposes?

Because every situation is different, no hard-and-fast rules can be drawn. Generally speaking, however, the following apply.

You should move beyond the norm for personal reasons. You have a potential to achieve on any job assignment you receive. If you put on the brakes before you reach your potential, you are frustrating yourself. Here is the way Wayne sees the problem.

When I reached the productivity level of the rest of the gang, I received a lot of pressure to slow down and relax. In fact, I was told it would be a good move on my part. At that point I gave the matter a lot of thought. Why should I bow to peer pressure of that sort? Why should I sell myself short after spending so much time and money for my education? I decided that the most important person to please was myself.

I believe that happiness and motivation come from a sense of personal achievement. Every individual needs psychological reinforcement. You need to receive a compliment now and then; you need recognition; you need to be involved in the decision-making process. To succumb to group pressure and be satisfied to just jog along with others is a cop-out, in my opinion. What was my solution? I decided to move ahead in the direction of my potential without being obvious about it. In other words, reaching my potential with co-workers' approval became my goal. But deep inside I knew I was doing this primarily for myself.

Better-than-average job performance is one way to draw management attention. All employees are measured in one way or another. In some skill-oriented jobs performance can be measured daily in a scientific manner. In management-oriented jobs measurement occurs, if at no other time, during the annual review period. The sooner you can be identified as a better-than-average employee, the more you will be talked about by management and considered for a promotion. There is some truth to the observation that, at least in some organizations, the average employee is "lost in the crowd."

Once achieved, above-average performance should be sustained. Those ambitious individuals who push for a high performance level that they are unable to maintain often do more harm than good to their careers. Sara made this mistake.

> I was so anxious to prove myself to management that I reached a performance level that was impossible to maintain. Sure, it got the attention of management but a few months later I knew I had made a serious mistake because they began to expect more from me than I could deliver. I wish now that I had raised my performance above the norm more slowly. Above average achievement can easily backfire if you blow hot one week and cold the next.

As you pass your co-workers in productivity, spend more time maintaining good relationships with them. A danger in pushing your performance above others' is that they may resent you and make your job more difficult. To compensate, it is important not to neglect relationships with these individuals. Sometimes you should help others in ways that contribute to their productivity instead of yours. The following story will make the point.

> Last year a new employee who was very capable came into our department. At first we thought that she would be a real addition and fit into our department harmoniously. In no time at all she was carrying her part of the load but, all of a sudden, she spurted ahead of the rest of us. We knew she was trying to get the attention of management, but this didn't bother us. When she began to push us around a little to keep her own productivity at a high level—in effect to show us up—we decided to teach her a lesson in human relations. Instead of doing what we could to get her promoted, we simply ignored her and let her make mistakes. It can be counterproductive to pull yourself above others unless you are sufficiently sensitive to build the right kind of relationships as you do it.

How far should you exceed the average performance level of co-workers? As long as you can maintain good horizontal working relationships with your co-workers, there is no limit. If you have the sensitivity to build the right kind of human relationships with them, co-workers will *want* you to excel. It is not always easy to be tactful, so caution is recommended. Based upon her recent experiences, Rita made the following suggestion.

> As you move from your starting level to acceptable standards, build yourself a strong human-relations base with everyone around you because, if you are ambitious, you will have to pass these people to

reach your career goals. There is a way to do this without incurring resentment and hostility, but it isn't easy. I believe this is the greatest challenge an individual faces in most organizations. If I had fully understood this a few years ago, my career progress would have been much better and faster.

How can you handle resentment caused by moving past a co-worker? Try to prevent resentment by creating such a good relationship with the individual while you are both at the same level that any jealousy or resentment is avoided or at least accepted without hostility. But if resentment is unavoidable, there are several solutions: (1) If you honestly feel the individual is capable, help him or her achieve advancement from your newly won position. (2) Discuss the matter openly in an attempt to dissipate hostility. (3) If the resentment is very deep-seated, your only solution is to proceed in such a mature manner that the individual cannot provoke you to irrational behavior.

Once you have reached the productivity of others, creative efforts are more acceptable. People will respect your ideas more after you have had some time and experience on the job. Once you have reached their level of expertise, they will be more receptive. In your efforts to reach your personal potential, your creativity should be released. You should develop and submit new ideas; you should recommend improvements. In short, you will not only be producing more as one member of a team, you will also be contributing more in the way of creative efforts. It is primarily through efforts of this nature that you will gain the attention of upper management.

In achieving your career goals, remember that it is often easier to be forgiven than to get permission. Most of the time it is best to get management approval before taking initiative—but not always. Sometimes managers cannot give you their blessing because it would be unwise for them to do so, yet they hope you will take the initiative to do something on your own. In other words, they would rather forgive you if you get into trouble than have you do nothing imaginative. As an example, a retail chain store manager decided to stock a locally made product for which many requests were received. He did not ask for approval, as stated in the company manual. The new product sold so well that the profit picture of the store improved and all was forgiven by management. In fact, the policy was eventually changed, and the image of the manager was enhanced by the action.

Discussion Questions

In these quotations, six employees express their attitudes toward productivity. Defend or criticize each quote.

1. "I have given myself six months to reach the productivity level of my co-workers, then an additional six months to raise myself above them so that I can get recognition from management. If I do not reach these goals under my time schedule, then I will know I am in the wrong job and the wrong organization."

2. "I figure that I reached the productivity standards of my job three months ago. At least I sensed at that time that my contribution was equal to that of others in the department. I think it would be unwise for me to push the measurable productivity aspects any further. It would just put me in a bad position with the people I work with. Rather, I think I will submit some ideas now and then, and create a good impression with management in other ways, to get my first promotion."

3. "My success formula is simple. Get your productivity up to, but not beyond, that of others; then depend upon your human-relations skills to get you a job as a supervisor. The worst way in the world to get promoted is to show others up."

4. "I am going to push my personal productivity up as fast as possible. When it equals that of others, I am going to move past them as soon as possible. If they want to follow me, okay; if not, then it is their funeral. I just don't buy this theory of being nice to them just because they want to sit on their duffs. I intend to set the pace, and if they do not care to follow, it's up to them. I am not trying to win any popularity contests; I am just trying to get ahead."

5. "This whole idea of measuring productivity is ridiculous. In almost all cases management measures an individual by value judgment. In other words, the impression they have of you is far more important than the actual work you kick out because they have no reliable way of comparing actual productivity between employees. Personally, I think you can get promoted from most jobs without reaching the productivity level of co-workers. All you have to do is create the impression you are contributing more."

6. "The people you work with are susceptible to good human relations. If you treat them well, they really won't care whether you carry your full load. Oh, I'm going to contribute to the total departmental productivity up to a point, but there is no need to reach the level established by others. Most employees are perfectly willing to carry another—as long as it's somebody they like.

Career Profile

Charles Bruce
Marketing Manager
Data Processing Division, IBM Corporation

When I was in college at the University of Detroit, the most important thing I learned was how to educate myself in a variety of subjects. There was a lot of competition for grades, and I felt that trying to guess what the teachers thought was important helped me study the right things. The process of planning my studying around my ideas of someone else's priorities helped me in school and has helped me ever since.

Math was my major mostly because there were no labs or term papers, and I had a knack for it. There was more time left over for other courses and extracurricular activities—mainly work, social life, and the fencing team.

The biggest mistake with my education was that I made no plans for what I'd do with it after graduation. I did so little career planning that I didn't even talk to the placement office or interview on campus. My career planning mistakes didn't hurt me much because I was saved by a stroke of good luck.

My older brother told me I ought to go to the IBM Data Processing Division to interview for a job and helped set up an interview for me. However, I don't think it was my brother's influence that got me a job offer. I think it was very good grades and a history of leadership roles as class officer and co-captain of some of the teams I played on.

At first, starting with IBM as a trainee wasn't much of a change for me because I went right into an extensive computer training program that was a lot like college. The big difference was that it was practical information, and I felt I was there to learn "for real."

My friends outside of IBM used to give me a hard time about conforming too much to IBM's corporate image with dark suits and white shirts. To me, though, suits with IBM just seemed natural, just as wearing a fencing uniform seemed natural when I was on the fencing team.

After I finished the IBM training program and six months' active duty with the National Guard, I was promoted to associate marketing representative and put on commission. Then luck struck again. I was assigned as the junior member of a three-man team in a very good territory. Then one teammate transferred out and wasn't replaced. The two of us continued as a team and had two years of very good sales and commissions.

During those two years I learned a lot. I learned about computers and what customers think are important. I learned that the customer may not always be right, but he's always the customer. I also learned I was at a tremendous disadvantage compared to experienced customers and IBM marketing representatives because they had broad computer backgrounds and I was new at the game. At first I felt overwhelmed competing with the more experienced people but I decided to rely on the lesson I had learned in school. I had learned how to educate myself, and I figured if I just learned all the new computer stuff, then in a few years I would have a better background than those who couldn't learn as well because the computer industry changes so rapidly.

My life-style went through a few changes during this period. I got married and bought a house that was close to work. I also realized that if I wanted continual career advancement, I would have to move out of Detroit someday and started selling my wife on the idea.

After my promotion to marketing representative, the skills I had picked up in college on guessing what teachers would ask on tests really started to pay off for me. Marketing computers was like taking tests in that I had to learn enough about what the customers cared about so I could show them how a particular computer approach could help them.

Then I was offered a promotion to advisory marketing representative on the regional marketing staff. It was a promotion with a salary increase but I was no longer commission. I took the job but had to give up the half of my income that came from commissions in order to advance my career for the long-term benefit. The area that I was to provide marketing assistance in was a very specialized one, and I was back to educating myself again. It was not much of a fun job since it had more travel away from the family, an additional hour per day commuting, more work, less satisfaction, and I started to lose contact with my old friends. However, it was very educational since it both increased my expertise in my specialty and broadened my exposure to more customers and more IBMers.

For the first time I learned that the boss isn't always right, but he's always the boss. I even learned that I wasn't always right as I saw how many different IBM people and customers could attack and solve problems in different ways.

Finally, after over a year of staff work (and seven and a half years since school), I got the big opportunity. A job as marketing manager was about to open up in Akron, Ohio, and I was a candidate. It would mean selling the house and moving the family almost immediately. I was concerned about moving away from my home town and my best friends, so I asked the manager who told me of the opportunity if he thought it would be good for me to take the job and not just good for IBM. He told me it would be good for my career if I did well. So I ended up taking the job and almost forgot to ask how big the raise would be.

When I started in Akron I was concerned at first because all but one of the people working for me were older and had more years of experience than I. Again, all my self-education paid off because I soon felt comfortable.

The manager role has been a very satisfying one for several reasons. First of all, there is a tremendous amount of freedom to make decisions. But there is also a tremendous responsibility. It was a unique experience the first time I formally appraised one of my employees on his performance, but it is an important human side of the computer business. There is also a certain prestige associated with the job, and that adds to job satisfaction.

When I look back to where I was in college I don't remember changes happening all at once. Certainly I feel I am the same person I was then. On the other hand, all the little changes have really added up over time. When I was in school I felt that I would probably do some important things in my life, but I didn't know what they would be. Now some of those important things have already been done. Also, I am sure now that I'll need to educate myself even more to accomplish these things, but I understand that necessity better now, too. I figure that as long as I can keep that learning going on, there is only one way to go. And that way is up.

Exercises for Part II

Six-Week Self-Assessment Progress Report

1. I am taking full advantages of my learning opportunities.   1 2 3 4 5   I am not taking advantage of my learning opportunities.

   Things I plan to learn in the next few months:

   _____

   _____

   _____

2. I am doing a superior job of building good relationships with my co-workers.   1 2 3 4 5   I am doing nothing to build relationships with co-workers.

   I plan to make these specific improvements in the next few weeks:

   _____

   _____

   _____

   _____

3. I have volunteered to assume as many new responsibilities as possible.   1 2 3 4 5   I haven't volunteered for any new responsibilities.

I plan to volunteer for the following responsibilities in the next two months:

_____

_____

_____

4. I have done
everything possible
to build a good
relationship with
my supervisor.

1 2 3 4 5

I have done
nothing to build a
good relationship
with my
supervisor.

To improve relations with my supervisor, I plan to do the following as soon as the opportunity presents itself:

_____

_____

_____

5. I have learned all
there is to know
about my firm.

1 2 3 4 5

I have learned
nothing about my
firm.

I plan to do some research to learn the following in the next two months:

_____

_____

_____

_____

6. I have raised my   1 2 3 4 5   I have been just
    personal   barely getting by.
    productivity as
    high as possible.

    I plan to do the following to increase my personal productivity:

    _____

    _____

    _____

7. My communications   1 2 3 4 5   I have made no
    have been superior.   attempt to
                                          communicate.

    I plan to improve my communications in the following ways:

    _____

    _____

    _____

8. I am making   1 2 3 4 5   I am at a standstill.
    outstanding
    progress.

    I plan to do the following to increase my progress:

    _____

    _____

    _____

9. Management   1   2   3   4   5   Management does
knows me and I am   not know me and I
building a good   have no image.
image.

I plan to do the following to improve my image:

_____

_____

_____

10. I am making   1   2   3   4   5   I have been wasting
maximum use of   time.
my time on the job.

I plan to do the following to make better use of my time on
the job:

_____

_____

_____

Case Study: Transfer

Kim, a communications major, was employed about six months
ago by the personnel department of the Mid-Continent Insurance
Society. She was given a one-day orientation program, then assigned to the statistical division because she had scored high on
a mathematics examination during her preliminary interview.

Her excitement ran high because she had been job hunting for
more than three months without luck and had almost decided she
would have to move away from home to get a good starting
position.

Her supervisor, Mr. Kelly, was extremely considerate from the
very first day. He saw that she received a sponsor who took a per-

sonal interest in her, taught her how to use all of the equipment, and assisted her on many mathematical concepts and procedures. As a result, Kim did very well and remained in the department for more than six months.

Then one day while she was having lunch in the corporate cafeteria, she heard that the assistant public relations officer had resigned. "At last," she said to herself, "now I can get into the work I really want to do, where I can use all of my special training in communications and experience with the media."

The following morning Kim made an appointment to see Mr. Kelly. She told him that she appreciated the experience of working under his supervision but that, after all, she was trained for other work. She then asked him the proper procedure to follow in effecting a transfer. His reply was, "Kim, we have spent a great deal of time and money to help you become effective in my department. To lose you now would mean starting over from scratch. I do not think this transfer request is fair to me or to the organization. You might as well hear it from me now. I will block your transfer in every possible way."

Kim was astonished. Imagine a progressive corporation permitting such behavior on the part of a manager! Shouldn't she be given the position where she could make her best contribution? Shouldn't she be permitted at least to apply for the position without prejudice? Kim talked the whole thing over confidentially with a close friend. What action should she take? What would be protocol? She finally narrowed it down to the following possibilities:

1. Submit a written request for a transfer and take her chances about getting an interview from the head public relations officer. In making the request, she would ask personnel to forward her original résumé.
2. Go over Mr. Kelly's head and talk to his superior regarding Mr. Kelly's attitude.
3. Go over Mr. Kelly's head and formally ask for a three-way meeting. Mr. Kelly, his superior, and Kim would be present.
4. Go over Mr. Kelly's head and formally ask for a four-way meeting. Mr. Kelly, his superior, a representative from personnel, and Kim would be present.
5. Initiate an affirmative action complaint.
6. Go straight to the public relations officer and apply for the position without communication with Mr. Kelly or his superior.

7. Go to personnel and ask for the opportunity to transfer.
8. Tell Mr. Kelly and *then* go to personnel and ask for an opportunity to interview for the job.
9. Submit a written request for a transfer; tell Mr. Kelly and his superior that she intends to go to personnel; tell personnel that she plans to contact the public relations officer on her own.
10. Submit a written request for a transfer to Mr. Kelly and send a copy to personnel and the public relations officer.

Which steps, if any, would you advise Kim to take? What other steps or choices does she have? Defend your answers.

Part III

ASSESSING YOUR PERSONAL PROGRESS

Objectives

Once you have finished this section you should have determined

1. When and how to assess your human-relations progress and why it will help you win a promotion

2. How to evaluate your organization and personal progress objectively

3. How to establish realistic organizational goals and why they are important

4. How to forestall or shorten "down periods" that might seriously impede your career progress

The Human Element

Part III is designed to help you balance your personal productivity (skills) with the way you are getting along with your co-workers and superiors. Both factors are extremely important as you chart and attempt to reach career goals.

PEOPLE

Are You Satisfied with Your Human-Relations Progress?

10

About six weeks after you report for work, you should assess your personal progress. Self-assessment is difficult because it involves self-criticism. As we have all learned, the individual who can accept criticism from others is a secure person who sincerely wants to improve. Self-criticism requires the same virtues, plus objectivity. Are you willing to discover some responsibilities you have neglected? Are you willing to discover your weaknesses and make changes? If you are not able to be honest with yourself, any self-assessing you attempt will be futile. You will go through the motions but no improvements or new actions will be forthcoming.

Why do you need to assess the progress you are making in building good relationships with people? Your human-relations efforts can make you or break you when it comes to a successful career. Are you building and maintaining the kind of relationships with others that will promote your career? Are you living up to your human-relations standards? How is the relationship with your immediate supervisor coming along? Are you building good horizontal working relationships with co-workers? If you are fully satisfied with your human-relations progress, you should concentrate on *maintaining* the relationships you have already built; if there is some doubt about what you have accomplished, then there is still time to make new efforts.

What constitutes a good, healthy relationship? A good relationship is one that includes dignity and respect on both sides. Communications are initiated and received frequently in a free, open, warm atmosphere—one that *feels* good to both parties. Many people say you can recognize a good relationship because there is a

135

"bond" between the two individuals; others like to use the words
empathy and *understanding*. Perhaps a better way to understand a
good relationship is to compare it with a bad one. A bad relationship is cool, uneasy, distant, and awkward. You always know you
have a poor relationship with a person you would prefer *not* to see
or work with. Sometimes a bad relationship is tinged with hostility
or prejudice. Often a bad relationship was a good one until something happened to it. Perhaps one person offended the other and
a communication breakdown occurred.

Most psychologists who deal with working relationships accept
the premise that it is easier to build a new one than to repair an
old one. Probably you have built mostly good relationships so far,
but it is possible you need to consider doing some repair work on
one or two.

How do you assess your human-relations progress? You could start
by using a chart similar to the one shown here.

Human Relations Progress Chart

Name and Position	I have already built a good relationship with this person	I need to work on building a relationship with this person	I have damaged this relationship and intend to make repairs
Clare F. Supervisor		X	
Carol J. Co-worker	X		
Sam S. Co-worker			X
Darlene R. Co-worker	X		
James K. Dept. Mgr.		X	
Sylvia K. Computer Chief			X

Names. The first step would be to list all of the people with whom you have been building relationships up to this point. This list should include everyone with whom you have frequent contact at work. Obviously, the list should begin with your immediate supervisor and all the co-workers in your department. But the list should go much farther. For example, it should include people in personnel, individuals you meet in other departments, and management people with whom you communicate. It should also include switchboard operators, guards, custodians, and secretaries to management people. The list can include from 30 to 40 people, sometimes many more. You may prefer to list them in the order of importance to your career progress as you see it.

Good relationships. Next, make checkmarks opposite the names of those with whom you feel you have already built excellent relationships. You would expect these people to go to bat for you should you get in trouble. They would be loyal to you. *You like to be with these people.* You also feel free to go to them and talk over problems of mutual concern. You have considerable respect for these individuals, and you would be loyal to them.

Relationships that need work. It is too much to ask that you have built excellent relationships with all employees in a short time. Chances are you have either *neglected* or *ignored* a few people. It is not that there is anything *wrong* with these relationships, it is just that they should be developed. Perhaps you should spend a little more time with these people or send them a few more friendly signals. It should be pointed out that you *do* have some kind of a relationship with anyone with whom you have frequent contact, either in person or by telephone. If you make the foolish mistake of ignoring someone deliberately (perhaps because this person offended or rejected you), you are not eliminating the relationship, but only intensifying it. There is no way you can avoid relationships with people where you work.

Relationships that need repair. It is quite possible that in the rather short time you have been on the job, you have already injured an important relationship or two. You may have done this unintentionally, but it happened nonetheless. Or it could be that one or two people are neglecting or ignoring *you.* You can almost hear them saying, "You are new in this organization and you will have to *earn* a good relationship with me. I was here first. I'm more experienced. I'm willing to have a good working relationship with you, but I'm not going to make it easy for you." After you have identified these relationships, each one will need to be analyzed and treated differently. Each will take time. You would make a mistake if you became impatient and took direct action too soon. It is often best to keep sending open and warm signals to these people until they finally respond.

Below are three cases that need either work or repair. They illustrate the kinds of human-relations problems new employees often face.

When Millie was first assigned to department C, she made the mistake of spending time with only three of her five fellow workers. In making her assessment after six weeks, she knew she did not have a good relationship with the two other women. Perhaps they thought she was frivolous (since both were more mature); perhaps she had hurt their feelings by ignoring them. Millie was also concerned that her supervisor might have noticed her favoritism and interpreted it as immaturity. At any rate, Millie decided to do something about it. After careful consideration, she decided to take the direct approach by saying, "When I first came into the department, I made a mistake by not getting to know both of you better. You have been very fair to me and I appreciate it. I hope I can earn your respect. I like my work here and I want to be a good member of the department and carry my full share of responsibility." Once communication was opened among the three people, Millie felt that both relationships improved substantially.

When Carlos was first assigned to the department six weeks ago, he got along well with everyone except Mr. Presson, who seemed to be holding a grudge for some unknown reason. After tolerating uncalled-for abuse for six weeks, Carlos sat down with Mr. Presson and discussed the matter openly. "This job is important to me," said Carlos. "I have been trying to get along with you to the best of my ability, but you have been rejecting me. What will it take for us to get along better?" Although Mr. Presson did not give Carlos any specific answers to his pointed question, Carlos noticed that he was a little more friendly the next morning.

John naturally put his supervisor at the top of the list on his Human Relations Progress Chart. It would have made him happy to check either of the first two columns in the chart (good relationship or one that needs work), but unfortunately John knew his most important relationships needed major repairs. Completing the chart made him realize that he had to take some action. The next day he asked his supervisor for a 15-minute meeting. His request was granted, and they actually spent 30 minutes talking things over. John did not confront the supervisor with the problem directly, but said: "I have been with you six weeks and I have learned to respect both my work and the organization. I would like to know, however, how I can improve. Please be frank with me. I feel I can take criticism. This is my first real career job and it means a great deal to me that I succeed." John is not sure what happened, but he feels that after he asked for help, the supervisor started to feel more positive toward him. He offered many suggestions, and John took them seriously. John now feels the relationship is in top order and that a major roadblock to his career progress has been overcome.

Once you have identified, analyzed, and developed a plan to maintain excellent relationships, work on those you have neglected, repair those that need it, and have confidence that you can make the plan work. The maintaining and repairing of human relationships is a continuous responsibility of all those in management. The more experience you gain early in your career, the better prepared you will be later on if management is part of your career plans. Human-relations skills can be developed through practice.

Should you join an organization working under one or more union contracts, you will probably have some additional human-relations responsibilities. You will interact with both union and management. How should you cope? You might, for example, consider doing some research into the history of previous labor negotiations so that you will understand current attitudes on both sides of the table. Researching specific conditions of present contracts might help you appraise what your own behavior should be toward various individuals and power groups connected with unions. Building sound human relations inside a union organization has added dimensions that need to be handled with considerable skill. Obviously, the stronger the relationships you build with people on both sides of the table, the more valuable you should be to the organization at a later date. This experience, in turn, will help your personal career progress.

Many individuals feel that there are certain minimum human-relations standards that should be observed by management and nonmanagement people alike. A few perceive these fundamentals as a human-relations "code." Now that you have survived the initial stages in your new role, you may wish to review the standards listed below.* If you agree that they are minimum requirements, you may wish to incorporate them into your own personal behavior patterns.

What is meant by the term *human-relations competency*? When can a person consider herself or himself to be human-relations *competent*?

Like other competencies, human-relations competency represents a certain acceptable level. It means that you have had enough

---

Minimum Human-Relations Standards

1. Treat each person as a unique individual.
2. Treat each individual with dignity and respect.
3. Do not spend too much time developing one relationship to the neglect of others.
4. Do not "bad mouth" either the people you work with or the organization you work for.
5. Do not let others intimidate you.
6. Recognize that communication is the life blood of all relationships.
7. Supervisors have the primary responsibility to develop good relationships with their employees, but employees have a secondary responsibility.
8. Employees have a responsibility to build and maintain good working relationships with co-workers.
9. Supervisors should periodically let their employees know how they are doing.
10. People should repair breakdowns in their relationships at the earliest possible moment.
11. People should be given credit when it is due.
12. When a human-relations mistake is made, an apology is in order.
13. One individual should not prejudge the potential of another.
14. Individuals should not start or spread false rumors.
15. When possible, management should tell people in advance about changes that will affect them.

---

*The standards are reprinted from Elwood N. Chapman, *Your Attitude Is Showing*, 3rd ed. Chicago, Science Research Associates, Inc.

training and experience in human relations to identify and solve problems, to live up to basic standards and operate effectively within groups of people. You should consider yourself competent in human relations under the following conditions.

1. When you seriously attempt to practice the basic human-relations standards acceptable within your culture. The list of standards in this chapter is only an example; you could easily extend the list according to your own beliefs. Remember, however, that these are *minimum* standards.

2. When you are relatively free of prejudice, willing to communicate, willing to listen, and sensitive to the frailties of others. Should you become so selfish that you ignore the needs of others, use others to enhance your own career, and ignore minimum standards, you have temporarily lost your competency.

3. When you recognize your own human-relations mistakes and take the initiative to make repairs.

Discussion Questions

Please comment on the following statements.

1. It is a waste of time for students to discuss self-assessment plans before they even have a job.
2. Taking time to assess your human-relations skills after you have been on the job for only six weeks is stupid—you need to work with people for at least a year before an evaluation is possible.
3. Less than 1 percent of all damaged human relationships are repaired because people don't have the guts to sit down and face the causes for such breaks.
4. Setting human-relations standards is ridiculous. The whole thing reminds me of being a Girl Scout ten years ago.
5. I reject the idea of using a chart to assess one's human-relations progress. It's too simplistic.
6. Over 70 percent of those who resign from jobs do so because of human-relations problems.

**Career
Profile**

Sally Graves
Newspaper Advertising Manager and
Creative Services Coordinator
Bullock's Department Stores

I graduated from the University of Missouri School of Journalism in June 1971. After spending the summer in St. Louis (my home), I moved to Los Angeles. My reasons were both professional (I didn't want to go to New York or Chicago, the other two most thriving advertising cities) and personal (my parents were not enamoured with my fiancé).

I immediately began looking for a job through an agency that specialized in communication positions and through the classified ads. It was not easy. Jobs were scarce and most required experience.

It was a great shock to my system to learn that after spending four years proving that I was bright and talented by actually having stories published, selling newspaper space, designing ads, and writing copy that no one wanted to give me a job.

So in order to eat (one must do that) I worked as a temporary typist while I continued to look. I was fortunate to be assigned for five months to a place that permitted me to get my work done in four days, which left me the fifth day to job hunt.

The enormity of learning to live in a strange city without a circle of friends and parental support is something I wouldn't want to go through again. When I left St. Louis, I gave myself a deadline of one year to become established in a job with some potential. If I hadn't made it by then, I'd decided to pack it back to St. Louis and hope that my college placement office could be more help in its geographical sphere of influence.

In April, I was hired as a receptionist in the advertising department of a major department store. I figured at least I could get my foot in the door and be around advertising people. My boss knew what he was getting—an ambitious, reasonably bright person. I think he grabbed me because he saw that I had potential. This job was my first break.

I worked as the receptionist for five months, getting to know the company, asking for special projects, and doing a good job at my assigned tasks. After five months, a copywriter position opened up. I applied and got the job—one year after I'd started my job quest.

This initial job-hunting period was very discouraging, and I almost gave up. After spending four years of proving myself, I had to start all over because I didn't have "job experience." The age-old problem (catch-22) of "We want someone with experience" but where do you go to get experience has always mystified me. So I adopted the "get your foot in the door" routine of taking any job in order to gain some visibility and get some advertising job experience for my résumé (which by the way is something everyone should have and keep up to date).

Briefly, I was a copywriter for five months, then media coordinator for two years, then fashion ad manager for a year, and now newspaper ad manager for a year. Each job opened up just about the time I was getting bored (which, by the way, is a sign for you to move on). The job I have now has almost unlimited possibilities, and I'm sort of creating as I go along. As you can see, being visible to management (or in the right place at the right time) is important in moving up the ladder.

To tell you what I've learned over the years would take another 2500 words, so I'll try to distill it into a few paragraphs.

1. Don't ever stop believing in yourself. You should know that you don't have all the answers (who does?) but you have to have some marketable input that someone wants. It's a matter of putting the right combination together—your knowledge and a business's need.

2. Never stop learning. That means not only in your particular area, but also in the broader area of general company operations. The more you know, the better decisions you'll make. It also means don't cut yourself off from the outside world. Your business doesn't operate in a vacuum, and neither should you.

3. Look up every six months at first, then every year, and evaluate what you're doing. Ask yourself: How happy am I doing what I'm doing? and Am I progressing? You spend the majority of your life working, and if you're not in it for fun or profit, what's the point?

4. Achieving success (good grades) at college is mainly an individual effort. Achieving success in a career is mainly a team effort. By that I mean that the higher up the corporate ladder you go, the more your success depends on your ability to work with other people, to motivate people who work for you, "to get the job done," to be a leader. Unless you become involved in extracurricular activities or were lucky enough to have a well-taught people-management course available *and* were perceptive enough to take it, very little is done to prepare you for the job of being a manager of doers rather than a rockbottom doer yourself.

In the business world, there isn't a system of evaluation as well-defined as grades. Sometimes you have to ask your boss how you're doing. Mostly you have to watch for signs of approval. But mainly you have to be objective and evaluate yourself in an ongoing fashion. Don't be too easy on yourself and don't be too hard. If the company had wanted an error-free computer for your job, they would have gotton one. Admit your mistakes and learn from them.

5. Learn to organize and discipline yourself. You'll be constantly shifting priorities in your day-to-day work. Don't let it overwhelm you because then your job will run you, you will not be running your job. As a manager, you're not supposed to do all the work yourself, you're supposed to see that it gets done.

6. Embrace change as a way of life. The only thing that's constant is change. Nothing is ever the same as before. Don't be afraid of change, or you can count on being unhappy the rest of your life. It doesn't mean that you don't need anchors of some nature, but even those must be re-evaluated periodically.

7. Find out your weaknesses and work on them. Mine is procrastination and I've had it for a long time. I always wrote papers the night before they were due—and got good grades. It's taken me two and a half months to get this profile out of mental card shuffling on to paper. It's a bad habit that I constantly have to fight. I'm getting better but I don't always succeed.

8. Don't let your work become your whole life. Believe me, it's easy to do. Once you're out of college, which for me was a 24-hour a day experience, you've got to make an effort to be with people. At college I lived with, "worked" (went to classes) with, and played with the same group of people. We all had something in common. In life, you don't always play with the same folks you work with. And in order not to become a hermit (which is deadly) you have to make an effort to keep in contact with the outside world.

I hope all of you have as good a working experience as I've had. A last bit of advice: Have a healthy sense of humor. Good luck.

ANALYSIS

Assessing the Organization You Joined

11

Although you may have taken a college course in organization and management, you probably want more specific information about the structure and policies of the organization you joined. How is it set up? (Line and staff? Committee?) What is the philosophy of top management? Do they support the classical, neoclassical, or systems analysis theory of organization? What leadership styles are most prevalent? Does your new company have a firm promotion-from-within policy? Is it aware of—and does it follow—current civil rights legislation? If you joined a government agency, have you studied the applicable civil service rules and regulations? If you joined an educational institution, have you read the certification or classification manuals?

You probably did not have time to get answers to all your questions during the employment interview or your first few weeks of employment. You were too busy adjusting to your job. From now on, the time that you devote to studying the organization will be a good investment because the more you know about it, the better progress you can make. The comment below from the personnel director of a large industrial corporation will give you the rationale for such an investigation and assessment.

We employ a large number of management trainees in our firm. Although many are business administration, engineering, and marketing majors, some come from other disciplines. We have discovered an amazing apathy in these graduates as far as learning about the company is concerned. Oh, yes, they do a little research before their employment interviews, but once they are on the payroll, they feel they will learn automatically. Very few ask for a copy of our annual report to stock-

145

holders. Few ask if there is any literature on the early history of the firm. Some do not even inquire whether we have a company library, which we do.

We do not have the time or the training budget to provide all of this information through counseling or in a classroom. We are forced to rely on their initiative. I wish they could understand how much it would help their progress if they would do some private research on their own. They would learn our local vocabulary, our philosophy, how we are structured, and how well we are doing in comparison to our competitors. If I was thinking about building a career inside an organization, I would learn everything possible about it, and the sooner, the better.

Assuming you agree with the personnel director, how will you go about educating yourself regarding the organization you have joined? What can you do in addition to reading annual reports, literature, and employee manuals? What can you do to understand the internal power structure and political pressures that will influence the way you build your career? Here are some possibilities for your consideration.

Learn from conversations with others. Your best source might be fellow employees both in and out of management positions. Without being too obvious, just by asking the right question at the right time, you can lead others into giving you both data and insights regarding the organization. Although your contacts with administrators may be limited, you will occasionally have an opportunity to direct a question to such an individual. If it is a good question, you will not only learn more about the organization, but you might also improve your image as somebody to "watch."

Examine the organizational structure. Because each organization is put together in a different way, each structure is unique. In many cases, authority moves in a straight line from the top executive to the rank-and-file employee (line organization). In other structures, there are many staff positions so that line managers can receive advice from experts in making decisions (line and staff). In some organizations, a single executive is replaced by a group of people who meet regularly to make decisions (committee). You will be able to observe the structure by studying the organization chart. Some firms pay a great deal of attention to organizational charts because they feel they can effect change through the realignment of a chart by giving some people more authority and others less (classical theory); other firms are more people-oriented and less chart-oriented (neoclassical theory); still other organizations conceive of the structure as a system that can be altered to meet changing needs (systems analysis).

As you study and analyze the structure of your organization, keep in mind the principles of decentralization, accountability, delegation of authority, and flexibility. Also give recognition to the problem of internal communication faced by all organizations. You may discover some fascinating aspects of your organization, some factors that will assist you in building your career.

Study the power structures inside your organization. Texts on organizational management and organizational behavior usually deal at length with the subject of "power structures." For our purposes, we will discuss the two that are most prevalent and can be found existing side-by-side in most organizations.

Formal power structure. Power, under this classification, is designated by titles. A vice-president has more authority (and presumably power) than an assistant vice-president. You get an overview of the formal power structure in an organization when you study the organization chart. The term *power hierarchy* is often used to designate the structure that will have the greatest influence on your career-building efforts. Perhaps 90 percent of all organizational power is found in these designated roles.

Hidden power structure. Through their strong personalities and activities, some individuals are able to build power roles for themselves *outside* the formal structure. For example, an individual in a front-line supervisory job could develop more power than his or her immediate superior. Or, as sometimes happens, an assistant supervisor has more influence than the supervisor. Through observation, you may learn that some people have built more power into their roles than their titles designate.

Obviously, it is incumbent upon you to recognize both structures. Suppose you have an innovative idea that you feel will enhance your image and promote your career. Your first step is to get it approved by management. You draw up the plan and submit it "through channels," which means through the formal power structure. You do what you can to persuade those in authority of the various advantages of the proposal. If there is a strong hidden power structure, you can, in addition, solicit the influence of those in hidden power roles. Perhaps a co-worker in your own department, a nonmanagement person in another department, a union agent, or a secretary could influence those in the formal power structure. Here is a comment from a recent graduate.

> When I was on campus we studied about power structures, but I had no idea that I would recognize them so quickly. I was amazed how many people had developed strength *beyond* that designated by their job titles. I also discovered that a few people my own age had already

developed little "power clusters" at the nonmanagement level. Believe me, any insights you can gather regarding power roles can be helpful to your career progress. You don't want to ignore anyone in a power position either in or out of the formal structure, and you don't want to waste time on an individual who still has a "power" title but has lost much of the influence that went with it.

Evaluate affirmative action programs. At this writing most organizations are involved in programs that will improve the mix of minorities and women at various management levels. Such programs could have a temporary influence on your career progress. For example, if you fall into a minority classification, you might receive an opportunity to hold a position of authority and responsibility sooner than you anticipate. On the other hand, if you are a nonminority, you might have to demonstrate more patience and understanding as you prepare for your opportunities. It will be up to you to evaluate how much progress your organization has made toward reaching its goals (sometimes expressed in percentages) of placing women and members of minority groups in management roles. Once these quotas have been attained, competition for higher positions should be open to all without the influence of programs that provide a temporary advantage to some. If the organization has not reached this level, a temporary advantage might still exist for a few people. There are advantages and disadvantages both ways. If, as a minority person, you receive a temporary advantage, you must still prove ability in order to hold the new job of additional responsibility and use it as a launching pad for further advancements. You must also be sensitive to those nonminority people you have temporarily left behind. Any individual, minority or nonminority, who leaves "bad feelings" behind in climbing an executive ladder will eventually pay a price. If, as a nonminority person, you are temporarily delayed in your progress, you must be sensitive to the possibility that the minority person might be better qualified than you (and would have succeeded without an affirmative action program) and that any resentment you develop might, in itself, impede your future progress.

Discover lines of progression. The traditional routes that employees follow from lower positions to top management jobs are called *lines of progression*. For example, it might be possible to move up to the presidency of an industrial firm from a starting job in production, research, accounting, or marketing. If you were in production and intended to move from that base, you would want to study the positions above you that you would eventually go through in your movement toward a top executive role.

Investigate the existence or absence of a PFW policy. If an organization has a firm promotion-from-within (PFW) policy, almost all new employees are hired at the bottom of the organizational hierarchy and given the opportunity to move slowly to the top without fear that the company will employ people for management positions from the outside. The illustration below describes PFW policy.

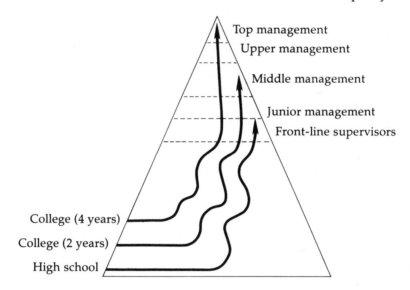

If your organization has a firm PFW policy and strives to live up to it, you can usually expect: (1) excellent internal training programs; (2) excellent job security and employee benefits; and (3) slow but steady progress to the top. If, on the other hand, your organization does not have a strong PFW policy (and many don't), then you can anticipate: (1) management might fill a position above you (one that you want) with an outsider; (2) employees within such an organization might be more assertive; (3) upward movement by ambitious junior executives might be faster; and (4) terminations might be more frequent.

You should learn just how the policy works in your organization because it can influence your present behavior and long-term career plans. If you should learn that your firm does not have a strong PFW policy, for example, and you prefer to work with an organization that does, this discovery could encourage you to make a change. On the other hand, you might prefer a firm in which an outstanding newcomer can advance more rapidly. Make some inquiries so you will know where you stand.

Give some attention to the leadership styles of superiors. You will not understand the structure of your organization unless you take into consideration the influence of the leadership that controls and directs it. Each supervisor and manager eventually develops her or his own, unique leadership style. Leadership style is basically the manner in which individuals work with employees who are responsible to them. There are many leadership styles that you can use as models as you start to put your own style together. Some leaders are strongly oriented toward authoritative or "control" styles, while others lean toward more permissive or participative blends. You can model your own leadership blend after studying those you feel to be most effective. The first style to study is that of your immediate supervisor. Does he or she draw a strong discipline line? Involve other people in decisions? Exercise too much control? Do you feel stifled working for this person? What are the good and bad parts of your supervisor's style?

Learn to distinguish between leadership style and personality. You will be more professional if you study only the style and refrain from dealing in personalities. It is a basic human relations principle always to try to make your supervisors look good; if you engage in gossip relating to a manager's personality, you may violate this principle. If, however, you talk to others about his or her *style,* you are talking about the manner or way one leads others, not about personal idiosyncrasies.

Inquire into available training programs. Many organizations help employees to continue their education. Such programs can be divided into three classifications: (1) formal, classroom training offered on company time; (2) correspondence courses that the firm has developed or is willing to pay for; and (3) financial aid to employees who enroll in courses at traditional educational institutions. Although most in-service training programs are operated on an "invitation only" basis, it does not hurt to let management know that you would like to qualify. You can usually discover whether correspondence courses are available through personnel or training departments. Organizations that provide tuition, textbooks, and transportation expenses for those who undertake and complete formal educational courses (usually at the college level) often provide brochures that explain all of the details of the program. Find out what is available as soon as possible so that you can dovetail the training into your career goals.

Joining outside professional organizations can increase your value to the organization. Many firms are willing to provide both expense money and time away from the job for those who can benefit from membership in a professional group. Your first step is to discover whether any organizations that will help you become more professional are available in your community. The second step is to get approval to participate.

If the organization you join does not support the expenses involved in belonging to an outside organization, *pay for it yourself.* If your superiors discover you are attending workshops, taking courses, or participating in professional organizations at your own expense, this fact will have a very positive influence on your career progress. It is very important that those above you know you are improving yourself.

Investigate internal organizations. You might be surprised at the number of internal organizations that invite your membership and participation. If you are a union member, you might wish to become more deeply involved in union activities. If you are in management, you might wish to investigate membership in a company-sponsored management club. Research company credit unions, recreational clubs, and other groups.

Evaluate ethical standards. It is vital to discover early in your work experience whether you can "live with" the ethical standards of your organization. If you have very high, rigid standards with little room for compromise, you may feel uncomfortable in some organizations. If this happens, you have two choices. You can leave, or you can decide to maintain your own personal standards and try to improve those of others. If all other factors you have investigated are positive, you might decide to remain. But if many other factors are negative, you might take the first option and resign. Do not make the mistake of staying with the wrong organization too long, as Gilbert did.

> My big mistake was sticking it out with the first organization I joined for three years. If I had really done some deep investigation the first six months, I would have *known* I was in the wrong place. I thought I had the right organization when I accepted the job, but all I really knew was what I picked up during the interview. It took me a long time to face up to the fact that I had made a mistake.

You should consider your first job an *exploratory* experience and make a serious investigation to discover whether or not you wish to stay. Although many people say you should wait a full year before making a decision, it is quite possible that you can make a sound determination within a few months. You are not doing either the firm or yourself a favor by hanging around if you *know* the organization is not for you. Once an individual has made such a decision, it is most difficult to keep up personal productivity and transmit a positive attitude.

The organizational checklist below summarizes this chapter. Using the checklist will help you decide whether you should stay with a given organization and prepare you for any employment interviews in your future.

**Organizational Investigation Checklist
and Evaluation Form**

YES NO

☐ ☐ Do I like the organizational structure?

☐ ☐ Will the "hidden" power structure help my career progress?

☐ ☐ Will affirmative action programs help my progress?

☐ ☐ Are the lines of progression good for me?

☐ ☐ Do I approve of the PFW policy?

☐ ☐ Am I pleased with the organizational leadership?

☐ ☐ Are the training opportunities good?

☐ ☐ Will I be able to join outside professional organizations?

☐ ☐ Are there some valuable inside organizations to join?

☐ ☐ Can I live comfortably with the organization's ethical standards?

As you continue your personal assessment of the organization you joined, please keep the following facts in mind.

Organizational structure influences human motivation and productivity. Some organizations may be so over-structured that people feel boxed in and stifled; others may be so unstructured that people feel lost and undirected. In all cases, the structure should be viewed in terms of its influence on the goals of the firm and the behavior of people who must work inside. Should you discover that the structure of your organization does not meet your needs or standards (and there is little you can do about it), then you will have a solid reason for moving elsewhere.

Organizational structures change more quickly in business than in government or education. The economic winds of change can influence a business corporation radically almost overnight. Because of the profit and loss system, often changes must be made immediately in order for a company to survive. Some business firms look outside for a new president who can come in and "save" the company, even though a complete reorganization may result. Government agencies and educational institutions are more protected against these "winds," and consequently change more slowly.

Nine out of ten employees must learn to live gracefully inside an organizational structure. After a few months inside an organization, many people dream of a job where they are 100 percent free and do not have to endure regulations and forced conformity. Some seek work outside organizational confinements, perhaps a business of their own or, if they are ready, a role as a consultant or outside salesperson. Some of these people succeed and are happy as "free agents" in our economic society. The vast majority of us, however, have no logical or sensible escape; we must adjust to some kind of organizational structure because our society is a culture of big organizations. For most of us there is no turning back. We must work and produce within organizational frameworks. Only our personal lives remain outside such influences. You may be interested in Anita's views.

I have always been something of a free agent in life. I love my freedom to make decisions and move about on the spur of the moment. When I finished college, however, the only work roles I could find to use my skills and earn a living were *inside* organizations. The first job I found drove me up the walls; the second was little better. I simply felt restricted, repressed, and depressed. I finally made up my mind, however, that I had to adjust. So the third time around I found an organization that understands my need for freedom up to a point, so I am relatively happy. It's not perfect, mind you, but it's better than the other two.

My advice is to look for the best possible organization to meet your needs and then make up your mind to live within it with enthusiasm.

Who knows, you might even discover that it's fun to try to make changes. One thing for sure, most of us must work in groups to accomplish our personal and societal goals, and there is no way to work with others without *some* organizational structure.

Discussion Questions

You are invited to defend or take issue with the conclusions made by the primary character in each of the mini-cases below.

1. Gerald prepared for three years to take over the job of his supervisor. He had received many signals that he would be chosen when the supervisor retired. When it happened, however, management selected an individual outside the company. Gerald was told, "Normally, you would have received the promotion, but we had this opportunity to employ Ms. Anderson and thought it would be for the good of the organization to do so. We hope you will cooperate with her 100 percent. Your opportunity will come soon." *Gerald resigned the following day.*

2. Mary Ellen discovered she was in the middle of a "power struggle" her second week on the job. Her designated supervisor had lost much of his power to an assistant, who was making most of the decisions and, without authority, controlling the department. Although Mary Ellen had no idea what management thought of the situation, or even if they knew about it, she sided with the assistant on the basis that the assistant would soon take over the department anyway. *Do you support her decision?*

3. Harry is a midmanagement employee with six first-line supervisors under his direction. Last week one of his supervisors resigned, and Harry was instructed to promote a minority person to improve the company's cultural mix. Everyone, including the person receiving the promotion, knows that Susanne is better qualified, has seniority, and deserved the promotion. Last night Harry decided that the only thing he could do was to take Susanne to lunch and talk openly about the situation. *Do you agree with this decision?*

4. Doreen is very ambitious and wants to earn her way into a management position with the United States Postal Service as

soon as possible. She has identified five *lines of progression* into upper management positions. Two of the five make use of her educational background. Progression track A is obviously faster than B, but her experience is limited in this area. Progression track B is obviously slower but fits both her education and experience. *Which line of progress should she choose?*

5. After six months with the Acme Corporation, Luis is pleased with his progress. In fact, only one thing bothers him. He has discovered that the corporation's ethics are not up to his personal standards. Some of his friends, who work for other organizations, have the same problem. Luis is not sure that *any* organization will completely satisfy him. Some limited compromise will probably be necessary. So yesterday Luis decided to stay with the organization and do what he can to improve its standards. *Is Luis a hypocrite?*

6. Last night Sylvia and two of her friends were comparing organizational structures. One of her friends is building a career inside a federal government organization. The other works for a nonprofit foundation. Sylvia works for a large industrial corporation. All three agreed that although the three structures are different, they are equally difficult to understand and adjust to. *Do you agree?*

JacqueLynn J. Eilbert
Research Associate
Career Information System of Iowa
Department of Public Instruction

**Career
Profile**

From the outset, I should tell you that writing about my first job is not an easy task. For me, a great deal of emotion is wrapped up in that experience. If I could only reduce it to quantitative terms like working hours and salary, it would be so much easier. But in writing about my first job, I'll be sharing feelings, many of which have helped to shape my professional attitudes.

My first (and present) job has offered me a twofold opportunity: growing as a person has been as much a part of this experience as my professional growth. I've been challenged to learn, to take initiative and work independently, to further develop my capabilities. It's been like being "educated" all over again, only better.

Many factors enhanced the learning/working environment. I was hired, along with three others, for a new educational program. Hence we were all learning together, exploring new ideas, and in the process helping each other grow. In addition, we were/are supremely committed to our task, that of developing the Career Information System of Iowa (C.I.S.I.) and making it available to students and other users all over the state. There's something very special and exhilarating about the creative process. Since C.I.S.I.'s beginning nearly four years ago, the excitement of creating new materials has taken on greater significance and has bound us together as a team.

The concept of teamwork has always been encouraged in our

unit. Yet, through working together, we grew as individuals. Of course, we have a leader, as most teams do: he's called Supervisor on the table of organization chart at the department. But he's really one of us. Mentor, friend, confidante, coach, all describe him.

It has been said, especially to aspiring women, that one should find a mentor to help expedite the climb up the career ladder. Mentors can offer the inspiration, interpretation, information, critique, and friendship often needed on a first job. Over the years, the mentor mechanism has been established for men through the "old boy network." Women, however, usually have to exert more effort and initiative in establishing these relationships. In any event, a mentor can be invaluable in career development, providing that encouragement to help you become acclimated, productive, and, hopefully, successful.

Another means of gathering forces is through a "support group." Again, this has already been happening for men, although more informally, through activities such as business clubs and golf games. Professional women are banding together in increasing numbers to share concerns about their jobs, to trade information about job prospects, and the like. I have been involved in the formation of such a group at the department. Through this group of women, a great deal of sharing, which had not previously been a part of our work routine, has taken place. I have many fond recollections of our gatherings. What a warm fuzzy!

Although not a direct function of my job, my participation in my professional association has certainly enhanced my knowledge and abilities. During my first year with C.I.S.I., I became active in the organization and shortly was able to develop a number of contacts that were helpful in doing my job.

The association with colleagues is extremely important, in my opinion, to the first job holder. Not only does it provide the opportunity to meet persons who have similar concerns, but hopefully, it also encourages professional growth and development.

Through this brief sketch of my first job experience perhaps I've raised some questions in your mind about your first job goals and expectations. Hopefully, you'll think about what job components are important to you. Have you determined what degree of commitment is comfortable for you? Do you like working as a team? How do you feel about having a mentor or being a part of a support group? What could a professional association offer you, or what could you do for it? These are very real considerations as you approach your first job. Take them seriously.

GOALS
How to Make Them Work for You

12

Once you have been with a new organization for a few months, you should be ready to set some personal goals or targets. If you are enthusiastic about the firm and your progress, you will be easily motivated to set such goals. But even if you are beginning to question the long-term possibilities with the organization you joined, establishing targets will enhance your career progress.

Self-motivation. Most people are goal-oriented for two very sound reasons: (1) Having a goal is motivating in itself; (2) reaching or accomplishing a goal is personally rewarding. Having reachable goals helps eliminate apathy. Saul W. Gellerman, who formulated the theory of Psychological Advantage, points out that workers constantly seek to serve their own self-interests (goals) to keep themselves motivated when management provides inadequate motivation.* A prime reason, then, for considering setting personal, work-oriented goals is that they will help to draw you toward your potential.

Establishing priorities. The very process of establishing goals helps you set up priorities. What goal should receive first call on your energy and abilities? Which targets should be farther down the line? There is clear evidence that those who become good at setting their work goals also manage their time better.

The satisfaction of accomplishment. Few things are more satisfying than setting a difficult goal and then reaching it. People who set goals seem to reap a deep inner sense of self-fulfillment when they accomplish what they set out to do. Some people say it is the same

*In *Motivation and Productivity,* Chicago, American Management Association, 1963.

158

feeling of exhilaration that mountain climbers and hang-glider enthusiasts talk about.

Fulfillment of inner needs. The recognition you get from reaching goals satisfies inner needs by enhancing your self-esteem. Social acceptance and praise can be achieved, along with monetary rewards (security). Here is the way Woody interprets goal-setting.

> For a long time I didn't understand the importance of setting goals. I thought it was a form of self-pressure I didn't want anything to do with. Then I discovered that it is the achievement part that makes it all worthwhile. Not only do goal-setters have more success in the work environment, but they also get more personal rewards from their efforts.

Better articulation with management. One of your superiors may ask you to discuss your career goals. It is also a possibility that management will invite you to write down your departmental goals—a procedure prescribed in those organizations that have adopted the Management by Objectives (MBO) philosophy. You will do a better job of articulation if you have *already* thought things through and are working toward some clear-cut goals.

Are there dangers in setting goals?

Yes! You can frustrate yourself by establishing goals that are beyond your capacity or by establishing firm time limits that, through no fault of your own, might have to be adjusted at a later date. To be effective and motivating, goals must be reachable. They may be difficult to reach (forcing you to live closer to your potential), but you must sense that you are making progress. There is also the possibility that you might create too many goals and attach unrealistic time limits to them. Pushing too hard could cause you to lose some of the flexibility you need in order to adjust to changes. Marti feels this way.

> I like short, reachable goals with no time limitations attached. You know, something I can accomplish in a week or so if things work out okay, but "no sweat" if it takes longer. I have come to the conclusion that there is a real art to goal-setting and that everyone must set them according to his or her own personality and style.

What kinds of on-the-job goals are there? Which ones would be best? How do you make choices? Career-development goals can be divided into three classifications. As you read about them, try to relate them to your present work or school situation.

Learning goals. Although they are somewhat difficult to set, learning goals are the safest and, in the long run, the most rewarding. As a new, career-oriented employee, you want to learn as much as possible about the organization and how to become human-relations competent. When you adopt learning goals, your attitude says, "I realize that I am an apprentice within this organization, but I have the potential to learn and make personal progress. The more I learn, the faster my progress will be; therefore, I will take advantage of every possible opportunity to learn from all available sources."

Ray, a new supervisor for a transportation company, follows this procedure.

> I try to have three learning goals going for me at all times. I write them down, and as soon as one is accomplished, I come up with a replacement. Right now, my three goals are: (1) learning the national safety code for highway drivers; (2) learning the new laws that govern truck highway transportation; and (3) learning the names and titles of the executives in my company. It usually takes me a few months to reach a goal I set for myself.
>
> The main reason I advocate learning goals is that it makes the job itself more interesting. My salary right now is not as high as I want it to be, but as long as I'm learning, I am gaining a benefit that will provide rewards at a later date. The problem with learning goals, and the reason most individuals do not set them, is that they are easy to forget because rewards are not immediate. Attending to goals that may help you get a new position three years from now is difficult for most people.

Position goals. Most people accept as good advice the idea of preparing for the job ahead of them on the line of progression to the top. If you are a nonsupervisor, prepare for the job of your immediate boss; if you are already a supervisor, prepare for the middle-management role above you.

What if your supervisor is nonpromotable? What if the firm reorganizes and eliminates a position you were preparing to occupy? What if people are frozen in their current positions because the company is not growing? It is probably wise to prepare for several different roles in an organization, rather than zero in on one exclusively, so that you are promotable in more than one direction. If possible, keep in touch with competing organizations so that opportunities to move up are not limited to a single firm. The biggest danger in preparing for a *single* position above you is the possibility that someone other than you may be chosen to fill the job when it becomes vacant, and your adjustment may be a bitter experience. Perhaps this advice from the personnel director for a large electronics concern is worth taking seriously.

Ambitious employees limit themselves when they prepare only for the position directly above them. It is better to prepare for horizontal, vertical, and staff positions all at the same time. When a management vacancy occurs, we feel obligated to review *all* people we believe to be qualified, not just those who have had a close identity with the role. In my opinion, it is also a good idea for anyone seeking a promotion to let personnel know they would appreciate consideration. Sometimes individuals are passed over because they fail to communicate their desires.

Money goals. Setting financial goals is a popular pastime for many individuals.

"I am going to give this company three years to get my salary above the $20,000 level, or I am going shopping."

"I expect to reach $30,000 by the time I am 35 either with this organization or a competing company. I think it is a realistic goal."

"I am going to be pretty disappointed if I don't get at least a $1,500 increase this year. Look at all the responsibility I have taken over!"

It is a natural phenomenon to equate organizational progress with income. The dangers, however, are many. When you set a money goal (say $20,000 per year) and then attach a time limit (such as three years) to it, you are placing yourself in a box that could cause needless frustration. Organizations must make promotions when the need occurs, not when advancement meets the goals of employees. Those who put time limitations on reaching certain positions (and the salary that goes with them) are being fair neither to their firms nor to themselves. Sometimes individuals leave a company because they did not receive a $2,000 increase, but if they had stayed another year, the increase might have been $5,000. In addition to salary, you must consider fringe benefits, such as medical insurance programs, retirement plans, and profit sharing. The organization's contributions to such benefits are part of your income. Here is the way a manager of a large retail store views the problem of unrealistic goals.

We lose some highly qualified people simply because they set impossible goals for themselves and then get upset because we can't satisfy them. I believe in goals. They are great motivators for most people. But if they destroy the flexibility one must have these days, they can do more harm than good. I have considered offering a seminar to help our people learn how to select and reach realistic, work-oriented goals. Of course, I believe that in setting goals you also learn how to establish priorities, which is equally important.

People set their personal-organizational goals either on an immediate, short-term basis or on a long-term basis.

Immediate goals. Research shows that most executives set daily and weekly priority goals. The president of a large utility follows this pattern.

> When I get ready to leave my office at night, I use the last ten or fifteen minutes to write out my priorities (goals) for the following day on my calendar pad. The list usually includes six or seven items. As I write them, I psych myself into believing that I am leaving these problems behind me so that I do not take my responsibilities home with me. When I arrive in the morning, I review and revise this list. Often this process starts on the freeway en route to my downtown office. These are my immediate goals, and although I constantly handle new problems during the day because emergencies occur, I still find the list motivating. I also believe in weekly goals, so on Monday morning I sometimes write out a few important things I want to accomplish before the week is over. I recommend this practice to all junior executives as long as they remain flexible and do not let their goals lock them in.

Surveys show that the majority of managers use some variation of the above system. They like the idea of setting targets that are reachable, and they feel they need to put first things first. Some declare that if a goal shows up on a list for two or three weeks in succession and has yet to be accomplished, it should either be taken care of immediately or eliminated. Those who adhere to this simple procedure claim that they not only get more work done (because of better motivation), but also arrange their tasks in better sequence.

Short-term goals. Inside an organization, a short-term goal is one that can be accomplished within a few months. This period could be from one month to six or more, but is seldom more than a year. When a new supervisor takes over a "sick" department where morale and productivity are low, for example, the supervisor might say, "I will give myself six months to turn this department around. By that time, I hope to have both morale and productivity on the way back up so that management will recognize my achievement."

Organizations that practice management by objectives (they mandate goal-setting procedures) usually ask their management people to prepare six-month objectives and submit them in writing.

Once reviewed, discussed, and accepted, these objectives become the official organizational goals of the manager for the period covered. These goals are expressed in such a way that results are *measurable*; that is, once the period is over, it is possible to evaluate how close the individual came to reaching expressed goals.

Long-term goals. Usually long-term goals are highly personal and unwritten and require more than a year to achieve. A business administration major, who joined a banking concern, set a long-term goal when she decided to earn her master's degree by going back to college on a part-time basis. Another long-term goal would be the ambition to move from junior management to middle management. Such goals will probably take several years to accomplish and, obviously, need not be written. Should a personal goal be kept private or discussed openly? If you discuss such a target, you may be embarrassed if you discard the goal later on. On the other hand, letting friends and associates in on it can provide motivation through strengthening your commitment.

Here are some special tips on how to set and revise goals to accomplish greater motivation.

Tailor your goals to your own needs and desires. Your goals may not be motivating to you unless you form them carefully and make them highly personal. They must be *meaningful* or inspiring to you. Other people, including your supervisor, cannot impose goals upon you and expect them to inspire you to great achievements.

Avoid setting time limitations except on very short goals. Setting time limits can be a good idea for weekly or monthly goals, especially when you can control your time. If you feel you must set a long-term time limit, why not make it a time range? Instead of saying "I will give this company one year to promote me," you might say "I will see what happens within the first few years before I make an organizational commitment."

Reward yourself to increase your motivation. Many individuals discover that if they reward themselves with a vacation, some personal purchases, or a special occasion of some kind, the goal becomes more motivating. Rewards are especially effective for immediate or short-term goals.

Try not to set too many goals. If you set too many goals, you may become confused, and your targets will have so little meaning that they are not motivating. Fewer than ten daily goals and one or two weekly, short-term, and long-term goals would seem reasonable.

Revise and up-date your goals frequently. Long-term goals, like completing your formal education, need not be revised in most cases. Daily goals, on the other hand, may need to be revised many times before the day is over. *Awareness* is an important factor involved in reaching goals. The goal must "pop into your mind" now and then to keep you inspired and headed in the right direction. The moment a goal is forgotten, it has lost its purpose. But you must be flexible enough to revise goals as necessary.

Block out some time to accomplish goals. After you have established your priorities, it is important to block out on your work calendar enough time to get the work done. Unless you take this step, you will not achieve your goals.

Establish a long-term plan. Once you have established your goals and time blocks, you might put everything into a general plan of action. You could ask a friend or co-worker to read your plan and make comments and suggestions. After this step has been accomplished, you follow the plan but continue to revise it as conditions change.

A significant hidden value of goal setting is that it helps you line up your priorities. As you decide on your goals, you often go through the process of elimination. Those goals that remain on your list become top priority items and help to determine the tasks you perform on the job. Those goals that you have considered but discarded probably represented a lower level of priority.

Long-term goals *transcend* organizations in most cases; that is, they are highly personal goals that have lifetime career implications and can be accomplished in one organization as well as another. To achieve their management goals, some people feel it is to their advantage to move from one organization to another as long as they make an upward step with each move.

Discussion Questions

How many of these statements can you support, if any?

1. "Finishing this book is a short-term goal for me. My motivation comes from the possibility that I might learn something that will help me reach the long-term personal and organizational goals I already have delineated in my mind."
2. "A goal provides motivation only when it helps a person to achieve a highly personal life-style. For example, I want to get into a management position not because I really want to be a manager, but because that is the only way I can make enough money to live the life-style I want. In short, there is no such thing as a motivating organizational goal."

3. "There is an automatic, inherent conflict between organizational and personal goals. Take my case. I am motivated to get a master's degree. Now, when I have it, I will be worth more to my organization; in the meantime, however, everybody thinks I am doing this just to improve my personal position in life, so the resentment factor is hurting, not helping, my career progress. There is just no possible way of eliminating or even mitigating the conflict."
4. "If you learn to set good short-term and long-term organizational goals, you have completely taken care of setting your priorities."
5. "When you find a goal that is meaningful to you, motivation is automatic."
6. "All highly successful organizational people are goal-oriented."

Robert Davis
Job Seeker

**Career
Profile**

It is difficult to evaluate my "passage" from campus to career since I recently quit the job I had for nine years and have not chosen a new one yet. The resignation was precipitated by moral and ethical conflicts with my employer, but I have never been totally committed to one profession. I always looked at my job as a vehicle to an end rather than a career in and of itself.

A year or two before I graduated from San Jose State with an Industrial Engineering degree, I began to realize that I was not totally satisfied with my major. I was already leaning toward business over engineering, but because of the draft situation at that time and my eagerness to begin a career, I finished in my major. In interviewing for jobs I relied on the San Jose State placement office and met with anyone who was remotely interested in the qualifications I had.

I chose the most interesting job with the highest *early* income potential. My thought was that the sooner I made a lot of money, the sooner I could do what I wanted to do. I kept this philosophy for nine years as a way of justifying staying with a job I did not like. And my wife and I did not practice the kind of financial management necessary to let me think about a lower-paying but more satisfying job. At the time, splurging seemed like a way of compensating for my lack of fulfillment in my job.

The job that I chose nine years ago was that of a commission salesman for an equipment manufacturer. I chose it because it did in fact offer income potential far above the average. Commission work also appealed to me because I felt that I was an above-average producer, and this was a way to be properly compensated. Finally, the particular job setup was similar to running a small business with some exposure to design work, bookkeeping, collection, service work, warranty administration, and a fair amount of clerical detail.

Not knowing where I will end up, I cannot really say if I stayed at this job too long. What happens in the next few months (or years) will give me a better feel for that. I know only that I was not ready before now to make the commitment to start over. I say start over, because I plan to completely leave the industry I am in, rather than move within it.

One of my biggest shortcomings has been my insecurity or feelings of lack of self-worth. I never made a true appraisal of my worth to the company. I underestimated the impact I could have in bringing about change. Earning an above-average income pacified me and did not motivate me to "stretch." I failed to make a realistic appraisal of what people my age with my background, qualifications, and ambitions had accomplished. It is important to compare yourself with people of similar ambition and with similar goals to properly evaluate your ranking or potential. You can always find someone you outshine if you only want to soothe your ego. Limiting your comparisons to people of your caliber and drive can be eye-opening.

This also relates to our homelife. Too often we compared our lifestyle, our possessions, our interests, our social life to everyone we were associated with. Naturally we were disappointed. We ignored the fact that couple A sacrificed their vacation to buy a car, couple B drove an old car so that they could afford a vacation, and so forth.

In retrospect I realize that I had been trying to compensate for an unpleasant job situation by making more money and having more "things." It didn't work! It sounds trite, but I learned money can't buy happiness.

At this point I'm happy where I am. I wish I had had more background in financial planning (just plain budgeting) in order to make my escape sooner. On the other hand, it's only been recently that I reached a level in my profession that gave me the self-confidence to do what I am doing.

I wish I had given myself a more realistic, short-term set of goals. I had been planning ahead ten years and not looking at today. I'm now committed to six-month goals as a means of more closely evaluating my position.

I feel I'm on track again.

DISENCHANTMENT
Successfully Handling Down Periods

13

For many graduates the transition from campus to career can be an up-and-down experience. You may have peak periods of involvement and excitement followed by temporary periods of review and reflection. A recent graduate explains it this way.

> I thought of myself as sufficiently mature to cope with everything and still stay in an upbeat mood. I soon discovered, however, that I had "down periods" like everybody else. These periods of reflection were not the fault of the organization I joined; in fact, I have come to the conclusion that they were necessary "lulls" that gave me a better focus on what was happening to me and the progress I was making toward my long-term goals. Stated simply, they are a part of the transition process.

The most important thing to learn about such periods of temporary disenchantment is that you can use them to help your long-term career progress. They can be disturbing, painful, and difficult to live through. You should take them seriously, but you can, if you wish, convert them into periods of self-assessment and value. Here are some thoughts, obtained through an interview, from an individual who has given the subject some close analysis.

> Organizational adjustment periods can be trying and difficult, but they do not seem to test us emotionally like things that hit us in our personal lives. They are best viewed as organizational hurdles instead of personal or career "blocks." I think it helps to know that they happen to almost everyone, they don't last long, and they seldom drift into forms of serious depression. In fact, from my observation, if a period of disenchantment turns into a serious long-term problem, the cause is probably outside and not inside the organization. I think they should be

interpreted as rest and re-evaluation periods along one's career path. They need to be understood and dealt with objectively, but they should not be indulged.

Why do these periods of review, assessment, and adjustment take place? Why are they part of the transition process? Here are five possible causes.

Campus and career may be farther apart than you think. Compared to campus life and leisure activities, the working world is often harshly pragmatic. Physical demands on your body can be painful until you get used to them; working hours can be rigid. At work there are more rules to live up to. Some jobs are "desk-bound" and confining. Competition can be brutal; human-relations problems can be shocking; management leadership styles can be difficult to adjust to; communication can be different and more demanding. The physical environment can be so different from that of campus life that a major adjustment is required. And, on top of all this, you are faced with developing a separate life-style away from work, since your college and personal life were probably blended together.

The "Disneyland syndrome" is perpetuated by some professors. Most educational institutions overprotect their students. First, they rightfully develop an academic climate that has the luxury of dealing with theory rather than reality; second, they assume a laissez-faire attitude and give students a very unstructured atmosphere; third, professors often paint a false picture about the business world—a world many professors have little contact with. Some go so far as to mislead their students into thinking they will qualify for higher level entry jobs than are generally available. Because it encourages fantasy, college has been compared to Disneyland. The following quotation is typical.

> Some professors prepare you as though you were going to stay on campus for the rest of your life. They have lost contact with the competitive world. They certainly don't do their students any favors. In fact, most of my down periods came while I was trying to get a job, not after I got one.

Some recruiters and interviewers oversell graduates. Although an opposing trend may be developing, in the past interviewers were often guilty of talking only about bright expectations instead of describing the demands of the job. Some graduates make comments like this.

After going through more than 30 interviews, I came up with three firm offers. I finally selected a company that appeared to have a great training program and many side benefits. From the outside it all looked very promising, but now that I've been on the inside for four months, I can tell you that it's not what I expected. Few of those dreamy promises made to me during the interview stage have materialized. I'm beginning to get the hang of things, but I was not prepared for the reality of corporate life.

A crucial financial adjustment period may occur. The majority of graduates discover themselves in a financial crunch when they leave campus and start their first career jobs. Why? Most students grow accustomed to relying on financial support from parents or scholarships. When this income disappears, the amount of money graduates make on their first jobs is not always sufficient to cover the expenses of getting started in the world of work. The following statement comes from a graduate who started her transition two years ago.

My folks supported me until I got my degree, but then it was over. The only job I could find was miles away, so I was paying for an apartment, taking care of my car, and spending extra money on the business wardrobe I needed. My beginning salary was very modest. Believe me, the financial pressure was much greater than all of the pressures from my job. My folks finally gave me a loan to help me through the transition. I think every graduate needs a few thousand dollars of transition money. Otherwise, we have to make two major adjustments at the same time.

Severing emotional ties results in loneliness. Many graduates are able to locate acceptable career opportunities without moving to a new geographical area some distance from their friends and relatives. If you can continue to associate with those you love, your adjustment will be less demanding. What about those who must move away? Here is a story told by a graduate from a small private college.

In order to get a suitable entry job, I had to move 200 miles away from home. This meant renting an apartment in an urban area where prices were highly inflated; it meant high transportation costs because I had to drive long distances and pay for parking every day. But mostly it meant I was alone and had to find a whole new set of friends and create a new social life for myself. Meeting people in a strange city was much more difficult than making new friends as a freshman in the dorm. Although I couldn't afford it, I made many weekend trips home during my adjustment period to get emotional reinforcement.

What can you do to avoid down periods? If you experience one, how can you get out of it quickly without damaging your reputation with the organization you have joined? Here are some suggestions that might help.

Isolate any value conflict that cannot be altered. For example, routine, repetitive, maintenance tasks cause some people to have down periods. A teacher may love classroom involvement but hate grading papers. A retail store buyer may love to work with merchandise but despise working for hours with computer print-outs. An outside sales representative may thrive on customer contacts but find it almost impossible to do the necessary paper work.

Every job or assignment has *some* undesirable, boring features. You might be willing to work with a 70/30 combination—70 percent creative or active work and 30 percent routine, repetitive work. You might *not* be able to avoid down periods in a 50/50 combination. Of course, if you are on a temporary job with an unfavorable combination, you might be able to live with it without becoming negative. If your job is permanent, however, you may need to consider a job change. You cannot afford to spend long periods of time in a work role that causes down periods no matter how hard you try to overcome them.

See the problem in proper perspective. Transition stress results from the need to make an adjustment, not from the faults of the organization you have joined. Accept the premise that going through small adjustment periods will help, not hurt your long-term progress. Remind yourself that down periods do not indicate an emotional weakness on your part.

Talk to a contemporary. Nothing lifts our spirits more than really talking things over with a friend. Mickey chose a friend going through the same adjustment process.

> I got through my first few adjustment periods by talking things over with a classmate going through the same transition with a different corporation. It is important to let it all out to somebody who is receptive. You feel much better when you realize you are not alone.

Enjoy the "fun" side of your job. Personnel people see new employees of all ages taking their jobs too seriously and, as a result, creating their own down periods. One interviewer speculated about causes and suggested a solution.

> I am not sure of the causes. It could be high expectations. Maybe employees expect too much of themselves, or simply dwell on the problem too long. The cause could be as basic as fear of failure. At any rate, the

best solution is to help them see the humorous side of the job. Work is not a "dreary" experience for those who can see the light side and enjoy the relaxation that comes from some fun and games. New employees, in their efforts to succeed, should learn not to take either their starting jobs or themselves too seriously.

Involve yourself in creative activities. Seek involvement with others in solving departmental problems and expanding possibilities. If you are fortunate, your supervisor will draw you into such exciting involvements; if not, you should make the effort yourself. Ben talked about the advantages of involvement.

> The only time I'm happy is when I'm busy and feel I'm part of a group in which there is lots of personal interaction. My periods of discouragement come when I'm inactive and have too much time to dwell on myself.

Balance your two worlds. Some new employees set an unrealistic work pace for themselves without providing enough release through social activities. Perhaps they try to make their jobs satisfy all of their psychological needs. Others relax so much on the job that they fall into down periods because they sense disapproval (which they have earned) from co-workers and management alike. Some balance is necessary, as another new employee testifies.

> Now that the transition is over, I can clearly see my major mistake. I put all of my energy into the job and did nothing to build an outside life for myself. Ultimately, I became disenchanted because I spent too much time working on job matters at home at the expense of social life. I guess I was so fearful of failure that I tried too hard.

Keep your long-term goals in focus. When you first join an organization, your immediate problems may become so overwhelming that you lose focus on your long-term career possibilities. You need immediate goals, such as trying to complete a training program with high marks, but you also need one or two long-term goals, such as earning your first assignment as a manager. Without a long-term goal, little problems magnify. The example below is from an individual who graduated with an M.B.A. degree three years ago.

> I got into a depression period because I temporarily lost sight of my long-term goal—becoming a successful mid-management person in a reasonable length of time. I thought I was being neglected, that my initial assignment was unfair, and that my supervisor was ineffective. I was so worried that I lost focus. Perhaps, without knowing it, I was

childishly seeking the treatment I had come to expect on campus. When I stepped back and got a better fix on where I wanted to be in a few years, things started to happen.

Create some new diversions for yourself. (1) Enroll in a night course to give your life-style a change of pace and your mind a new challenge. (2) Become involved in a job-related professional group or a community organization such as a dramatic club. (3) Take a mini-vacation. (4) Change your personal image by having your hair styled differently. (5) Make a big effort to make *somebody else* happy. (6) Do something unusual that has a "humorous touch" to prove to yourself you are not taking yourself too seriously. (7) Learn a new art or craft. (8) If your job is sedentary, try a new sport or enroll in an exercise class.

Evaluate your job. Sometimes, without knowing it, an employee permits the negative factors in a job to outweigh or overshadow the positive ones. Then a period of self-examination takes place. Am I in the right job? Did I join the right company? Some people use this period for job evaluation. You might divide a sheet of paper into two columns, then list positive factors in one column and negative factors in the other. The example below shows how this simple exercise might help you become more objective and return to a more balanced perspective.

Job Evaluation

Positive Factors

Interesting work
Opportunity to learn
Freedom to move
  around
Can wear nice clothes
Satisfactory pay
Medical plan great
Company pays for night
  classes
Air-conditioned building
Super company cafeteria
Good promotion
  possibilities

Negative Factors

Supervisor distant
Little recognition so far
Difficult to park
Old equipment
Commuting expensive
Not a prestige company
Company no longer
  expanding
No profit-sharing

This exercise forces you to view the positive factors that exist in every job but are sometimes overlooked. Many individuals experience periods of discouragement because they have lost sight of the advantages that surround them.

Employers recognize that new employees, especially recent college graduates, need to explore the first organization they join and that down periods may result from this process. The old ideal of immediate loyalty, whether or not it is deserved, has gone by the board—and rightfully so. Many people try three or four companies before they find the one that is right for them. Still, many beginners leave their first jobs without giving the job and the company a fair chance. How will you know when you have found the right career unless you give each employer a fair chance to meet your needs? Try to look for all the positive factors and ignore the negative ones for at least a few weeks. Combine positive thinking with maximum effort to do your job well. After the trial period is over, continual awareness of negative factors is probably a signal that you are in the wrong job and should start looking elsewhere. Searching for a suitable vocation is part of the developmental process of young adults who are still formulating values and seeking identity. Perhaps this quotation from a personnel director will help.

> We retain less than 50 percent of our college graduates a full year. I don't mind people leaving when they *know* they are in the wrong spot, because it is best for all concerned. What worries me are those who walk away when the first dark clouds appear. Often they become "job hoppers" and damage their careers. I have heard many personnel people and college placement directors say that the new employee should try the organization for at least one year before deciding to stay or leave.
>
> I disagree because I don't think it's just a matter of time. Deciding whether to stay should be like making a major, sophisticated market survey; all of the facts should be gathered, considerable communication should take place, and the final decision should not be made in haste or on an emotional basis. Many people jump out too soon and then make the same mistakes all over again with another organization. Applicants need to do *more* research *before* making a job commitment.

Why is it so important to keep your down periods to a minimum and recover from them quickly when they occur?

Periods of discouragement can damage your career progress in three ways. First, during such periods your relationships with management and co-workers may deteriorate through neglect. Second, such periods can cause you to make bad decisions. For example, you could become so discouraged that you might resign your position and regret it later. Third, unless you control such periods, they may cause you to lose your long-term goals, which, in turn, can destroy your self-confidence.

Discussion Questions

You are invited to defend or criticize the following statements.

1. "Ninety-five percent of those who go through down periods during their transition to the world of work do so without letting it show either in their attitudes or productivity."
2. "I reject the idea that down periods are inevitable for all new employees during their adjustment period."
3. "I do not think it is possible either to shorten or to pull yourself out of down periods; they are physically and emotionally based cycles that everyone goes through. These moody periods may spill over into the job environment, but they were not created by it."
4. "Periods of discouragement and frustration are caused by the goal-setting process. When we are blocked from reaching goals, a down period is precipitated. Eliminate goals and you eliminate such periods."
5. "The idea that something good can come from living through down periods is garbage; they do nothing but slow down your career progress."
6. "Down periods are goal destroyers. They cause people to lose sight of their career objectives, which, in turn, destroys self-confidence. Such periods should be treated more seriously."

Career Profile

Inge Krieg
Director of Housekeeping
Bonaventure Hotel, Los Angeles

In viewing my passage from childhood and schooling in Germany to my current position as director of housekeeping for the Los Angeles Bonaventure Hotel, I have realized something that many students and teachers do not recognize—that the academic life does not always prepare you for what is to come and that students are sheltered and protected. I would probably consider this the biggest obstacle a person must overcome when moving from academia to the world of business.

The manner in which a student is prepared for the future has a great deal to do with his or her instructors. Fortunately, I had a teacher (in hotel school) who helped me by teaching the proper French service; but he always stressed that he never wanted to hear of his students telling an employer that they could not do something because that was not how they were taught. That instructor knew that you have to bend and conform to each situation.

And that is where the real problem lies with the educational world. The experiences there often are not translated into real-life language—things are not related to day-to-day practical living.

But one also discovers things in school that become invaluable in later life. Because the hotel where I received my practical training was small, and because I was willing to spend extra time beyond my required hours, I learned things about the business that the other students did not. I found out that your education doesn't always come in between 8 A.M. and 5 P.M. And I carried that experience with me from school into the real world, where I found that if you want to accomplish more than your neighbor, you have to spend extra time, you have to work for it, and that when you start out you are never paid for the effort you put into reaching your goal.

After graduating, I left Germany to become a governess in New York. I just wanted to visit the United States and see how things were done there. I intended to go back. Once here, I decided that I had at least one foot in the door, and I wanted to collect experiences and references before going home.

One of the main problems I encountered on entering the business world, other than realizing that you must relearn things with each new organization you work for, was a language barrier. I applied for a front-desk job, the only position that was available, with a San Francisco hotel. I tried to tell the manager that I wanted to think about it and would return in the evening with my answer. I returned and the job was gone. We hadn't made ourselves clear to each other, and I lost the job.

I finally found a position in housekeeping with the St. Francis Hotel, part of the Western International Hotels chain. Nine months later I became assistant director. A year later I was director of that department.

In the summer of 1975 I served as director of housekeeping and opened the Peachtree Plaza in Atlanta. And in the summer of 1976 I took over my present position as director of housekeeping for the Bonaventure.

To open a hotel the size of the Bonaventure, I worked about 15 hours a day. I spent nights in the hotel and often came down on Saturdays and Sundays. I learned from mistakes I made at the Peachtree Plaza, but new problems arose here. And again I made a discovery—that you learn from each new experience and that you cannot be fully prepared for it.

I head the department in the hotel which spends the most money. I head a staff of about 250 people, and I must work to achieve harmony between this and all the other departments in the hotel.

My experience exemplifies one of the great pluses of the hotel industry; you can start from the bottom and move up. And by doing that, you serve in all capacities of the area you eventually hope to head; thus you do everything at least once yourself and can better understand the responsibilities and problems of your employees. I will not ask anyone in my department to do something I would not do myself.

I really feel, too, that you have to know yourself and what your own limitations are—and that you can't be completely honest with yourself at first. You must set high goals, higher than you can accomplish, and when you have achieved 98 percent of those goals, then you should realize that you have made it, that you have done a great job.

And I am doing things I always wanted to do, but didn't think I could achieve. Design, teaching, and the fashion world all interested me when I was younger. Through a counselor I turned to the hotel industry—and now I work on the interior design and decorating of the hotel, pick out uniforms for the employees, and each day I deal with people and instruct employees.

So I am 30 years old. I had set a goal for myself that by the time I was 30 I would have worked for the three largest hotels—and I did. I opened the largest addition to a hotel, the tallest hotel, and the largest hotel on the West Coast.

My puzzle has been put together. I now hope to give someone else advice, and I want to see my assistants grow as I did—through the help of others.

Exercises for Part III

Three-Month Self-Assessment Progress Report

(If your answer is number 1, you need not complete the second part of each evaluation factor.)

1. I am fully motivated   1   2   3   4   5   I am totally without
   on my job.   motivation.

   I will start looking for another job or motivate myself to
   do the following:

   _____

   _____

   _____

   _____

   _____

2. I have met the   1   2   3   4   5   I have not tried to
   dress standards set   meet the dress
   by my co-workers   standards set by
   and superiors.   my superiors and
                                                co-workers.

   I intend to do the following to improve my visual image:

   _____

   _____

   _____

   _____

3. Since I took this   1 2 3 4 5   I need help to
    job, my personal   improve my self-
    confidence and   concept and my
    self-concept have   self-confidence.
    improved 100
    percent.

    I intend to do the following to improve my self-concept on
    the job:

    _____

    _____

    _____

4. The ethical standard   1 2 3 4 5   There is total lack
    of my work   of harmony
    environment is   between my values
    harmonious with my   and the ethics of my
    personal values.   work environment.

    Listed below are the personal values that are in harmony
    or disharmony with my organization's ethics.

    Harmony   *Disharmony*

    _____   _____

    _____   _____

    _____   _____

5. I like the   1 2 3 4 5   I am completely
    organization better   disenchanted with
    now than when I   the organization.
    joined it.

If I decide to stay with the firm, I plan to do the following in an attempt to appreciate its good points:

_____

_____

_____

6. I am getting all of   1   2   3   4   5   I have been totally
the recognition I   neglected.
deserve.

If I decide to stay, I am going to earn recognition in the following ways:

_____

_____

_____

7. I can be completely   1   2   3   4   5   I deny that I have
honest about the   made any mistakes
mistakes I have   so far.
made so far.

I plan to eliminate the following mistakes in the future:

_____

_____

_____

8. The people in this   1   2   3   4   5   The people are
firm are sensitive   hostile, and I can't
and I get along   get along with any
with them well.   of them.

I intend to do the following to build better relationships with co-workers and managers:

_____

_____

_____

_____

9. I would rate my   1 2 3 4 5   I have made no
   progress as   progress.
   superior in all
   areas.

I want to improve my progress in the following areas:

_____

_____

_____

_____

10. I am proud of my   1 2 3 4 5   I haven't made an
    efforts to adjust to   effort to adjust.
    this organization.

I believe the following efforts on my part will enhance my adjustment in the future:

_____

_____

_____

_____

Case Study: Isolation

Michelle's secretarial skills were extremely high in all areas. Although she had not completed her junior year in college, everyone recognized her potential. Still, after less than three months, Michelle's supervisor was ready to ask for her resignation.

Why?

Michelle worked in the management office for a large shopping center. There were only eight people, including the manager, in her office. The climate was very relaxed, and everyone was expected to "pitch in" to meet deadlines and accommodate the tenants of the center. Despite this need for cooperation, Michelle had built a psychological wall between herself and others. She was slightly rude when others interrupted her work and unfriendly when tenants asked her for favors. She never initiated any communication in the office, and was cold and negative on the telephone.

Her supervisor (the assistant manager of the office) put it this way.

> Michelle has kept herself in a box; she wants to work as an isolate in an office where isolation is impossible. As a result, we all feel uncomfortable around her, and we sense the tenants are beginning to react to her in a negative way. We deeply appreciate her skills. In fact, she turns out more work than anyone else if she is left alone. She is the most efficient person I have ever known. But unless we can communicate to her that she must join the group, we will eventually have to take some corrective action. I honestly feel Michelle would be in trouble in any office environment. Yet, I really want to save her for our organization and help her see the opportunities beyond her present position. How do I go about doing this?

Assume that you are Michelle's supervisor. Which of the following steps would you consider and why?

1. Have a serious, open talk with her and tell her that she will either have to break out of her self-imposed shell or seek employment elsewhere.

2. Suggest that she take a course in communication skills at a local community college and offer to pay all expenses involved, including transportation.

3. Take her to lunch and get to know her better. After you have built a good relationship with her (and have learned a great deal

more about her), set up a three-way counseling session with your-self, the manager, and Michelle. Use the approach of compli-menting her on her skills before introducing the communication problem. Then, at the right time, ask her what she is going to do about it.

4. Have a secret staff meeting with everyone but Michelle pres-ent. Introduce the problem and ask everyone to pitch in and help bring her out of her shell.

5. Take her to lunch and ask her if she will accept professional help if the company pays the bill.

6. Take the slow approach; that is, make more attempts to get to know her, talk with her, and slowly help her eliminate the box she has put herself in. You realize this may take months, but you feel any form of threat would only cause her to raise her barriers higher.

7. Ask her to make a survey that would require her to contact each tenant on a personal basis, thus forcing her to come out of her shell.

8. Do some research into her background by contacting a pre-vious employer and school officials. Refuse to take any step until you have more personal data. Then, using your own skills, try to probe deeply into the matter for a sound solution.

9. Be satisfied with her professional skills and work things out so that her isolation will increase the efficiency of the office and will not require any communication from her.

10. Accept the premise that she has a problem you will probably not be able to solve and give her notice.

(Note: You may use any combination of the above procedures or revise them to meet your needs. You may also develop procedures of your own.)

Part IV

USING AND IMPROVING YOUR SKILLS

Objectives

After you have completed this section you should know

1. Whether you should speak up more—or less—and how to improve communications

2. How to become a better listener

3. Whether you should take a reading improvement course and why such courses are helpful

4. Whether you need to improve your business writing skills and if so, how to start

Preparing in Advance

As you read and study Part IV, please remember that preparing for career success ahead of time (as you are doing) may be the best way to get a good job in the first place. Why might this be true? (1) Knowing more about what employers expect can give you more personal confidence during the interview period. (2) Anticipating certain problems in advance can give you some insight regarding questions you may be asked by an interviewer. (3) Obtaining a reservoir of information about the transition period can greatly improve communication between you and an interviewer.

COMMUNICATION
Are You Speaking Up Enough?

14

Surveys show that a serious and common mistake among new, ambitious employees is their failure to communicate verbally as much as they should. Here are some typical comments from communication specialists and consultants in government, educational, and business organizations.

> Many employees think they are communicating sufficiently when they are not. They pass up opportunities every day. These individuals need to understand that failure to speak up leads to misinterpretation. If you don't know what a person is thinking, you may assume the wrong things.

> No one has sold the recent graduate on the basic premise that communications is the life blood of a working relationship. Two-way communication between people is essential; I think it is better to talk too much than too little.

> We want people to voice their creative ideas around here. We also want to know their frustrations and their gripes. It's not healthy for employees to keep their feelings bottled up. They may not know it, but it hurts their productivity and their career progress when they hold too much inside.

In the box on the next page are seven simple questions. Please answer them as honestly as possible. When you have finished, total both the Yes and No answers on the next page.

If you added up four or more Yes answers in the quiz, chances are you should concentrate more on developing your speaking skills because the possibility of being misinterpreted may be hurting your career progress.

Communication Quiz		
	YES	NO
1. Have you avoided public speaking courses while on campus?	☐	☐
2. Would you rather listen to others than speak up yourself?	☐	☐
3. In a classroom, do you frequently hope you will not be called upon?	☐	☐
4. Do you hesitate and feel embarrassed to introduce yourself to strangers?	☐	☐
5. Do you envy those who volunteer to speak in group settings?	☐	☐
6. Would you like to feel more confident about speaking up?	☐	☐
7. Would you refuse an invitation to be a chairperson for a group discussion?	☐	☐
TOTAL	☐	☐

How can you be more assertive in a verbal way? How can you sense and take advantage of communication opportunities where you work? How can you build the reputation of being a skillful communicator with something significant to say? Here are some suggestions.

Initiate more job-related and personal communications with others on an informal basis. Since some of your co-workers may not go out of their way to communicate, you may have to take the first step. You can easily do this by sending some informal verbal signals, like "hello" or "good morning," and follow up with some casual comments regarding on-the-job changes, sports events, or even the weather. Remember that verbal signals can show warmth and friendliness. *They show that you are willing to communicate.* Your fellow workers need to know that you are receptive. If you refuse to initiate any communications, they may feel that you prefer to be left alone. In the event that you have already created some psychological barriers with a few co-workers (by not communicating), you might want to make a special effort to restore and improve these relationships through more communication in the immediate future.

Speak up more in staff and training sessions. If you did very little speaking in groups while on campus, you may have to make an extra effort now. You will understand the need if you remember that you are now playing for keeps. We are not talking about passing a course; we are talking about your income, your position, and your career. Few things can slow down your career progress more than an unwillingness to communicate.

Make your contribution fit into the discussion. For example, if a manager or co-worker has just made a point, you can quickly pick up the conversational trend by saying, "I would like to add to that" or "Could we look at the problem from a different angle?" It is easier and sometimes better to supplement the thoughts of others than to start a whole new trend of thought. Try to volunteer your thoughts without waiting for the group leader to pull them out of you. Once you get over the temporary feeling of self-consciousness that results from being the center of attention, your personal confidence and skill will increase quickly.

Refuse to let others freeze you out in group communication sessions. Those who talk too much may eventually hang themselves, but those who talk too little may be ignored by management or, even worse, interpreted as having nothing worthwhile to say.

If you have had previous group experiences, you understand the impact of interpersonal relationships in group dynamics. You should also understand that there may never be a perfect time to intervene with your comments. Sometimes you just have to take the initiative and assert yourself, even though you may feel awkward in doing so. In most organizational group sessions, the verbal competition from others can be intense. A few people, therefore, may push you into the background unless you speak out. Here is the transformation Martin went through.

> When I first started to work, I told myself to stay on the sidelines until I had more to say and could learn from observation how to say it better. I kept thinking I would embarrass myself and do more harm than good if I spoke up. After waiting much too long to jump in and assert myself, I realized that making a few awkward attempts was far less damaging than not contributing at all. Now I can hold my own with the best of them, and I feel much better about myself.

Set up more private communication sessions. You have a perfect right to arrange interviews with those above you and others in key positions if you do it openly and do not hurt relationships with supervisors by going over their heads without their permission. In fact, if you are taking your career seriously, you have an *obligation* to keep upward lines of communication open. You should feel free occasionally to set up conferences with your immediate supervisor, the personnel officer, and co-workers on your same level. Under certain circumstances, you also can set up interviews with those above your supervisor, including a top official, providing you go about it the right way and have an appropriate matter to discuss. For example, if you had been with an organization for two or three years and you had a creative idea to submit to management, you could write a letter asking for permission to discuss the subject with a high superior and his or her staff. You could introduce the subject in the written communication without going into detail.

Could this action be interpreted as presumptuous on your part? Could it backfire and hurt your career progress? There is always some risk in initiating written or oral communications, but if the idea to be submitted can contribute to the organization, and if you are going through channels, it could be worth the risk. Here is the way one executive puts it.

> In my opinion, it is better to initiate communications that do not result in any action than not to create any at all. Every organization *needs* information and ideas to flow from employees upward to management. Sure, I know about using proper channels and the possibility that feelings can get hurt, but if such communication is initiated in the right way, the risk is worth taking. Most people who get lost in organizations are afraid to take the risk of communicating positive ideas from where they are. In other words, they often stifle themselves.

Once you can sense *why* and *when* you need to speak up, you might want to consider ways to improve your verbal skills. Described below are certain conditions that may or may not apply to you. If a situation *does* apply, the suggestions that follow may help you either solve a problem or increase your effectiveness.

When personal confidence is still a problem. If you need special help to build your confidence to speak up either in private or in group situations, you should enroll in a course in public speaking or communication skills. The Dale Carnegie courses are an example. You may be critical of the techniques used by people who teach such courses, but the *results* are more important than the technique used or the price paid. For self-help, you might practice speaking every night on your own tape recorder until you develop the necessary confidence. Perhaps the comments made recently by one college graduate to another, a close friend, might motivate you to take action now instead of waiting around until your career is damaged.

> Look, Yolanda, you are an adult and you can no longer afford to indulge yourself with this misguided lack of confidence that says you can let others do the communicating. You speak well, you have an excellent vocabulary, and you organize your ideas well, so why don't you do yourself a favor? Start talking and let your fellow workers and management benefit from what you know.

When voice improvement would help. Some people speak too softly, some have voices that are irritating to others, some talk too loudly, some have speech impediments that can be corrected, and some habitually mispronounce words. Most colleges have speech therapists who can give you professional help, if you need it, without any cost to you. If you are hesitant to ask for help, remember that Eleanor Roosevelt took diction lessons after she became First Lady of the United States. Voice improvement is another way to build your self-confidence.

When you find yourself talking too much. Individuals who have the habit of excessive talking in both private and group situations usually fall into one of three categories: (1) They are unaware that they are overtalking. (2) They are compulsive talkers; that is, they know they have a problem but can't seem to stem the flow of words. (3) They deliberately use verbal assertiveness to intimidate others. In each of the first two cases (after the individual accepts his or her problem), controlling the amount of talking is a matter of self-discipline. You can limit the amount of talking you do if you have enough determination. Try to become a better listener. Elisabeth views it this way.

> You can learn to talk less and build better relationships if you learn to be a better listener. You can't talk and listen at the same time. In private conversations, I talk about 50 percent of the time and listen the other 50 percent. In group situations I attempt to make my presence known by saying the right things at the right time, but I keep my contributions to a minimum. It is the right combination of talking and listening that everyone needs to work on.

When learning a new vocabulary is necessary. Perhaps you have joined an organization where a special language is used—not a foreign language, but words you have not yet added to your vocabulary. Medical facilities, legal offices, and technical firms, are examples of work situations in which you may have to learn new words in order to communicate. Naturally, you will be handicapped until you "learn the language." If you need to learn a new vocabulary, you might make a master list of new words, look up their meanings in a dictionary, and weave them into your communications gradually. Terminology can be learned also from reference books, glossaries, and individualized courses.

When you need more on-the-job opportunities to speak. The more you speak up, the easier it will become, but at this point in your career, you may have to learn how to recognize opportunities or how to make them. For example, if you are scheduled for a 30- or 60-day formal appraisal, make certain that you take advantage of this opportunity to tell the appraiser how things are going. When you get a chance to be the leader of a discussion group, don't hesitate to do it. The next time someone is overtalking, wait a reasonable length of time and then intervene with your comments.

In your exuberance to become a better communicator, you must be careful to pick the right time. You *do* want to choose your subject and contribute something of significance. You also want to build good relationships with others. However, you do not want these goals to keep you silent. Remember that it is great to be a good listener as long as you also communicate.

When you have an opportunity to counsel others. One excellent way to improve your ability to communicate is to learn how to be a sensitive advisor or counselor. You can practice with a co-worker or a personal friend. In counseling, one must learn when to listen and when to speak. The balance is crucial. But counseling is primarily "talking things over" in a private setting where two people are comfortably seated and have time to interact. Melinda improved her communications skills by making an unusual transfer.

> I made an interesting discovery about myself a few months ago. I was very quiet on the job, but when I went out to dinner or had a few drinks with a friend, I communicated like you wouldn't believe. I guess I was holding things inside on the job and opening up in the social one-to-one setting. I decided to make a transfer by speaking up more on the job and listening more off-the-job. Guess what? It worked.

To improve communications, in either one-to-one counseling or a group situation, it is often better to ask a question than to make a statement. Sometimes the most effective communicator is the one who does the least talking. In other words, you might improve your ability to communicate by improving your skills in asking questions. Learning about the three basic kinds of questions might help.

The directive question. Directive questions are ordinarily used (sometimes by the group leader) to bring out a topic that needs to be discussed. A directive question is one that calls for greater clarification: "Henry, I would be interested in hearing what you have to contribute on this matter." "Hazel, would you mind stating the problem as you see it?" "Miguel, let's hear your opinion on the topic to help us get started."

The open-ended question. The open-ended question places less limitation on the person invited to respond. Such questions are often heard in both group and private counseling: "Maria, I would be interested in hearing any comments you might make regarding your experiences with our training program." "Jeff, what do you think of the progress we have been making so far?" "Lloyd, is there anything you might like to add before we close up shop this afternoon?"

The reinforcing question. Sometimes a question is designed to keep someone else talking until you understand his or her concept or problem. "Serina, I liked what you said a moment ago, but I am not sure I fully understand everything you said. Could you expand on it for me?" "Helen, I believe I got the general idea of your proposal, but it would help me if you could provide some specific suggestions. You may be onto something." "I would like to go back to what Richard said a few moments ago. Perhaps if he could talk a little more about the idea, I could give him my support."

This chapter emphasizes *verbal* communication, perhaps at the expense of other forms. Some of the feedback you receive from your verbal contributions may be nonverbal in nature. A raised eyebrow, a frown, a turned back, or a noticeable loss of attention also communicates.

Silence itself is a form of communication. It can, of course, mean that one is not listening. It can, however, indicate that a person is concentrating, trying to help defuse an emotional situation, or simply keeping quiet so that another person will continue talking. Attentive silence is the chief attribute of a good listener.

It is very difficult to be a good listener. Research tells us that we listen at an effective rate of about 25 percent and that a great many of the communications breakdowns in organizations occur because of poor listening. We need to listen for instructions, directions, clarification, and understanding. We also need to listen for empathy. The process of listening is so vital that it will be dealt with separately in the next chapter.

Discussion Question

Assume that you are the supervisor of an excellent employee who has yet to learn how to speak up effectively. The potential of this individual is so high that you are already thinking about having her replace you when you move up. You have decided to make a major effort to help her.

Your analysis tells you that she comes from a quiet family, was not assertive during her college years, and is often misunderstood. You feel she must learn to communicate more frequently and openly if her progress is to continue. As a result, you have listed five possible plans to pursue. You have to decide which one would be best.

Plan 1: Advise her to take a special course in communications. If necessary, persuade the firm to pay for a course that will bring her out of her shell.

Plan 2: Put her on the spot daily by asking her more and more questions that demand replies. Continue the questioning until she shows more confidence.

Plan 3: Loan her a book on communications from your personal library.

Plan 4: Start a "teasing" campaign to break her out of her shell.

Plan 5: Appoint her chairman of a research committee.

Plan 6: Initiate a series of counseling sessions.

Which plan, in your opinion, would be most effective? Why? Are there any combinations of the six plans that you would support? Which plans, if any, might do more harm than good?

Adelina S. Silva
Guidance Associate
San Antonio (Texas) College

**Career
Profile**

When I decided to go to college, I realized immediately that I needed money. I decided to stay home and attend a local junior college, and to apply for every form of financial aid the school had to offer. I was awarded a "tuition and books" scholarship and immediately started seeking a part-time job. It just so happened that my freshman counselor hired me to work in the Counseling Center.

So, I was all set—and on my way. My job in the Counseling Center turned out to be very interesting and rewarding. I liked people, especially helping them. I wanted to be an English teacher, and this job gave me enough exposure to people to make me feel I could work with students as a teacher. Little did I know at the time that this job was going to open my eyes and mind to all sorts of information about jobs, job markets, and job satisfaction. Students with bachelors degrees would often come in to ask counselors questions about retraining for technical jobs because either they couldn't get a job or they hated what they were doing. Now more than ever, I didn't want to waste my time getting a degree that might not help me later.

Nevertheless, I paid little attention to the tight market in my own field. I stuck to my teaching major and felt that qualified people weren't getting jobs because they just weren't outgoing or assertive enough. I failed to see that many good people couldn't get jobs just because there were few openings in particular areas. I was very lucky to be able to find a teaching job after college. I could have fallen right on my face expecting so much.

After a few months of teaching, and especially after a few months of the depressing teachers' lounge, I started to wonder why I had wanted this so much. I enjoyed the students, teaching, and our growing experiences, but I wasn't very fond of the assemblies, schedule changes, surveys, collecting dues, and all that.

After a little soul searching, I knew I wanted out but I couldn't afford it immediately. I was now married and my husband was attending college. I did, however, know that I wasn't stuck there. I never lost sight of that. And I think I benefited from my experiences in teaching. I learned much more about myself and what I could do. I also saw from other people that conforming too much to the point where it stifles your personality and potential may not be worth it. One should realize that you can make career changes as well as job changes throughout your working life.

So again I analyzed my personal situation. I liked working with the students and helping them cope with the ups and downs of adolescence. This reinforced and confirmed the thoughts that had been in the back of my mind all along. My experiences in the Counseling Center at junior college came back at once. This was what I really liked. I was now sure. It was time to go back to school.

Because I was working and going to school evenings, my job change did not happen overnight. It took me almost one and a half years to obtain my MA in counseling, but I started applying for jobs long before I graduated. I tried twice and didn't get either job, but the second time I came very close. At the time, I was very upset to think I wasn't good enough to get the jobs, but later on I realized that just to be in the finals meant that I was truly competitive and well qualified. I eventually applied at the Counseling Center where I had worked as a student assistant in junior college. I was fortunate in that the director, my former boss, knew how I could perform. Now, however, I was a professional and had much more experience and confidence in myself and in my work. I knew I brought many assets to the job. I could plan, organize, and carry out projects and presentations as well as do counseling. I was the right person, and they soon agreed.

The job was exactly what I had thought it would be, and I loved it. The people were different. They had changed since I had last been there, or maybe it was because I had changed. My new position changed my former superiors into colleagues, and that in itself was an adjustment for all of us. But any personal adjustment I had to make was outweighed by the rewards of the job itself.

It took me almost three years to find a job that made me truly happy. Years have passed like days since I found that job. I meet new people with new problems. I see mature students returning to school and can empathize with their need for retraining. I also get a lot of visits from my former high school students, who now more than ever realize the value of education. As a guidance associate, careers and the world of work plays a major role in my position, and I can truly see its importance based on my particular experience and those of students I see. All in all, my position holds the best of many worlds, and I am fascinated by it.

However, I never lose sight of my feelings and attitudes. I have to be honest with myself at all times. During low times, I re-evaluate my situation and make decisions that affect it when needed. Now that I feel I have found my career, someday I may want another job in the same field. I have reached my goal, but there is always room for growth and the possibility of change. I invested years of my life in this transition from college to my career, and it was well worth it. Time and effort are well spent when you eventually are able to benefit from them.

CHALLENGE

Improving Your Listening and Reading Skills

15

Few things will hurt an individual's executive image more than gaining a reputation as a poor listener. If communications is the life blood of a sound relationship, then the inability or failure to listen causes anemia.

Would you like to know how others rate you as a listener? If so, you may wish to use the survey on the facing page. A number of people have used it with revealing results. If you decide to use it, please follow these steps.

1. Reproduce a minimum of five copies of the questionnaire on a standard copy machine. Provide an envelope for each copy.
2. Distribute these to individuals with whom you communicate frequently (members of your family, close friends, co-workers, or perhaps your immediate supervisor).
3. Tell these individuals that you are doing research on listening and want each person to rate your own listening effectiveness on the questionnaire. Inform each one that the questionnaire should not be signed, that at least four other individuals will fill out the questionnaire, and that you will be happy to share the results.
4. Ask each person who fills out a questionnaire to put it in the envelope you have provided, seal it, and return it to you.
5. Ask another person to total the results and summarize the answers for you.

Such a survey can give you an idea how well you have been listening. If you were rated 1, 2, or 3, you should feel complimented and motivated to keep on trying. If you were rated 4 or 5, you will know that improvement is needed. By studying

---

Listening Survey

Dear Friend, Fellow-student, or Co-worker:

In order to become a better listener, I am asking you for assistance. Based upon the communications we have had in the past, complete the survey form below. First, through a comparison with others with whom you have verbal contact, please rate me on the listening scale provided. Second, please place a check in any box that you think is *applicable to me and will help me improve my listening skills.*

Once you have finished, place this letter in the envelope I have provided and seal it. I will, in turn, give your envelope (along with others) to a third person who will provide me with a summation sheet. Your anonymity will be protected.

Listening Scale

Outstanding   1 2 3 4 5   Extremely poor
listener (best I   listener (worst I
know)   know)

Suggestions for Improvement

You might consider talking less.   ☐

Refrain from interrupting so much.   ☐

Be less defensive in communications.   ☐

Try to stop forming a reply before you hear me out.   ☐

Relax more when you communicate.   ☐

Slow your mind down so that you won't anticipate
what I say before I say it.   ☐

Be more attentive and send me signals so I know
you are listening.   ☐

Improve your concentration.   ☐

Other suggestions:

the answers to the questions, you may be able to identify some of the problems that prevented you from achieving a higher rating. The survey might improve your relationships with the people who participate because they will respect you for your willingness to evaluate yourself and try to improve. It might even make them more aware of their own listening habits. A few might even want to do a survey on themselves.

As the questionnaire brings to light, there are many bad habits that cause people to be poor listeners. The three examples below may give you some additional insight.

The accessible executive. The general manager of a large retail store continually made statements like these: "The office door is always open." "I always try to make myself accessible to those who work under me." "I attempt to set a psychological climate that encourages my people to come to me with both their creative ideas and their complaints." Still, his secretary noticed that very few people crossed the threshold on a voluntary basis. Why? Because once they took advantage of his invitation, they learned he didn't listen. Frequently he rudely shuffled papers in front of them while they were talking; at other times, he interrupted them in a way that proved his mind was elsewhere. Eventually his inability to listen destroyed so many relationships that productivity dropped and he was replaced.

The insecure supervisor. A young man was promoted to his first supervisory position because he had earned the right through seniority and hard work. Everyone expected him to be successful, but it didn't turn out that way. Apparently he was so anxious to succeed that his mind raced ahead of his ability to communicate and listen. When he was invited into the office of his superior, he was so anxious that he overtalked. His manager finally had to sit him down and lay the cards on the table.

> Robert, you are trying too hard. You are so enthusiastic that you are talking when you should be listening—sometimes you are so nervous that your lips move while I'm talking to you. You are going to have to slow down. I figure that if you're not listening to me in my office, you are probably not listening to your employees in the plant. I'm not a communications specialist, but my guess is that your mind gets into a "runaway" condition in the presence of others. Your inability to concentrate results in failure to hear what you *need* to hear. Whatever the cause, I want you to read some books on being a good listener or talk to an expert. The inability to listen is the only characteristic that will keep you from becoming a successful manager.

The emotional worker. The mutual-reward theory of sound human relations claims that for a relationship to survive in a healthy state over a sustained period of time, both parties must come out ahead. That is, the relationship must be mutually beneficial. Sandy, apparently, had never heard of the theory, because in her relationships with others, she almost always dominated the conversation. Most of the time she did more than 75 percent of the talking. What happened? She would quickly make new relationships and get them off to a good start, then she would kill them off slowly by talking too much and listening too little. Why? For the most part, it was an emotional reaction on her part. She liked people so much that she became energized around them and this seemed to cause her to talk excessively.

What can you do to improve your listening skills? There are many books in the library that can be of assistance to you. Meanwhile, here are a few suggestions that you may or may not have picked up in your survey. They should help you get started.

Be an active listener. Active listening means letting the speaker know you are getting the message: (1) Respond at the *feeling level* by saying something like "Yes, I'm hearing what you're saying and trying to react in the most objective manner possible." (2) Respond at the *behavioral level* by saying something like, "Do you mean you feel it would be best for me to call you once a week?" (3) Respond through nonverbal signals such as a hand gesture, nod of the head, or eye contact. Active listening reassures the "sender" that you are hearing what is being said and that communication is working both ways. Obviously, an active listener is a courteous listener.

Listen with your eyes. If you watch people as they communicate, it will help you concentrate on what they are saying, and the temptation to let your mind wander will decrease.

Discipline your mind from racing ahead. Many highly intellectual and creative people are poor listeners because they can't seem to slow down their minds while others are talking. They get bored and lose their concentration.

Hold your enthusiasm in check. Some people become so involved in a subject that they cannot seem to apply the brake to their minds. As a result, they are so caught up with their own thoughts that they do not hear what others are saying.

Now that you have evaluated your listening skills, you are invited to examine your reading ability with the same degree of objectivity. Strange as it may seem, it is possible for a marginal or poor reader to get through college. On campus there are ways to compensate, such as taking good lecture notes, getting personal assistance from fellow students, and avoiding heavy reading courses. But in business, especially in management levels, you may be faced with the necessity of reading an abundance of material in a hurry with no way to compensate. Suppose some morning you are invited to a meeting that afternoon to discuss a new field of development your company is entering. You have only a few hours to become knowledgeable about this new field by reading as much as possible. Under such conditions, you will need all the reading skills you can muster.

Chances are you fall into one of the three reading categories explained below.

High level. If you can read at the 650 to 750 words-per-minute range, you can consider yourself in the 9-to-10 level of a 1-to-10 range. At this level, with comprehension of 80 to 90 percent, you have a distinct advantage because your reading efficiency is so superior that you can quickly read all in-house materials, keep up with trade publications applicable to your position, and continually expand your knowledge in areas that might mean a promotion for you later on. As an additional example, you should be able to read this entire book in 2 to 3 hours. If you are already at this level, you will want to concentrate on maintenance by keeping your skills sharp through practice. Without use, reading skills deteriorate quickly.

Good level. If you read at 300 words per minute with comprehension at 80 percent or above, you are average and should have little trouble keeping up. You will not have the time efficiency of those with reading skills above you, but you will not be noticeably handicapped in most organizations. You could, for purposes of comparison, read this book from cover to cover in 5 to 7 hours. Any improvement, of course, would help your career progress. According to reading specialists, if you can read at 300 wpm, 700 wpm is *attainable* through training, especially in the techniques of skimming and scanning.

Weak level. If you fall measurably beneath the 300 wpm level, you may be handicapped to some extent. Surveys show that many adults who admit to reading difficulties fall around the 170 wpm level. These people should find help if they wish to enhance their careers. Here is how one knowledgeable reading specialist views the problem.

Evidence is strong that the need for improved reading skills is greater inside organizations than on campus because optional compensatory sources of information are not available. Those in beginning management jobs need to improve their skimming and scanning techniques so that they can quickly identify information that requires concentration. Many adults easily face up to the fact that spending extra time to improve their reading skills is a good investment. But usually they make this discovery *after* they move into their first management positions. With good teaching and improved concentration, their efficiency increases measurably. Although there are private reading clinics for adults, the best place to contact is a local community college. Of course, some progressive organizations still conduct reading improvement courses for their employees on company time. Anyone lucky enough to have this opportunity should certainly take advantage of it.

Why should you consider action that would improve your reading skills?

The higher up the management ladder you climb, the more reading you must do. Because a more responsible position usually means keeping better informed in more areas, reading efficiency at a high level is not only an advantage but sometimes a necessity. Teresa had this experience early in her career.

> My entry job, which I occupied for more than a year, required almost no reading. When I was promoted to my first supervisory job, my reading skills had deteriorated. It became apparent that it would be to my advantage to take a refresher course. It was one of the best decisions I have made so far.

You must keep up with the information explosion. In many occupations the problem of keeping up with advancements, new procedures, and pending changes is demanding. Those who fall behind in their reading cannot make the same contribution as those who keep up.

The legal implications of decision making are growing. As society becomes more complex and sophisticated, more of the decisions that organizations make are regulated by state and federal laws. Reading is the best way to keep informed on developments that influence decision making so that costly mistakes can be avoided.

Being a fast reader on the job reduces the need to take materials home. Many executives complain because they have to take materials home to read. In many cases a jump from 300 wpm to 500 wpm would eliminate the need to take home a briefcase of materials to read every night.

Improved reading skills can free you for more people contact. Often executives complain, "If I could somehow get rid of this paperwork, I would be able to improve communications with my people." For some executives, the best way to eliminate excessive paperwork is to learn to skim and scan more effectively. The president of a manufacturing firm summarizes the feelings of many top executives.

> If our company were large enough and our profit picture were better, I would employ a reading consultant to work with all of my junior management people. As it is, all I can do is pay their tuition, books, and transportation if they take an evening course. Believe me, I appreciate their taking off-duty time to improve their reading skills because they become much more valuable to themselves and to our firm.

Discussion Questions

1. If you participated in the listening survey presented in this chapter, how did you benefit, if at all, from the results? Would you or would you not recommend it to others? Why?
2. If you participated in the survey, have you noticed any improvement in the relationship between you and someone who completed a questionnaire? If so, how might you account for this improvement?
3. Defend or argue against the idea of an employee having her or his immediate supervisor complete the listening survey.
4. Name and discuss a minimum of three major reasons why people are poor listeners.
5. If you were in charge of a large organization, would you approve a plan to sponsor a reading-improvement clinic for management personnel on company time? Justify your decision.
6. Under what circumstances or conditions should an ambitious full-time employee enroll in a reading improvement program at his or her own expense? Be specific in your answer.

Willie Young
Control Data Corporation

**Career
Profile**

I had gotten into a rut in my campus life. I was no longer sure of my desire to attain the goals I had set for myself. I became disillusioned with my major and decided that I did not want a degree in theater arts. I dropped out of school to reassess my position and to figure my next move.

I made a short and unprofitable stab at a theatrical career, and my part-time job as a taxi driver became a full-time pursuit.

I had some background in electronics that began in the military (U.S. Navy) but because of time spent away from that field while pursuing studies, I found it extremely difficult to gain employment in this field. I had not considered more training for I felt my abilities were sufficient, but potential employers voiced concern that my abilities may have been inadequate because of the time spent outside the field.

I was interested in the computer field, but I had no training in digital electronics. I saw a television advertisement for training for careers in the computer industry being offered by Control Data Institute. Desiring more information, I telephoned and received several brochures in the mail which I looked over, discarded, and forgot about. A short time later I received additional correspondence which I ignored.

Meanwhile we went on strike at my job and economic conditions became severely strained. I received an invitation from a CDI representative for a get-acquainted tour and interview. I went, took some examinations, and found that I qualified to enter the class in computer technology which began two weeks previously.

I completed the course in the upper third of the class, and received three job interviews with Control Data Corporation that resulted in my being offered two positions. From these two offers I accepted my present position.

I may have made a mistake in my job seeking by not looking more, but I feel I made the right decision, for it's a good company to work for with opportunities for career advancement.

The most difficult thing for me in the passage from campus to my present career was to take the first step, which in my case was a simple telephone call.

The organization I work for does not have a lot of pressures to conform to. As long as I do the job that I'm paid to do, I can adhere to my own style and values.

I was lucky to have been chosen for a team that is developing a new product, and I have many chances to travel. I guess I was in the right place at the right time.

REPORTS
Showcasing Your Writing Skills

16

Although your verbal, listening, and reading skills may not fall in the upper 10 percent, perhaps you have excellent ability to communicate in writing. If so, you have a definite career advantage. If, on the other hand, your writing skills are somewhat less than adequate (perhaps inferior to your other skills), you may wish to do something about it.

Why can writing skills be so important to your career future?

You'll find a great deal of written communications in most organizations. In many firms you find a "paper mill" of written communications—everything from simple office memos to formal reports on sophisticated research projects. Data processing is a vital part of organizational life. The typewriter and the computer are symbols of the corporate and bureaucratic worlds. So, as important as your verbal skills are, at times you may be restricted to written communications. You will need to prepare business letters, formal evaluations, computer data interpretations, research projects, and other written communications—many of them to be sent to your superiors.

Others are critical of written communications. Some people who have excellent writing skills are "picky" when it comes to the writing of others. They like to analyze grammar and sentence structure, and they can't resist pointing out errors in spelling. You may find a "literary critic" in any organization. Verbal communication soon disappears, but written forms of communication remain behind for others to evaluate. Once sent through channels, a written communication cannot be hidden within an organization. If you have made an embarrassing mistake, someone will probably discover it, and it may come back to haunt you. Here is a progress report from a recent graduate.

> On my first job, I tried in every possible way not to expose my lack of writing ability. I would try to use the telephone instead of memos. I would walk to the other side of the building to avoid sending a written note. I would spend hours on important reports and then have them typed by a commercial establishment so that I wouldn't give myself away at work. Well, all of this got tiresome, so I enrolled in a business English course in a local college, where I found an outstanding teacher. After taking two courses from her, I feel I have raised my writing skills to a high level of competency. Now I use written communications of all kinds with full confidence.

Those who excel in writing skills impress top management. Sooner or later, employees receive or can create the opportunity to submit their ideas in writing to their superiors. Those who have high skills have a chance to make a good impression. Those who do not and have to rely on others may hurt their reputations. These comments from a city government official are appropriate.

> We thought we had an outstanding junior manager on our staff until we received a research report from him. His lack of writing skills was so obvious that, even though we tried to pass it off, he could not overcome the negative impression he had made. We kept wondering how he managed to get a college degree.

Although some organizations require more written communication than others, most management people find themselves preparing more reports than they anticipated when they were still on campus. The following comment from an English major is relevant.

> As an English major, I had a really difficult time finding a job. I often thought that I should have gone into accounting or engineering. But after I found a good position, I was happy to be an English major. Why? Up till now I have been spending more than 50 percent of my time preparing written reports. I still can't figure out why they were so reluctant to hire me. Perhaps they needed an English major more than they knew.

What should you do if you feel your writing skills are marginal or substandard? The first step would be to set a personal goal to overcome the handicap. As we learned in Chapter 12, once a problem has been given the proper priority, a goal is good motivation. The fact that you still have the handicap at this stage of your life should make reaching the goal more urgent. Why not put improving your writing skills at the top of your priority list?

Today there are specialists on campus who understand the psychology of overcoming writing handicaps. Most are English teachers; others can be found in learning skills centers. See one of these people. Talk openly about the handicap. One thing you have going for you is a *readiness factor* that may never have been present before. The fact that you were not able to overcome certain psychological blocks in the past does not mean they are still inside you. The fact that you can concentrate on your writing skills now, while you hold down a promising career job, is an advantage. Another advantage is the opportunity to practice writing skills on the job. Here are some specific suggestions.

Take a business English course. Some colleges have outstanding teachers who prefer to instruct courses in practical business English rather than courses in creative writing or literature. Such an individual can teach you fundamentals as well as proper business forms and procedures. Even if you are already a college graduate, you can benefit from one of these courses.

Improve your typing skills. Learning to type, or improving your typing speed and accuracy, will help you improve your written communications. If your penmanship or printing is not legible, typing skills are even more important.

Learn to write more like you talk. In business correspondence you are not seeking a Nobel Prize in literature, but rather the ability to communicate in concise and understandable terms. If your writing skills are low but your verbal skills are high, try to write more like you talk. You can learn to do this by saying the words to yourself before you write them down.

Have someone proofread important communications. Probably you know someone who would be good at proofreading—a co-worker, your spouse, or a personal friend. Find out what kinds of mistakes you make most frequently. Your writing skills will start to improve immediately if you concentrate on the mistakes you have been making and learn how to correct them. If improvement is not your goal, it may be necessary for you to have communications proofread during your entire career.

Buy and use a dictionary. Improving vocabulary and learning to spell are lifetime pursuits for most people. Top-flight executive secretaries and specialists in business communications know the value of a dictionary. If they use one regularly, why shouldn't you?

Practice your writing skills. Your skills may be marginal because you were not required to do enough writing during your school years. The more you write with a desire to improve, the greater progress you will make. You will improve more rapidly if you welcome opportunities to communicate in writing, instead of dreading them.

How can you capitalize on your writing skills once you raise them up to acceptable standards? Or if your skills are already above average and no special improvement is necessary, how can you showcase your written work to enhance your career?

Take pride in your written communications. Many people who have superior writing skills are nevertheless "sloppy" in their writing because they refuse to take the time to do the work carefully.

Look for appropriate times to use written communications. Telephone conversations, face-to-face communications, and group meetings have many advantages and should be used when appropriate. There are times, however, when a written communication is more suitable. For example, when people need to study a suggestion or proposal, they need to have it in writing. When an important document (such as rules and regulations) is being revised, it should be submitted in writing so that additional changes or interpretations can be made. When an individual wants to submit a plan so that it will reach top management, a well-prepared written communication is the only answer. Obviously, those individuals who do not have English competency will avoid such opportunities to save themselves embarrassment. The more skilled individual has a better opportunity to communicate his or her ideas and innovations.

Submit a suggestion every six months. Although there are many jokes about suggestion boxes, many organizations still find them effective. You should consider submitting a carefully prepared suggestion now and then, especially one that can save the organization time and money. Accept this opportunity whether or not a reward is involved because it is the best way to communicate your ideas. Neil submitted a fresh, creative idea every six months. Although his first few were not accepted, everyone, including the president, knew that he was involved and thinking. Of course, a few people thought Neil was wasting his time, but when his fourth suggestion was accepted and saved the company a lot of money, these same people changed their attitudes. During the process Neil also had showcased his writing skills.

The following quotations from successful managers illustrate the point: "The first real recognition I received in my organization ten years ago came from a carefully prepared report I submitted on a voluntary basis." "Some managers hesitate to submit suggestions because they feel that they will not receive serious consideration. In the vast majority of cases this is not true."

Pay special attention to research papers. You may be assigned to do some research early in your career or you may want to do research on your own initiative and submit a report on a voluntary basis. Research papers need to be professionally prepared to be effective. If you are not an expert in the preparation and submission of statistical data, perhaps you should seek help from a librarian. Charts and other graphics can make or break a research paper.

Submit articles to your house organ. Most large organizations have monthly magazines or newsletters and encourage written ideas from employees. Take advantage of such media by submitting something for publication.

Thank-you notes can be effective. It is easier to thank people verbally, but there is often a special impact to a well-written thank-you note. Organizational life will give you many opportunities for this form of communication.

Provide copies to interested people. One advantage to written communications is that an extra copy or two can be made to keep others informed. You can demonstrate or showcase your writing skills by circulating extra copies.

Are there any special tips one should follow in business communications? You will find an abundance of excellent suggestions in a good business English book. Here are a few "do's" and "don't's."

DO	*DON'T*
Be direct and to the point.	Be glib.
Use simple language.	Be wordy.
Follow model forms.	Be academic.
Keep sentences uncomplicated.	Use "literary" words or expressions.
Use short paragraphs.	Be overly creative.
Always check spelling.	Try humor unless you are good at it.
Make sure type in typewriter is clean.	Rush.
Make sure typewriter ribbon is not worn.	Show hostility.
If necessary, have it proofread.	Violate normal procedures or channels.

Here are two quotations from graduates who measurably improved their writing skills *after* they had started their careers.

> I returned to college to take a course in business English because I discovered that—just like doing maintenance on an automobile—one needs to do maintenance on writing skills. You do this by writing, not by reading about it, and I needed the discipline and motivation that comes from being in a class.

> I improved my writing skills 100 percent from a self-study program. You can find good business English books at most commercial book stores to help you reach such a goal. These books provide excellent model letters. I started to improve my letters after studying these models. I also accumulated a few good ones from company correspondence. They really helped.

This chapter can be summarized by two suggestions.

If your writing skills range from good to outstanding, *showcase* them. Take advantage of your skills by introducing written communications into organizational channels when possible and appropriate.

If you feel your skills range from fair to poor, do something about it now so that you will not be at a disadvantage in the future.

Discussion Questions

1. What are three typical reasons graduates give to excuse their poor writing skills? How valid is each of these excuses?
2. Why does a college graduate working full time in a career role have advantages over a full-time student when taking an evening course in business English? Explain fully.
3. What career handicap, if any, does a college graduate with *average* writing skills have in a typical organization? Defend your answer.
4. How would you reply to the student who claims, "I know my writing skills are below average, but as a manager, I'll have a competent secretary."
5. Please respond to the following statement: To get your writing up to acceptable standards and keep it there, you have to *write*. Every skill requires maintenance.
6. Assign a priority (1, 2, 3, or 4) to each of the skills below and defend your choices.

    _____ Listening   _____ Reading
    _____ Writing   _____ Speaking

Career Profile

Kathy Kelley
Assistant Manager, Personnel
Ohrbach's Department Stores

When I started college in 1969 my goals were high. I wanted to get my elementary teaching credential and my B.A. degree.

I went to L.A. Valley College my first two years and received my A.A. degree. I transferred to California State University, Northridge, in 1971 and graduated with a B.A. degree in English in 1973. My fifth year was spent student teaching and taking the appropriate related elementary teaching classes. My fifth year was also spent looking for a permanent teaching position. CSUN placement center was very helpful in setting up interviews with various districts. I also wrote a résumé and sent copies to many school districts. Nevertheless, the summer of '74 came to a close, and I had no job. The L.A. district was offering no contracts; the best I could do was substitute. I substituted for a few months. The assignments were sporadic, and made life hard to cope with financially.

It was at this point I faced my first reality: five years of college, two degrees, a credential, and no employment. I was forced to make a difficult decision: either seek employment in another field or take a chance on an out-of-state teaching job. While I was attending college I had worked for Ohrbach's. In fact, my Ohrbach's career had started at the same time my college career did. I worked part-time evenings and weekends as a salesperson in the children's division.

While I was student teaching, I was promoted to a night manager in the Sportswear division, and sometime later I became a night manager in Lingerie and Accessories.

In December 1974 I decided to look for full-time employment

outside of teaching. The problem was that I didn't know what I wanted to do. For as long as I could remember I wanted to teach, and I wasn't really prepared for any other profession.

Our store manager found out I was looking for full-time work and offered me a manager's position in Accessories, Jewelry, and Gifts. The most difficult thing I had to cope with at this point was giving up a prospective teaching career for a career in retail.

During my first year as a full-time manager, I became frustrated and argued with myself about my future. The most impressive argument that kept popping up was: I'm a college graduate, I have a teaching credential, and I'm not using my skills. For a time I kept my eyes and ears open for news of openings in the teaching profession and left my name on the substituting list. A second argument hit me at this point, and I decided that I should turn my aspirations full force toward a retail career, do my best, and go as far as possible in my new career. In February 1976 I was moved to the Wilshire store and promoted to assistant buyer in the Fashion Jewelry department. Six months later I became assistant buyer in Fashion Accessories.

In February 1977 the company went through a major reorganization and the positions of buyer and assistant were eliminated on the West Coast. Where at all possible, people were placed in other positions throughout the company. At that time I was offered two different positions. The first was a senior manager job in a branch store and the other was a personnel assistant manager job at Wilshire. I felt the need to learn new things, so I made the transition from merchandising to operations and took the personnel job.

As a personnel assistant I work with the people throughout the store, training, counseling, and disciplining. I'm also involved with recruiting, interviewing, hiring, employee benefits, and unemployment insurance. I'm happy with what I'm doing. It's a real challenge, and it's almost like teaching again. I'm anxious to get as much experience as possible in my present position. Then I'll be ready for a more responsible job in the personnel field.

My major transitions were (1) going from education to retail, and (2) going from merchandising to operations in retail. My personal growth areas have been primarily in communication with people, first as a teacher, then as a manager in retail. The entire transition took approximately three years, even though I've been with Ohrbach's for over eight years.

When you talk about luck, I guess I was lucky in that I was at the right place at the right time. When Ohrbach's needed me I needed Ohrbach's. My life-style is my own, and I think because of the way I am I fit into the organizational mold of the company well.

Exercises for Part IV

Six-Month Self-Assessment Progress Report

(If your answer is number 1 or 2, you need not complete the second part of each evaluation factor.)

1. My on-the-job   1 2 3 4 5   I have yet to learn
    vocabulary is   a new word on this
    increasing by leaps   job.
    and bounds.

    I plan to do the following to increase my job-related word power:

    _____

    _____

    _____

    _____

2. I have maintained   1 2 3 4 5   My writing skills
    high writing skills   are still poor and
    since I took this   not improving.
    job.

    I plan to do the following to improve my writing skills:

    _____

    _____

    _____

    _____

    _____

3. I think I am the   1   2   3   4   5   I think I am the
   best listener in the   worst listener in
   firm.   the firm.

   I plan to do the following to improve my listening skills:

   _____

   _____

   _____

   _____

4. I am reading 800   1   2   3   4   5   I am reading below
   words per minute   150 words per
   with excellent   minute with poor
   comprehension.   comprehension.

   I intend to bring my reading speed up to _____ words per
   minute by taking a reading improvement course in the
   next two months.

5. My verbal skills   1   2   3   4   5   My verbal skills
   with co-workers or   with co-workers or
   customers are   customers are very
   outstanding.   weak.

   I plan to do the following to improve my verbal skills with
   co-workers and/or customers:

   _____

   _____

   _____

   _____

6. My verbal skills   1 2 3 4 5   My verbal skills
    with management   with management
    are outstanding.   are very weak.

    I plan to do the following to improve my verbal skills with
    management personnel:

    _____

    _____

    _____

7. My human-   1 2 3 4 5   My human-
    relations skills are   relations skills are a
    superior.   serious handicap.

    I plan to do the following to improve my human-relations
    skills:

    _____

    _____

    _____

8. My equipment or   1 2 3 4 5   My equipment or
    machine operation   machine operation
    skills are superior.   skills are poor.

    I plan to do the following to improve my machine or
    equipment operation skills:

    _____

    _____

    _____

9. My math-related   1 2 3 4 5   My math-related
    skills (bookkeeping,   skills are below
    working with   acceptable
    figures, doing   standards.
    problems) are
    superior.

    I plan to do the following to improve my mathematics
    skills:

    _____

    _____

    _____

10. A communications   1 2 3 4 5   A communications
    expert would rate   expert would rate
    my telephone skills   my telephone skills
    as outstanding.   as unacceptable.

    I plan to improve my telephone communications in the
    following ways:

    _____

    _____

    _____

Case Study: Pride

Joel is a well-disciplined, hard working, and extremely ambitious
individual. He grew up in a fatherless home where he became
self-reliant at an early age. He takes great pride in handling his
own problems. Some people who meet him in a social environment feel he is difficult to know. He is always courteous, however,
and always willing to pick up a check.

Since his graduation from college, Joel has made outstanding progress with a national restaurant chain that specializes in steak-lobster dinners, an active bar, and disco dancing. He is now managing a large unit that often serves more than 500 dinners in one evening.

Joel's first supervisor was very difficult to deal with and was eventually released. But Joel has lived through some tough problems with the company and has some good contacts with top management. He has had to handle some tough terminations involving dishonesty and has built a reputation for operating a "tight ship." In addition, Joel has gone through a divorce that few people even know about. He has never sought the help of others. He has always drawn from his own inner strength.

But Joel has a different kind of problem this time—*a serious morale problem*. Without being aware of it, Joel has become more autocratic, more solitary, more impatient with others, including the 38 people on his staff. He spends much more time in his office working with figures than he used to. At other times, he sits at the end of the bar watching staff members, but saying very little to them.

Although once Joel was popular, he is now avoided. Joel knows something is wrong. He thinks about it often, but he just doesn't know what the problem could be. Could it be the fault of the assistant manager? Is it just a sign of the times? At any rate, Joel figures he will get a promotion soon and be able to start all over at another location. Still . . . perhaps he should talk to somebody about the problem. "No," he tells himself, "that would be foolish. I can work it out. Just give me more time."

You are the district manager for the chain. You have recently learned about Joel's problem. Already the restaurant is showing a decline in net profit. You know that something must be done. You want to save Joel for the organization, yet you sense he will not come to you to talk about his problem openly because of his personal pride.

Putting yourself in the manager's position, please answer the following sets of questions.

Set 1: What is the nature of pride? Why is Joel so hesitant to seek help? What are the dangers of excessive pride? How often is pride the downfall of a good manager? Why can't Joel *see* that his problem is a lack of communication with his staff?

Set 2: As Joel's manager, what action should you take? If you decide on counseling, how would you go about it? What approach would you use? How many sessions? What are the dangers of counseling a person with excessive pride? Could he be encouraged to take a course in communications?

Set 3: Assume that after many counseling attempts, the manager is successful; Joel honestly senses what has happened and feels that he can restore communications and repair all relationships. Should Joel be permitted to remain or transferred to another location? Take a firm stand on one position or the other.

Part V

CREATING YOUR OWN PROMOTION OPPORTUNITIES

Objectives

After finishing this section you should know

1. When and how to ask for more responsibility

2. What is involved in developing your best leadership style

3. What you can do now to prepare for a supervisory role tomorrow

4. Whether you should stay with your first (or present) organization

You're Ready for Promotion

Part V assumes that you have made an excellent transition to the organization you joined (after one or two years), and you are now ready to prepare for and win a more demanding position. It might or might not involve supervising others, but it will provide you with greater financial rewards and substantially enhance your organizational "image."

RESPONSIBILITY
Why Not
Ask for It?

17

The transition from campus to a career role of responsibility may continue for a number of years. It sometimes takes the recent graduate a few months or longer to "land" the best starting job available and then a much longer time to earn a position with authority and meaning. Most starting jobs can and should be considered internships to the more responsible positions that lie ahead. You probably won't feel you have really "arrived" as far as your career is concerned until you have

1. Earned a position important enough to give you a strong feeling of accomplishment and identity.
2. Held down a position that has some degree of responsibility and influence within the organization.
3. Moved up in your organization to the level where you are making sufficient income to live the life-style you had in mind when you started.

Of course, most graduates do not move into such positions as quickly as they would like to. Quotations from recent graduates tell the story.

> The most difficult thing for me was playing the corporate waiting game. As I slowly moved upward from one job to another, I always felt I was ready long before anything happened. I have since learned that almost everyone must live through such plateau periods.

> I was underemployed for my first two years out of college. I was assigned what management called a series of "learning stations," which would, they said, prepare me for my first job as a supervisor. Looking

back, it seems to me that a considerable waste of time could have been avoided.

I thought I would never rise above those routine, unchallenging, clerical jobs so frequently occupied by women. I had a degree in business administration but nothing to administer. I would not want to live through that period of my career pattern again.

In a recent in-service management seminar for beginning supervisors, students were invited to list the most unexpected and difficult problems they had experienced during the transition from their starting jobs to their first important roles. Here are the answers listed in order of frequency.

1. The excessive length of time needed to make the transition.
2. The low pay during the transition period.
3. Not knowing what the next step might be.
4. The jealousies (tender egos) of those already employed with the organization.
5. The poor supervisors it was necessary to work under.
6. The need to be aggressive in order to get anywhere.
7. The degree of pressure.
8. Not being taken seriously as a married woman seeking a career.
9. Maintaining a good self-image.
10. Adjusting to reality.
11. Being on my own financially and emotionally.
12. Just being patient.

Is there anything you can do to speed up the transition? How can you learn to live through the inevitable plateaus with more grace? How can you get into a salary bracket that will permit you to live the life-style you want without waiting until you have lost your motivation? Although answers to these and other questions will depend in part upon the organization itself, here are some ideas that may be worth consideration.

In most organizations your chances improve when you demonstrate that you are capable of accepting more responsibility. Build an image as a person ready for and capable of assuming responsibility. One way to communicate this readiness is by accepting more and more responsibility in your present job without asking for more pay or special favors.

In accepting more responsibility, make sure you maintain good relationships with co-workers. If you desire and are given more responsibility than your co-workers, you can easily incur human-relations problems. First, you might encourage jealousies and animosities among those who sense that you are trying to leave them behind. Second, after accepting more responsibility, you may begin to feel that you are carrying more than your share of the departmental work load and get impatient with your co-workers. Either or both of these conditions can do your career progress more harm than good. If you are willing to assume more responsibility than your co-workers in order to move yourself into management sooner, then you must recognize the double importance of keeping good relationships with these same fellow workers.

When should you ask for more responsibility? The best time to seek new duties and more experience is when you have some extra time, when you are not working up to your potential, and when you have exhausted all other possibilities of learning. As long as you are still learning in a job, it might be too soon to ask for more responsibility. In other words, you need to demonstrate that you can handle every responsibility that has been assigned to you before asking for more.

Why should you ask?

Here are four of the many good reasons to ask for more responsibility.

1. Individuals learn and grow at different speeds, but supervisors frequently forget or ignore this fact. A gentle reminder from you that you'd like to learn more might be not only appropriate but also effective.
2. Asking might cause a supervisor who is stifling you to see you in a different light.
3. Asking for more responsibility can open channels of communication to your immediate supervisor and beyond.
4. A request from an individual who is ready for more responsibility is difficult to turn down. In short, your chance of getting more responsibility by asking for it is excellent.

Whom should you ask?

To request more responsibility, you may approach other managers in addition to your supervisor.

Ask your immediate supervisor first. Obviously, if you are to remain in your present position, the person who can add responsibilities to your job is your immediate boss. If you have tried this a few times without success, then you have two alternatives left.

Seek a horizontal transfer. If you have joined a firm with a personnel department, you can always ask personnel for a new assignment where you can learn more. It should be made clear, however, that you are not running away from your present supervisor or department. Also, you should not go to personnel without talking over the possibility with your supervisor and seeking permission.

Go to upper management. Going above your supervisor to discuss learning possibilities for yourself can sometimes be accomplished without hurting relationships with him or her if you go about it in the right way. First, ask permission from your supervisor. Second, restrict your request to new learning opportunities, not to such factors as a salary increase, job transfer, or job reclassification.

How should you make your request?

Assuming that you have demonstrated that you are ready for more responsibility, the following steps are recommended.

STEP 1: Make an appointment with your supervisor.

Ask your supervisor for "fifteen minutes of your time to discuss an important matter." Asking for a specified amount of time often gives the request more importance and makes it possible to sit down in a private setting to discuss the matter without rushing through it.

STEP 2: State that you are pleased with your learning progress so far.

Start out by discussing what you have learned in a positive manner and then attempt to move the conversation in the direction of what you want to learn in the future. Make it clear you are not seeking a new position at this stage, just more responsibility so that you can prepare for future positions. Try to limit such a discussion to 15 minutes.

STEP 3: State why you feel you are ready for more responsibility.

Without being negative or defensive, it is important to communicate that you have really learned all that is possible and that your personal productivity is at a high level and will remain there. Now you would appreciate new assignments, duties, or experiences. You might add that you do not want to put your supervisor in a position of providing you with special privileges that will hurt his or her relations with others, and that you will do your part to see that this does not happen.

STEP 4:   If possible, make a specific suggestion.

If you have two or three specific suggestions in mind, so that your supervisor will know what things you would like to do, such a request will be much easier to grant.

Your supervisor might grant your request immediately. In some cases, however, a delay will occur while the supervisor works out a new assignment and makes necessary adjustments. You should also be prepared for the possibility that the request may be denied.

Even if the request should be denied, much might have been accomplished if the request was made as suggested in the four-step approach. The supervisor would know that you are ready for more responsibility, have demonstrated a good learning attitude, and have communicated upward in a professional manner. The comments below are from graduates who completed their formal education at least five years ago.

Asking for more responsibility did more for my career progress than anything else. Not only did it build a better relationship with my immediate supervisor, but it also made me better prepared for a promotion than my contemporaries.

It is a good decision to seek more responsibility providing you are prepared to do an excellent job of whatever is assigned. You have to be ready, able, and willing to produce, or it can all backfire.

In looking back, I feel that I was not as aggressive as I should have been. I followed the practice of doing a good job, working on my human relations, and waiting it out. At first it did not occur to me that within many organizational structures, you have to *create* your opportunities. After waiting around too long, I started initiating upward communications and openly asking for new assignments. I went about it in a quiet way, and I was pleased with the results. The more managers became aware that I was willing to take on responsibility, the more attention I received. I think it is a mistake to sit back and assume that upper management knows when you are ready; they don't. You have to let them know and keep on letting them know.

For a fresh and stimulating point of view on how to make progress inside corporate walls, you are invited to turn to Appendix II, where an article, "How to Stand Out in a Big Organization," is reprinted from *BankAmerican*, a publication for Bank of America employees in Los Angeles, California.

Discussion Questions

1. If asking for additional responsibility is such a good idea, why don't more employees do it?
2. Assume an employee asks for and receives a few additional responsibilities. Does he or she benefit more from what is *learned* from performing the new duty or from demonstrating the ability to handle responsibility?
3. Can a supervisor reach a point where it is impossible to delegate more responsibility to an ambitious employee? If you claim it is possible, please provide an example.
4. Under what conditions, if any, would it be counter-productive to ask for and receive additional responsibility?
5. What are the advantages and disadvantages of seeking and receiving a horizontal transfer? Explain fully.
6. Defend or criticize the four-step procedure on pages 226–27. What changes, if any, would you recommend?

**Career
Profile**

G. Michael Milhiser
City Manager
City of Montclair, California

After high school, I entered a community college to pursue my interests in two areas—education and basketball. Two years later I transferred to a Christian-oriented liberal arts college in Southern California. I was able to accomplish there what I had intended to do at the beginning of my college career: to graduate with a Bachelor of Arts degree in political science and to participate in basketball all four of my undergraduate years.

The Vietnam war was also a factor in my education. Because of the 2-S deferment (which enabled college students to continue working toward their degree as long as they took a full load of courses), I made a decision that I am not sure I would have made otherwise—to get a masters degree in public administration.

I didn't get the first job I wanted—an entry-level government job in Washington, D.C. Following this disappointment, I went through a period of deep disillusionment. When I got my act back together again, I decided that perhaps I could gain experience in a local municipal or county government in an entry-level, general-administration-type position.

Fortunately, Lady Luck happened to come my way. A city near the graduate school I attended was advertising for an entry-level administrative assistant position. I made several appointments to see the department head who was actually in charge of hiring for this position. I was fortunate enough to be hired for my first "real" professional position in the profession I had chosen—municipal government. I was later told by the man who hired me that my aggressiveness in arranging interview appointments and the enthusiasm I showed during the interviews were important factors in my being hired. I think that anyone graduating from college now, with all of the competition, should display an eagerness to work. It might be the edge in gaining initial employment.

For the first four and a half years of my employment, I was an administrative assistant, a position that involved duties in several different areas. During those years, I was generally included in top management's discussions of issues, and it was easy for me then to "tell it like it is or how it should be." I did not have to take into consideration any other major department within the city, since I was not responsible for running any of them. However, that quickly changed a year and a half ago, when I was promoted to assistant city administrator, a job that carries with it the responsibilities of managing administrative services—which includes general administration, finance, personnel, and duplicating.

In the brief year and a half that I held that position, I became much more aware of the role that compromising and compromise itself plays in city government. This is certainly not to say that one needs to compromise any particular principle, but that in order to resolve disputed areas of conflict on any issue that may be discussed, compromise may be necessary. Recently I was made City Manager, a position that will present a whole new set of responsibilities and challenges.

One of the most difficult decisions for me to make in my short career in municipal government was to try to determine what the chances of upward mobility would be for me. Normally, an entry-level administrative assistant position is good experience in one agency for approximately two to four years. After that period has passed, if you have not either advanced through that agency or left to gain broader experience in another agency, you may find yourself becoming much less motivated. The worst thing you can do is to become resigned to the fact that you may not get promoted. You become much less effective and lose substantial interest in your job. However, it is always a constant battle to not let your job become routine. Generally, once you are promoted, supervision becomes part of your job—which provides you with the opportunity to use some of your college courses dealing in human behavior and relations. Perhaps the one aspect of my current and previous positions that was not touched upon enough in my college days was how to become an effective supervisor.

I am sure many times you have heard different people stress the importance of goal setting. Although sometimes it is difficult to do, or you feel self-conscious in doing it, goal setting is important and should take place at least every two years. Everyone, of course, will include different objectives in their goal setting, but some that I would recommend as certainly important are:

1. *Professional Growth*   How far do you expect your career ladder to extend? Don't rely on fate to be kind to you. Try to guide your job. Don't let your job guide you totally.
2. *Financial Growth*   If you want to be financially independent, you certainly need to monitor your financial growth closely. Don't be afraid to set that as a goal, if it is what you want.
3. *Professional and Personal Goals*   Professional and personal goals should be assessed on an ongoing basis. You never know what might happen any day, week, or month that might radically change them. In other words, don't just write them down and put them away for a year or two and think that you are done. Always review them and keep them up to date, if changes occur.

At first, I wondered if a job would give me the same kind of personal satisfaction that my college career had. I must confess that at first it didn't, but it wasn't too long before I realized that I had taken a major step forward and that I was now putting to use the knowledge I acquired in school. That provides a sense of satisfaction. Work is a major change. Soon you have experience you can use in future years as you expand your professional career. Even if you make a radical departure and change professions at some point, you at least have substantial experience to rely on, most of which will be helpful to you in a new career or new job.

LEADERSHIP
Developing an Effective Style

18

Somewhere not too far down the road, your career may lead you into a leadership role. Many graduates are quickly placed in supervisory positions that they did not expect so soon. With this in mind, this chapter assumes that you are currently developing your leadership style for such an eventuality.

What is meant by *leadership style?*

Leadership style is the individual's way of leading others. Your personal style includes your approach to achieving productivity from others and building good human relationships with those under your guidance. Leadership style involves setting and maintaining good discipline, counseling employees, delegating authority, setting priorities, and many other factors. Your leadership style is the manner in which you will handle your first role as a supervisor.

The style you ultimately develop will be a manifestation of your personality, but managing others requires more planning than most other, more personal roles in your life. When you are in a supervisory role, you have different responsibilities. You are responsible for the productivity of others, and you must accomplish your goals *through* others. You must plan, organize, motivate, control, and appraise results from a position of authority. The development of a good leadership style, then, should be one of your most interesting challenges as you build your career. The time to start is now because what happened to one recent graduate could also happen to you: "I was offered a supervisory position three weeks after I started. I would have been far better prepared had I known this could happen."

One way to prepare in advance is to observe how managers operate and how their employees react to them. For example, when you hear complimentary comments similar to those below, employees are describing the leadership style of their manager.

"Hank is a tough boss to work for all right, but he's always fair. That's more than you can say about some other supervisors."

"Mrs. R. is so busy it's hard to get an appointment to see her. When you do get one, though, she will really listen to you, and if there is anything she can do to help, you can depend upon her following through."

"When he says he maintains an open-door policy, he means it. He's the most accessible manager I know."

"I like and appreciate her leadership style because it's consistent. You always know what you can expect. She doesn't manage by impulse, according to her moods."

"What I appreciate most is the way Ms. Carroll buffers the pressures we know she's getting from above. She passes very little along to us."

"The thing I like about the style of Mr. S. is that he tells you immediately if he doesn't like something you've done. He doesn't withhold resentment until he explodes in front of you, where everyone can hear."

"The best thing about her style is the way she teaches employees. I have never learned so much from a supervisor before."

"He has an excellent approach to management because he always lets you know how you stand. If you are doing well, he will let you know; if not, you will get the message in a hurry along with suggestions on how to improve. He makes me feel very secure and comfortable in my job."

A popular way to discuss leadership styles is through Theories X and Y.* Theory X is the more autocratic style, which supports, to a limited extent, the premise of *management by control*. This theory claims that management is responsible for organizing the elements of productive enterprise in the interest of economic ends. Through strong supervision, the behavior of employees is modified to fit the needs of the organization. Control is essential.

Theory Y, on the other hand, is a more permissive style, which

*Douglas M. McGregor, *Human Side of Enterprise* New York, McGraw-Hill, 1960.

supports the premise of *participative management*. This theory claims that people are not by nature passive or resistant to organizational needs. The essential task of management is to arrange organizational conditions so that people can achieve their own goals by directing their own efforts. Theory Y supports a process of creating opportunities, releasing potential, removing obstacles, encouraging growth, and providing guidance.

A leadership style is always a *blend* of the two theories. There is no such thing as a pure, 100 percent X or Y style. A manager who was 90 percent X-oriented would stifle the productivity of others. A 90 percent Y manager would be so easygoing and permissive that people would take advantage of their freedom. So the leadership style that you eventually develop will be a blend of the two orientations. You may favor the Y theory and build a reputation as an effective Y-oriented leader, but chances are your style will be no more than 80 percent Y. *Some control will be necessary.* Should you favor the X orientation, you might be able to achieve a blend of 60 percent X and 40 percent Y that would be effective for you.

The blend you develop between the two orientations will determine to a large extent your leadership style, as these quotations from young managers indicate.

> I eventually want to have about a 60 percent Y and 40 percent X blend because I feel this ratio fits my personality and my beliefs. I think it will help me achieve greater productivity. I would like to be about 70 percent Y, but I don't think I could pull it off too well in my kind of organization.

> I believe my most effective style will be about a 50–50 blend, because this is where I see myself now, and I am very comfortable with it. I want to give my people as much freedom as possible, but I think they will be happier and more productive with some strong leadership and discipline to go along with it.

> I have worked under both X and Y styles, and I believe that I will be more effective with a blend of about 60 percent X and 40 percent Y. Considerable discipline is needed in my type of organization, and if I moved too far in the direction of Y, I might have a hard time meeting quality standards.

From the above comments, it is obvious that each individual must come up with his or her own blend. It is also obvious that the key to effective leadership is the *discipline line* that the manager creates and maintains with his or her style.

What is a discipline line?

A discipline line is an imaginary line that a supervisor establishes to set standards of acceptable behavior for employees. It is, in effect, the *tone* of the working climate. It tells the worker how much freedom he or she has in which to operate. If the line is too high and rigid, the worker feels restricted; if it is too low or loose, the worker takes advantage of the supervisor.

Discipline lines vary according to different work environments. For example, a production line in a factory, because of precise work schedules and safety factors, might require a much higher discipline line than a research laboratory where scientists need freedom to be creative. The following interpretations of the expression *discipline line* may help you understand it better.

> I operate an isolated training school where a very strong discipline line is necessary. Most of our students have been in some kind of trouble and resent authority figures. If we didn't establish a very firm line from the very beginning, students might take advantage of the situation and the amount and quality of learning would diminish.

> One key to operating a successful publishing house is giving people the freedom to be creative. With this in mind, I try to set a very low, but clear discipline line. I want people to work, as far as possible, in an unrestricted climate because they will produce more; this does not mean, however, that the line is eliminated.

> Because I was so young when I first became a manager, I made the mistake of setting my discipline line too low. I thought that I could be about 75 percent Y-oriented. I soon discovered that it wasn't working. My employees, especially those near my own age, took advantage of me, thus forcing me into raising the line. I wish now that I had set a higher line to begin with.

Every manager walks a tight rope daily as far as his or her discipline line is concerned. Some supervisors are able to set a graceful line and be consistent with it. Others have so much trouble that they eventually decide to forgo a management position.

What are the factors involved in setting discipline lines? As you look ahead, what considerations should you analyze in establishing a discipline line of your own?

Many people seem to be highly successful with a 60 percent Y, 40 percent X blend. Many young managers apparently have been able to set a rather open and free discipline line without sacrificing productivity. They seem to sense that their employees need freedom in order to be responsive and motivated, yet the discipline line must be drawn clearly at a certain level. These successful managers believe in participative management, in which employees are involved in making decisions and everyone works as a group, yet they can still set a line beyond which employees know they should not go. The line is not too high or rigid, but it is respected and seldom violated.

It is usually better to set a high discipline line at the beginning and lower it later, rather than the other way around. Employees resent having freedoms and privileges taken away from them. Those who have had experiences in taking over departments as new managers claim that it is better to set a rather high line at the beginning and then lower it to the point where maximum productivity is achieved. Some managers have found it impossible to raise lines that were initially too low.

Employees who are stifled produce less and resign sooner. The danger of a rigid discipline line is always present. Although strong control may cause employees to produce at a higher rate for awhile, hostility and resentment can lower long-term productivity. In addition, many employees will move to another organization rather than endure supervision that is too tight and restrictive.

You should not permit the styles of leaders above you to determine the blend that is best for you. It is possible that your best combination could be 60 percent Y and 40 percent X, but your immediate supervisor operates from a reverse style. In such cases, some adjustment on your part may be necessary on a temporary basis, but you should gradually develop and protect your own style. What is right for you (once you find it) should be maintained insofar as possible because it is the prime factor in determining the long-range productivity of those who work for you.

Upper management may select those with strong discipline lines (X-oriented) for promotions. Although all organizations are different and it is dangerous to generalize, there appears to be a tendency among top management people to select for promotions those who have learned how to set strong discipline lines. In some organizations lines seem to grow stronger as one moves up the organizational structure. Perhaps top management feels more secure with an X-oriented blend of leadership. The preference of top management is a factor that should be taken into consideration in building a career within a given organization.

It is considered professional to analyze leadership styles, but unprofessional to analyze personalities. Once you have moved from campus to a work environment, you will have the opportunity to study leadership styles as models. Observing your superiors will help you reach your best personal blend at a later date. You should not, however, confuse the leadership style with the personality traits or idiosyncracies of a manager. To attempt to understand the style and discipline line of a manager and learn to live with it gracefully is a professional endeavor. To discuss personality traits in a critical manner (bad-mouthing) is unprofessional.

Your leadership style is reflected in the way you counsel. As a manager, you will need to counsel with your employees on many matters. Most of the time, you can take a Y-oriented, positive approach as you pay compliments, motivate people, and help them set goals. At other times, however, difficult problems involving discipline and possible termination may cause you to be more X-oriented. The way in which you handle such problems not only contributes to the total discipline line you set but also determines the kind of relationships you are able to maintain among your employees.

Productivity should be the final yardstick. If the employees who work for you produce more than those in similar departments, the message will eventually reach upper management. You should adjust your style, then, to this primary goal.

Although it may seem premature for you to be concerned with your own personal leadership style, a management position may be thrust upon you sooner than you expect. With this in mind, you should not only study those above you, but also start forming an image of the way you intend to manage when the opportunity presents itself. In addition, learning as much as possible about leadership styles should help you to adjust to whatever style of supervision you experience in your entry job.

Discussion Questions

Listed below are short descriptions of six different leadership styles. Please read them carefully and make these choices: (a) Assign a Theory X–Y blend to each style. For example, if you feel style 1 is a 60 percent X, 40 percent Y blend, write these percentages in the blanks. (b) Fit each style into the most appropriate work environment: military, atomic plant, factory, creative research, retail store, restaurant. (c) State your personal preferences by assigning a priority (1 through 6) to each style.

Style 1: Quiet, conservative, and very sensitive to personal needs of each employee. Maintains a firm and consistent discipline line. Achieves modest productivity and has little

personnel turnover. Has reputation of being fair, consistent, and steady, but not a good motivator.

a. _____ X   _____ Y

b. _____

c. _____

Style 2:   Open, direct, frequent communication with all employees. Expects and receives high productivity. Style is
strong, forceful, consistent. If a problem develops, it is
discussed immediately. Has reputation as a good
motivator.

a. _____ X   _____ Y

b. _____

c. _____

Style 3:   Free, easy, and permissive with employees. Low or soft
discipline line. This individual is very protective of employees as far as upper management is concerned. Spends
considerable time discussing their personal problems.
Involves employees in decisions. Has reputation of being
"easy, yet effective."

a. _____ X   _____ Y

b. _____

c. _____

Style 4:   Sets very high standards. Employees always know where
they stand. Provides recognition, develops unusual pride,
and has the reputation of being a strong leader. Has outstanding safety record.

a. _____ X   _____ Y

b. _____

c. _____

Style 5: Very employee-oriented; helps them set their goals. A superior teacher with great patience; willing to change work schedules. Almost always grants personal requests coming from employees. Modest productivity but has the lowest turnover in the organization.

a. _____ X   _____ Y

b. _____

c. _____

Style 6: Takes pride in developing a work-hard, play-hard attitude among employees. Feels an X style is best during peak periods of productivity when the pressure is great; likes Y style during slow periods. Maintains high productivity level but personnel turnover is high.

a. _____ X   _____ Y

b. _____

c. _____

Career
Profile

Elizabeth Dowell
Asst. Vice-President, Credit Administration
Bank of America NT&SA

Most people begin their careers after going to school. Elizabeth Dowell reversed this process. She began her career with Bank of America and then decided to get her Master of Business Administration Degree from the University of Southern California.

"I felt I could make it in the bank without a degree, but I knew it would help. And, besides, it was very much a matter of my own personal fulfillment. So I did it."

Currently assistant vice-president in credit administration at the bank's Southern California headquarters in Los Angeles, Dowell joined the bank as a clerk and began working her way up through posts of increasing responsibility. She was also taking courses from the American Institute of Banking (AIB).

"AIB courses are very good. But I figured if I was going to school, why not go ahead and get a degree?"

As a matter of fact, she got three: Associate of Arts from Citrus College in 1970, a Bachelor of Arts from California State University at Fullerton in 1974, and her MBA in 1976. All of this while working full time at the bank and advancing to the position of assistant manager at one of the bank's branch offices.

"One of the first things I learned was how to manage my time. I had to, because I was usually taking twelve credits at school in addition to handling the responsibilities of my job. I had already learned some time management as an assistant manager, but that was an idle stroll compared to the pace needed for working and going to school at the same time. I think this is critically important for anyone in business, on and off the job.

"Never let work be your total life. Be involved with other activities or groups. It's good for you in terms of mental stimulus, and it's good for you as a whole person. And I think you'll do a better job at work, too.

"It's a matter of setting priorities—of deciding what you want to invest your time in. You have to be perceptive to changing needs so you don't get stuck in a rut. And you have to be able to say no in those situations where you feel your time would be either wasted or not fulfilling to you as a person."

Following graduation from USC, Dowell was promoted to her present post as assistant vice-president in one of the bank's regional credit administration departments.

"This has been a fascinating change from my duties as an assistant manager of a branch. The stimulus is different and so are the needed skills. I'm getting experience with a variety of different types of loans.

"So far, every different job I've had with the bank has been a learning experience. That, too, is important to anyone in business. Whatever the assignment is, approach it with the idea that you can learn from it.

"Also, approach it with full confidence in yourself—confidence that not only can you do the job, but do it well. You'll find that the learning aspect becomes a part of that confidence and also of doing the job well.

"Here are some other observations that might be applicable to a person just beginning a career.

"Think for yourself. By this, I don't mean ignoring the advice and counsel of your superiors or people with more experience than you have. It's a matter of critically analyzing the information you receive and not slavishly following or accepting what someone else says. Trust in your own analytical abilities.

"Be a self-starter. This may be a related aspect of approaching a job with confidence, but don't sit around and do only what you have been told to do. In any position, there are always other things that need to be done. So, analyze your job, figure out what needs to be done, and then do more.

"And finally, as mentioned earlier, don't let work become your total life. If you do, you'll soon become a drudge and develop a narrowness of vision that will impair your personal relationships as well as your ability to do your job. There is more to life than nine to five, so make sure you live that part, too."

ANTICIPATION
Your First Supervisory Position

19

Assume you were fortunate enough to win an excellent starting position with a progressive organization six months ago. Since that time, you have made rewarding personal progress. You are fully adjusted to the environment and your new job, and you have more respect for the organization now than when you started. Yesterday, after a serious debate with yourself over a period of several weeks, you decided to seek a beginning management position. *This is a firm decision on your part.* As a result, you have already notified your supervisor and the personnel department that you would like consideration for any openings that might occur in the future.

How should you go about preparing for this position in advance? Reading the 20 profiles in this book will provide a valuable background. Here are some additional suggestions.

Improve relationships between yourself and your co-workers now so they will accept you in a role above them at a later date. Don't over-do it. If you become too friendly with a co-worker and then become his or her supervisor, the change in your status can affect the relationship. But don't start pulling away from co-workers in anticipation. Be as sensitive to their needs as possible. Make sure you do your share of the disagreeable jobs, avoid unnecessary absenteeism, and above all, keep your business and personal worlds separated. The respect you earn from your co-workers now will follow you if you become the new supervisor. Once you have been promoted, your future, to a considerable extent, will be in their hands.

Imagine yourself in the role of supervisor. Starting immediately, try to get the "feel" of what it would be like to supervise your department. What practices will you continue? What changes might you make? How will you go about building better vertical relationships with your former co-workers? Through a careful analysis of the relationship between you and your supervisor *now,* you might be able to sense how you could do a better job should your turn arrive. Has your supervisor given you the recognition you have earned? Is he or she a good teacher? Have you always felt free to discuss a problem? Has your supervisor involved you enough in departmental problems? Did he or she always tell you about changes in advance? Although you cannot anticipate exact circumstances, you can and should prepare yourself mentally for the new role. You must make this preparation secretly, however, because any premature change in your outward behavior could damage your progress.

Find yourself two or three exciting management models to study. Your own supervisor may or may not be a good model. Compare your supervisor with others, perhaps an officer in personnel, your supervisor's supervisor, and any top management person you have contact with. Study these people. What makes them effective? In making your evaluation, consider everything from grooming to leadership style. Find out how they communicate with others, conduct themselves in formal situations, prepare written communications, and use the telephone. If you choose good models, you can improve your behavior and prepare yourself in advance for similar roles. The following quotation is applicable. "I don't think that Ms. Travis ever suspected that she was my executive model for almost two years. She had a positive influence on my career progress, but I never got around to telling her about it."

Take a college course in management. If you have already had courses in management, take a more advanced one. If you have never had a formal course in management, supervision, or human relations, it is imperative that you take one as soon as possible if you are serious about becoming a good manager. Here is a comment from a young supervisor who supports this view. "I completed my first course in supervision at a local campus just two weeks before I was promoted. Looking back, I doubt whether I would have survived without it."

How can such courses help you? Here are several benefits.

1. Your readiness factor is high at this point, and you could absorb both theory and technique quickly.

2. The specific techniques learned in such courses could prevent you from making mistakes.
3. Your personal confidence should improve as a result of taking such courses.
4. You will meet others who are preparing for management roles, and you can learn from them.

Most community colleges offer a wide variety of courses in supervision in their evening programs. If you already have a four-year degree, you might be able to take a graduate course in management at a local university. You should investigate all courses available to you as soon as possible so that you can complete enrollment procedures in time for the next term.

Do some reading on management practices. Why not do some advance preparation by getting acquainted with periodicals that deal with supervision and management? You have two basic sources, the organization for which you work and your nearest library. It might help you build better relationships with people at work if you ask them to recommend trade magazines and other materials. Your supervisor or your personnel officer might be willing to lend you periodicals. Your organization may have a library with up-to-date materials on management and supervision. In most college and public libraries you can find considerable current data on management trends, practices, and techniques. The author of this book is also the author of *Supervisor's Survival Kit,** which was written primarily for the new supervisor and is used both on and off campus. It is a mid-management primer, now in its second edition.

Start managing your own time more efficiently. One way to prepare for a mangement role is to learn to manage your time better. As an employee, you can rely on your boss to provide directions. When you become a supervisor, these same directions must come from you. You will determine your own objectives and decide how to achieve them; you will assign priorities to your duties. You will delegate specific tasks and make sure they are accomplished, establish standards of performance and see that they are met. You will also need to appraise results. Your effectiveness in accomplishing these multi-responsibilities will depend on how well you manage your time. You can start now to improve your productivity by eliminating some time-wasters (like talking too long on the telephone), by setting daily goals for yourself, by scheduling your time so that you can get extra work accomplished. Another way

---

*Published by Science Research Associates, Inc., Chicago, 1976 (2d ed.).

of learning to manage your time better is by scheduling your personal off-the-job duties in a more organized manner. Perhaps you can make a list of Saturday chores to accomplish by "clustering" to save time and driving.

Study the appraisal system within your organization. When you start with an organization, it is the responsibility of your manager to appraise your personal progress. When you become a manager, the tables will be turned and you will appraise others. Appraisal, an important function of all supervisors, must be accomplished in a professional manner because many laws govern such practices and because salary increases and possible promotions are affected. Begin now to prepare yourself for this responsibility.

1. Obtain and study a copy of the appraisal form your organization uses.
2. Discuss the techniques and pitfalls of appraising with your supervisor or someone in personnel, or both.
3. Do some reading on the subject in management periodicals.

The more you understand about performance appraisals in advance, the easier it will be to make them. Try to keep a positive attitude toward the procedure because, done professionally, appraisals have great value to the organization and to the individual. An appraisal properly handled can strengthen the relationship between an employee and a supervisor.

Start analyzing decisions more carefully. As an employee, you are not in a position to make many decisions. As a supervisor, you will make decisions daily. One way to prepare is to pay more attention to the decisions your supervisor is making now. Can he or she separate the big decisions from the little ones? Are employees involved in decisions that affect them? Are the possible side effects of decisions always considered in advance? Is your supervisor guilty of procrastination when it comes to making decisions? As you have learned in your educational experience, the scientific process follows a three-step pattern. First, get all the facts; second, weigh the facts to determine the best answer to the problem; third, make the decision and follow through to see whether it works. The more you study and analyze the decisions (good and bad) made by others, the better prepared you will be to make decisions when your turn arrives.

Start a personal log of "do's" and "don't's." Start building your own leadership style formula by making a list of plans. For example, to improve communication in your department, you might decide to install and use a bulletin board as a communications center to provide messages for your employees. You might add to your list those things you will try not to do. For example, you might decide against having lunch or coffee with your previous co-workers because you feel they need privacy and would prefer to enjoy free time without your supervision. Instead, it could be productive for you to have lunch with other supervisors and discuss common problems informally. Such a list will be useful whether you become the supervisor of your present department or of any other department.

Work harder than ever to improve your technical knowledge. Once you become a supervisor, the people in your department will depend upon you for information about new developments, trends, and technology. Teaching will be part of your role. Although a supervisor gets the job done through others, he or she must be able to show people how to do their work safely and efficiently. Much of the respect that employees feel for their supervisors is derived from the knowledge and know-how the supervisor transmits. When you become a supervisor, will you be able to train a new worker in the department, or do you need to learn more about the skills performed? If so, today would be the best possible time to start. The following example might show you the way to proceed.

> I discovered early in my career that you achieve a great deal of job security when you learn every skill in a department. I would work hard to gain some free time so I could help my co-workers and learn their skills in operating special machines and performing specific tasks. Later, when I became a supervisor, I was in an excellent position to train new employees throughout the department.

Since an organization cannot be expected to satisfy the *personal time schedule* of every employee, you might follow all of the steps outlined above and then be forced to wait for your first supervisory assignment. On the other hand, you might become an "instant supervisor" long before you have completed these steps. The idea is to be prepared as soon as possible. Nothing is more injurious to career progress than to receive an opportunity you are not prepared to undertake.

Discussion Questions

1. If you were in top management, would you recommend that an employee be promoted to supervisor of the department in

which he or she is now working? Or would you make it mandatory always to move a person to a new department for his or her first management experience? Take a firm stand either way.

2. Suppose an employee prepares for a supervisory role in advance, then is forced to wait for a year or more. Could this delay destroy the individual's morale? Might it be better just to wait patiently without any advance preparation?

3. How would you select an executive model? What will you do if you can't find a model who meets your standards?

4. Select the profile (model) in this book that you feel can help you most in achieving your management goals. Justify your choice.

5. Which profiles, if any, should be eliminated as possible supervisory models? Justify your position.

6. Which of the 20 profiles do you identify with the most? Would this profile be a good or bad model for you to follow? Why?

PROGRESS

Could You Be Doing Better Elsewhere?

20

There are many excellent reasons why you might decide to leave one organization and join another. Your career may be stalled with little hope for future progress. You may have made so many human-relations mistakes that it is unwise to remain with the organization. Often greater opportunities, including better pay, are available elsewhere.

There are frequently some real advantages in starting fresh in another organization. One employee, upon meeting a former co-worker, referred to his fresh start as "therapy." "Pete, leaving your firm was the best decision I ever made. Since I last saw you, everything has been going right instead of wrong for me. I think the new environment is the therapy I needed. I wish I had quit two years before I did."

On rare occasions a competing organization hears about your talents and seeks you out. In most cases, however, you will have to initiate the contact yourself.

When *should* you move to another organization? For most individuals, this is an agonizing decision to make. The Career Progress Evaluation Form has been prepared and tested to help those in the decision-making process. If you are presently employed, even if you are not seeking a new organization, you are encouraged to complete it for experience and evaluation purposes. If you are not presently employed, become acquainted with it so that you can refer to it if you are faced with such a decision in the future. Studying the form now could prevent you from starting your career with the wrong organization. It can also give you additional insight into the job interviewing process.

Career Progress Evaluation Form

This form was designed to help you decide whether you should stay in your present position or seek a fresh start with a new organization.

First, rate your job on a scale of 1 to 5 for each question.

Second, write *why* you have selected this rating. Your explanation could provide additional insight and help you (or your teacher) to evaluate the quality of your answer.

1. What are your present opportunities to learn?

    I have great   1 2 3 4 5   I have no opportunity
    opportunities to   to learn on this
    learn on this job.   job.

    State why you rated yourself as you did.

    _____

    _____

2. Are you utilizing your skills and talents?

    I am working close   1 2 3 4 5   I am working far
    to my full potential.   beneath my
                                                 potential.

    Why? _____

    _____

3. How do you rate your job in comparison to your qualifications?

    I have the best   1 2 3 4 5   I have the worst
    possible job   possible job
    considering my   considering my
    qualifications.   qualifications.

    Why? _____

    _____

4. What are your long-term career possibilities?

    Prospects are   1 2 3 4 5   Prospects are zero.
    outstanding.

    Why? _____

    _____

    _____

5. How motivated are you by your job?

    I wake up eager to   1 2 3 4 5   I wake up hating to
    go to work.   go to work.

    Why? _____

    _____

    _____

6. Have you considered resigning?

    I have never   1 2 3 4 5   I think of resigning
    thought of   every day.
    resigning.

    Why? _____

    _____

    _____

7. Are you involved in decision-making?

    I am highly   1 2 3 4 5   I am never involved.
    involved.

    Why? _____

    _____

8. Does your job give you the recognition you need?

   I get all the   1 2 3 4 5   I get no recognition
   recognition I   at all.
   deserve.

   Why? _____

   _____

9. What is the quality of the leadership in your organization?

   Outstanding   1 2 3 4 5   Worst possible
   leadership at all   leadership at all
   levels.   levels.

   Why? _____

   _____

10. Are there any dangerous physical risks on the job?

    No risks.   1 2 3 4 5   Heavy risks.

    Why? _____

    _____

    _____

11. How do you rate your physical work environment?

    Physical working   1 2 3 4 5   Physical working
    conditions fine.   conditions
                                        unbearable.

    Why?

    _____

    _____

    _____

12. Do you receive all of the on-the-job freedom you need?

    All possible   1   2   3   4   5   Completely stifled.
    freedom.

    Why? _____

    _____

13. What are the financial rewards?

    My salary is the   1   2   3   4   5   My salary is the
    highest for my kind   lowest for my kind
    of role.   of role.

    Why? _____

    _____

14. Are human relations satisfactory?

    Highly harmonious.   1   2   3   4   5   Continual dissension.

    Why? _____

    _____

15. How fulfilling is your role?

    I am completely   1   2   3   4   5   I am completely
    fulfilled.   unfulfilled.

    Why? _____

    _____

16. How do you rate the geographical location?

    Ideal.   1   2   3   4   5   Couldn't be worse.

    Why? _____

    _____

17. How would you rate you present supervisor?

My supervisor is   1 2 3 4 5   My supervisor is
excellent.   inadequate.

Why? _____

_____

_____

18. What are your promotional possibilities?

I expect a   1 2 3 4 5   I never expect a
promotion   promotion.
immediately.

Why? _____

_____

_____

19. How good are the fringe benefits?

Best benefit   1 2 3 4 5   Worst benefit
package around.   package around.

Why? _____

_____

_____

20. What kind of formal training, if any, is your organization
furnishing?

Excellent formal   1 2 3 4 5   No formal training.
training.

Why? _____

_____

21. Is your organization expanding so that you will have more opportunities?

    Expanding at a fast   1 2 3 4 5 Getting smaller at a
    pace.   fast pace.

    Why? _____

    _____

22. Does your job offer creative opportunities?

    I have many   1 2 3 4 5 I have no creative
    creative   opportunities.
    opportunities.

    Why? _____

    _____

23. Does your organization promote people from within?

    My company   1 2 3 4 5 My company always
    always promotes   goes outside.
    from within.

    Why? _____

    _____

24. Considering your length of service, will you lose much seniority if you make a move?

    My length of   1 2 3 4 5 I have been with the
    service is   company a long
    insignificant.   time.

    Why? _____

    _____

    _____

25. Has your organization lived up to all promises?

My company has   1   2   3   4   5   My company has
lived up to all   not lived up to any
promises, both   promises.
expressed and
implied.

Why? _____

_____

Add up your total points: _____

Divide your total by 25 to get your average: _____

If your average for the 25 questions was 4 or above (a total of 100 points or more), you should seriously consider moving as soon as possible because your needs as an individual are not being met. If your average is close to 3 (a total of 65–85 points), most of your needs are being satisfied, and you should consider doing whatever is possible to improve your status *within* the organization. If your average is 2 or less (under 50 points), you are extremely fortunate and might have trouble improving your situation elsewhere.

Making a move from one organization to another is complex when it involves selling a home and moving a family to another area, leaving friends and relatives, and making a major change in your life-style. All of these factors, and many others, have a tendency to keep people within the organizations they join initially. This pressure to maintain the status quo and remain in a secure job has probably hurt the career progress of many individuals far more than they realize. There are, however, certain cautions or factors people should carefully evaluate before making a move.

Normal let-down periods. It is natural and expected that following the initial adjustment to a new organization, a psychological let-down may occur. To leave a company during such a period of discouragement could be a mistake because the same let-down can happen elsewhere.

Personality conflicts. Studies show that more people leave organizations because of human-relations problems than for any other cause. Often resignations result when employees cannot build good relationships with their immediate supervisors. Such personality conflicts may be ample cause for moving, but evidence shows that often they can be resolved without a resignation. One experienced personnel officer stressed the fact that resolving a conflict is a valuable learning experience.

> I hate to see someone leave a company on a personal conflict matter, especially if the employee is satisfied with the job itself and with the company. Most of these situations work out, and the employee learns more by staying than by leaving

Poor health. Sometimes the cause of dissatisfaction is not the job itself, but a health problem that the employee has not yet recognized. For example, Olga, a legal secretary with excellent skills, moved from job to job over a period of three years. Although she was never terminated, she began to realize that employers were not sorry to see her leave. Why? She finally discovered that she had a health problem that was causing her to be lethargic and unmotivated. Once the problem was corrected, she started to make excellent progress. Further moves were unnecessary.

Negative influence from co-workers. A small number of negative insiders will, if you permit them, try to convince you that you have made a mistake by joining the company. Often these "gloom and doom" employees have made some serious mistakes but lack the courage to start fresh elsewhere. They try to pull you into their camp instead of letting you make your own evaluation.

Dissatisfaction over low pay. Serious down periods can result from acute financial pressure caused by pay scales that do not keep up with rising consumer prices. Unfortunately, some of the diversions (like vacations) that help to relieve such depression also cost more today.

If financial pressure has been a persistent problem—in spite of genuine efforts to live within your salary—ask for an increase with finesse and confidence. At the same time, actively seek a better paying position elsewhere. People today are more open, more comfortable, and more assertive (without being aggressive) in seeking pay increases. If you are timid about this matter, it may be time for you to change your behavior.

The best time to seek a substantial increase is during the formal appraisal period (if there is one), but if this period is only an annual affair, a mid-period discussion might be in order. If low pay is causing you to produce at a lower rate and creating inner hostilities, it is time to talk about it. One should learn to introduce the problem of higher pay in the same nonthreatening manner used in seeking a particular vacation period.

Apply for a raise on the basis of your current productivity and your future worth to the organization. Obviously, if your recent contribution has been below acceptable standards, you are at a strong disadvantage. Start out by saying that you "would like to investigate the possibility of a pay raise." Try to avoid the following:

Any hint of inner hostility toward the organization or any individual. If you put the superior on the defensive, communications will be defensive, communications will be influenced and the possibility of success will diminish.

Any reference to a possible resignation. This is a form of intimidation and adds nothing to the investigation. The fact that you *are* actively engaged in finding a better role elsewhere need not be introduced.

The temptation to tell *why* you need more money. It is more professional to base your request on what you are doing and what you can do for the organization; the fact that you have a big dental bill to pay off isn't the main issue.

Any reference to a specific amount or a time limitation. It is better to let management come back with an offer after they have had time to consider all aspects of the problem. If they come back with too little (or nothing), intensify your outside search.

Organizational loyalty is a value many people respect, but your first loyalty is to yourself and your career. If your behavior has been professional and your contribution high, then moving to another organization to gain a salary increase might be advisable. You may belong to a group (perhaps a union) that will do your bargaining for you; if not, the more experience you get in bargaining for yourself, the better.

Availability of a better job. Most placement advisors believe that it is best to stay in your present position while you are searching for a better job. They point out, of course, that it is advisable to keep your personal productivity high while you are searching because you do not want to leave a poor reputation behind. Experience shows that a substantial number of people who resign their jobs without making other arrangements live through long periods of unemployment. Loss of income is especially difficult when unemployment insurance is not applicable because the individual resigned for personal reasons. Here is the advice of one young executive who recently made a switch.

> There is nothing unprofessional about seeking and finding a better assignment with a new organization while you stay on the payroll of the old one. It is a common and accepted practice. I recently made such a switch myself. Of course, while I was going through interviews with others, I didn't neglect my job. I worked hard and gave the customary two-weeks notice. You can't always leave a good image behind when you quit, but it is always worth a try.

Once an individual has made the decision to move, the following steps are recommended.

When possible, arrange interviews during off hours, days off, or vacations. If this cannot be worked out, there is nothing wrong with asking for a day off "for personal business" without pay. The practice of using up sick leave for interviews is not recommended.

A request for confidentiality from a prospective employer will almost always be honored. It is accepted procedure to ask that interviews and applications with outside organizations be kept confidential. You need not advise your present employer that you are seeking employment elsewhere.

State your desire to give your present organization notice. Almost all organizations will respect and honor the need for an employee who is joining them to sever relationships with a previous concern on a professional basis.

Depart in the most professional manner possible. Ask for a face-to-face exit interview, return all equipment, and take any action required on retirement plans, profit sharing, or medical insurance programs.

No one, including you, should attempt to predict just what your "career passage" might look like some years from now. Certainly it will be different from those you have read about in this publication. *Your* career, for example, could be built inside a single organization (large or small), but chances are it will be built inside many. You may never return to a campus for "upgrading" or further degree purposes, but most likely you will. You may or may not move away from the special career or general career area you prepared for originally. Your personal passage may not be smooth, but with the right attitude on your part, it should be exciting and rewarding.

There are many surprises in store for you. Twenty years from now, you should be able to look back and describe with pride the mobility and flexibility you have demonstrated.

Discussion Questions

1. What are some of the emotional and psychological problems that keep employees in an organization when it is obvious that their career progress would be better elsewhere?

2. How valuable is the Career Progress Evaluation Form in this chapter? Would you actually use it if you were considering a job switch? How might it help you? Would you recommend it to a friend? Why?

3. Could some of the questions in the Career Progress Evaluation Form be used during the interview process? If so, which ones would be most applicable? Why?

4. What is your opinion of the familiar statement that an individual should not transfer from one organization to another unless a substantial pay increase (say $2,000 per year) is involved? Explain your position.

5. Why is *hindsight* frequently so much better than *foresight* when it comes to changing jobs? Explain fully.

6. What is the probability, in your opinion, that an individual who resigns a job with an organization will be welcomed back at a later date? What are the factors for and against such an eventuality?

Exercises for Part V

General Self-Assessment Progress Report

(If you answer number 1 or 2, you need not complete the second part.)

1. I am doing a great   1   2   3   4   5   I am doing nothing
    job of creating my   to create my own
    own promotion   opportunities for
    opportunities.   promotion.

    I am either going to quit this job or do the following to create my own personal promotional opportunities:

    _____

    _____

    _____

2. I have learned all   1   2   3   4   5   I have learned
    about my   nothing about my
    supervisor's job,   supervisor's job,
    and I am 100   and I couldn't
    percent capable of   survive in it.
    taking it over.

    I plan to spend more time observing my supervisor and learn the following:

    _____

    _____

    _____

    _____

3. I have made such   1 2 3 4 5   I have made so
    good progress on   little progress on
    this job it would be   this job I had better
    foolish for me to   leave.
    leave.

    If I decide to stay with this job, I intend to do the follow-
    ing to improve my personal progress.

    _____

    _____

    _____

    _____

4. My human   1 2 3 4 5   I have been so
    relations progress   unskillful at human
    has been excellent.   relations that I
                                              should resign.

    If I decide to stay with this organization, I intend to do
    the following to improve relationships with others at all
    levels:

    _____

    _____

    _____

    _____

5. I have done my   1 2 3 4 5   I haven't done
    best to develop my   anything to
    leadership   develop my
    potential.   leadership
                                              potential.

I plan to do the following to improve my leadership potential and prepare myself for a promotion:

_____

_____

_____

6. My assertiveness has been "just right."   1 2 3 4 5   I have been much too quiet (or far too aggressive).

I intend to do the following so that I will be assertive in the right degree for my organization:

_____

_____

_____

7. I have not in any way permitted my supervisor or management to intimidate me.   1 2 3 4 5   I have permitted my supervisor and management to "scare me to death."

I plan to take a stronger stand with management in the following ways:

_____

_____

_____

_____

8. At this point, I am   1 2 3 4 5   I am totally
    fully motivated to   apathetic, and there
    excel in this   is no hope for
    organization.   improvement.

    If I decide to stay with this firm, I plan to motivate myself
    in the following ways:

    _____

    _____

    _____

    _____

    _____

9. Working for this   1 2 3 4 5   I have learned so
    firm is a continual   little, the job has
    learning   been a waste of
    experience.   time.

    If I decide to stay with this firm, I plan to establish the
    following learning goals for myself:

    _____

    _____

    _____

    _____

    _____

10. I have not had a   1 2 3 4 5   I have serious
    serious down   down periods
    period with this   frequently.
    firm.

I plan to do the following to help me eliminate down periods in the future:

_____

_____

_____

11. I chose the best   1 2 3 4 5   I made a very
     possible   serious mistake
     organization when   when I joined this
     I chose this firm.   firm.

☐ I plan to leave this firm and start over.

☐ I plan to stay with this firm and try harder.

An Exercise in Goal Setting

Please read the following story as background material before completing the exercise.

"My name is Carl Henderson, and I am the president of a large corporation. I have six vice-presidents who report to me, and our operation is national in scope.

"I have always been a goal-oriented person. I still am. For example, each night as I get ready to leave my office, I write out my goals for the following day. I usually have from five to seven on my list, and I arrange them in order of their importance to the smooth operation of our corporation. You might call them my daily priority list. I have discovered, over the years, that by writing them out I can 'psych' myself into leaving all of my problems at work. It may sound like an oversimplification for the president of a company to do this, but I don't want to take problems home with me any more than other people do.

"The next morning when I drive to work (I commute more than 30 miles each way), I start recalling my priority list and perhaps make some revisions, which I transfer to the list when I arrive.

These, then, are my work goals for the day. Of course, I may revise the list many times as a result of developments, emergencies, and so on. In addition to my daily goals, I also have weekly work goals. I usually write them out on Monday mornings and cross out those I have achieved by Friday. Obviously, my daily goals often assist me in reaching my weekly goals. Because I am responsible to the board of directors, we also have a long-range corporate goal list, which I must refine and articulate to them.

"I also believe strongly that each manager in my organization should develop targets for his or her department or division, so we have incorporated the management by objectives philosophy into our organization. It works this way for us: Each manager submits his or her goals in writing every six months. The goals are carefully reviewed and revised by the superior above, and all of these plans slowly make their way to my desk. I then review them and incorporate some of the ideas into our total corporate plan, which I submit to the directors. On the six-month target date, I ask each manager to sit down and discuss the outcome with the supervisor who submitted the plan. How close did the individual come to his or her plan? What changes should be made next time? We always try to take into consideration any factors beyond the control of the supervisor that have made his plan out of date. We do, however, take these goals into consideration as far as promotions and pay increases are concerned.

"So you can see I am a highly goal-oriented individual. I like the premise that an individual who must struggle to come up with a good plan may find it most motivating. In setting goals, however, I always keep these rules in mind:

1. Keep goals flexible so that changes can be made quickly.
2. Job goals should be communicated, but personal goals might best be kept private.
3. Keep the number of goals to a minimum. Too many goals become confusing.

"I strongly recommend to anyone who wishes to move into management roles that he or she start experimenting with a goal-setting process as soon as possible."

Now is the time to start setting goals. If you have a full-time or part-time job, complete the exercise by writing goals that apply to your work. If you are a student, write goals that apply to your studies. An example is provided for each step.

Work-Oriented Goals

Daily Goals: Write a minimum of three work goals you hope to accomplish tomorrow.

Clean out my desk

Weekly Goals: Write a minimum of three work goals you hope to accomplish before the end of the week.

rearrange the stockroom

Monthly Goals: Write a minimum of three work goals you hope to reach by the end of the month.

eliminate 50% of mistakes in calculation

Personal Goals

Short-Term: Write a minimum of three personal goals or targets you would like to accomplish in the next year.

trip to Las Vegas

new car

Long-Term: Write a minimum of three personal goals you hope to accomplish in the next three years.

Complete my master's

program

Case Study: Calculation

In an effort to increase the number of women at the executive level of the San-Firm Corporation, Melvin Dooer, the recruiting officer, employed Alice and Audrey from the same graduating class. He felt both had outstanding potential to reach management levels. After two weeks in an intensive management training program, the two women were given similar assignments.

After sizing things up carefully and deciding that it was a typical, large, male-oriented corporation, Alice decided to follow a highly calculated course in her bid to reach middle-management as soon as possible.

I intend to be openly aggressive as I act upon corporate procedures, problems, and protocol. I intend to be sensitive about the timing, but aggressive, nevertheless. For example, I intend to speak up firmly on issues when I think I am right and will be effective. When appropriate, I will use mild forms of intimidation. If management begins to wonder whether they have employed a militant, it will work to my advantage. If they start to worry about an affirmative action suit should I be terminated, so much the better. I want to gamble on my future; I want to scramble. I want to live on the razor's edge with rules and decisions. Why worry about making a few enemies when it is inevitable anyway? I will be subtle or bold depending on the circumstances, but I will quickly demonstrate my ability to lead. They will know I am around. I will be talked about. Wouldn't it be fun to be a vice-president before you are thirty?

Audrey, after sizing up the company as being somewhat typical and conservative—a "do-it-by-the-book" organization—decided to make her bid for a middle management position in a different manner.

I am going to play the corporate game the way management expects it to be played. I am going to win using *their* rules. I will be assertive at times, but I will stay strictly within accepted procedures and protocol. I want to build the image of being safe, predictable, easy to communicate with, and reliable. I will make decisions slowly to achieve the reputation of being a good, sound decision-maker. I will communicate with people on a pick-and-choose basis. I will avoid creating waves unless appropriate, and then only little ones. In addition, I am going to protect myself from every angle. For example, I don't expect to create a single enemy if I can help it. My career and personal worlds will be kept 100 percent separate so that I will never be vulnerable to any form of criticism. "Safe, steady, and sure" will be my career motto. Sooner or later, they will discover I am efficient, always sure of facts, capable of making tough decisions, and a safe leader. In short, whenever management gets together and starts looking around for a woman to promote, most will support me. My personal goal? I am not in any big hurry and I don't have a personal time schedule, but I plan to become the first woman vice-president for San-Firm.

If both individuals stay with the firm for five years, which one would you expect to be at the highest management level? *Justify your position in detail.*

APPENDIX I

Career Awareness

ACCOMPLISHMENTS To assess what you consider to be your accomplishments is an important step in helping you understand your skills and values as well as your likes and dislikes. In a word or two describe your accomplishments in the space provided. This may seem difficult at first but if you take the time to think about your past experiences, you will be able to do this. An accomplishment is something you feel you have done well. For example, you might have succeeded in a course which was a great challenge to you. Or you might have planned a very successful social event.

1. College Accomplishments (academic or extracurricular)

a. _____

   _____

b. _____

   _____

c. _____

   _____

2. Volunteer Accomplishments

a. _____

   _____

b. _____

   _____

c. _____

   _____

Note: The Career Awareness form is reprinted from a brochure entitled *Plan Your Career with Atlantic Richfield* published by Atlantic Richfield Company, Atlantic Richfield Plaza, 515 South Flower St., Los Angeles, CA 90071.

3. Work Related Accomplishments (including part-time and summer)

a. _____

b. _____

c. _____

4. Any Other Areas (family, sports, hobbies, recreation)

a. _____

b. _____

c. _____

ACTIVITIES In addition to your accomplishments, you participated in many other activities that may have provided a good learning experience. To consider these activities is *also* important in understanding yourself. In this section you should list these activities. As an example you may have worked on a factory assembly line or you may have attended a movie or lecture that greatly influenced you.

1. College Activities (academic or extracurricular)

a. _____

b. _____

c. _____

2. Volunteer Activities

a. _____

_____

b. _____

_____

c. _____

_____

3. Work Related Activities (including part-time and summer)

a. _____

_____

b. _____

_____

c. _____

_____

4. Any Other Areas (family, sports, hobbies, recreation)

a. _____

_____

b. _____

_____

c. _____

_____

SKILLS Now that you have identified some of your accomplishments, you should determine the necessary skills (abilities) involved. Many of the skills you have successfully used in the past will aid you in future endeavors. For *each* of the accomplishments listed on pages 269–70, state what you feel were the important skills used. If the same skill was used in more than one accomplishment, list it under all appropriate areas. In the example of succeeding in the difficult course, a response to this section might look as follows:

College Accomplishments—Skills

Communications skills
(Oral & written), Ability
to grasp new concepts,
Organizational skills

1. College Accomplishments—Skills

a. _____

b. _____

c. _____

2. Volunteer Accomplishments—Skills

a. _____

b. _____

c. _____

3. Work Related Accomplishments (including part-time and summer)—Skills

a. _____

b. _____

c. _____

4. Any Other Areas (hobbies, recreation)—Skills

a. _____

b. _____

c. _____

INTERESTS (LIKES AND DISLIKES) In your experience there are some things you enjoyed and others you did not. In order to relate your interests to future career possibilities, you need to identify the things you like and dislike. For each of the accomplishments you identified on pages 269–70, write down what you liked and disliked about the accomplishment. You may find the same likes and dislikes in several areas. Repeat them where appropriate. In the example of succeeding in the difficult course, the response might be:

College Accomplishments

Like

Challenge,
Competition

Dislike

Amount of reading,
Class participation

Like   Dislike

1. College Accomplishments

a. _____   _____

   _____   _____

b. _____   _____

   _____   _____

2. Volunteer Accomplishments

a. _____   _____

   _____   _____

b. _____   _____

   _____   _____

3. Work-Related Activities (including part-time and summer)

a. _____   _____

   _____   _____

b. _____   _____

   _____   _____

4. Any Other Areas (family, sports, hobbies, recreation)

a. _____   _____

   _____   _____

b. _____   _____

   _____   _____

In the same manner for each of the activities listed on pages 270–71, list what you feel were the important skills used in that activity. Again repeat all skills where appropriate. In the example of the factory work, the response might look like this:

Work Related Activity—Skills

Working with others, Meeting deadlines & quotes, Knowledge of equipment, Keeping records of time & materials

1. College Activities—Skills

a. _____

b. _____

c. _____

2. Volunteer Activities—Skills

a. _____

b. _____

c. _____

3. Work Related Activities (including part-time and summer)—Skills

a. _____

b. _____

c. _____

4. Any Other Areas (family, sports, hobbies, recreation)—Skills

a. _____

b. _____

c. _____

For each of the activities you identified on pages 270–71, list the likes and dislikes as you did for the accomplishments. The example of the factory job might appear as follows:

Work Related Activity

Like

Money

Dislike

No challenge,
Dirty, noisy

Like   Dislike

1. College Activities (academic or extracurricular)

a. _____   _____

b. _____   _____

2. Volunteer Activities

a. _____   _____

b. _____   _____

3. Work Related Activities (including part-time and summer)

a. _____   _____

b. _____   _____

4. Any Other Areas (family, sports, hobbies, recreation)

a. _____   _____

b. _____   _____

VALUES Values are those things you believe in. They are basic and important, yet often difficult to identify because you may not consciously be aware of them. The purpose of this section is to stimulate you to identify some of your values in order to help clarify their importance to you. Some examples are freedom, meaningful human relationships, importance of education, respect, integrity.

In the space below, list as many values as you can.

1. _____   11. _____
2. _____   12. _____
3. _____   13. _____
4. _____   14. _____
5. _____   15. _____
6. _____   16. _____
7. _____   17. _____
8. _____   18. _____
9. _____   19. _____
10. _____   20. _____

Now that you have listed some values, rank the top five from most important to least important.

1. _____
2. _____
3. _____
4. _____
5. _____

YOUR SKILLS AND INTERESTS SUMMARY In this section you are to identify related skills. You have already listed the skills associated with a number of experiences. As a next step you need to review pages 272–73. Ususally there are patterns to the skills listed. Some skills may be written down for several of the accomplishments and activities. If you find very few, or no instances where the same skill is repeated, you may have used different words to represent the same skill.

In the space provided below, write down the five skills which appear most frequently; again look for different words meaning the same thing.

1. _____

2. _____

3. _____

4. _____

5. _____

Similarly, review your interests (likes and dislikes) listed on pages 272–73. In the space below, write the five likes and five dislikes which appear most frequently.

Likes   Dislikes

1. _____   _____

2. _____   _____

3. _____   _____

4. _____   _____

5. _____   _____

Career Action Plan

The previous exercises have concentrated on your experiences to help you understand yourself better. As you make plans to enter the world of work, your chances of success will be enhanced if you consider your alternatives based on what you know about yourself.

The following section includes important items you should think about in this phase. Most of them focus on the question, "What do you want to do?"

JOB FACTORS From the list [below and on the following page] rank the five most important job factors for you. Think only in terms of what is related to the job.

1. Opportunity for advancement
2. Challenge
3. Security
4. Salary
5. Training program
6. Direct job assignment
7. Hours worked per week
8. Size of company

9. Type of industry
10. Autonomy of action
11. Travel
12. Educational opportunity
13. Results of job seen
14. Prestige
15. Work environment
16. Co-workers
17. Type of boss
18. Frequency of moves
19. Job location
20. Responsibility
21. Variety of work
22. Others (list)

Job Factors Ranking

1. _____

2. _____

3. _____

4. _____

5. _____

Considering the job factors you have ranked above and keeping in mind your skills, interests and values, describe the characteristics of an ideal job for you:

_____

_____

_____

_____

_____

_____

NON-JOB FACTORS There are other items that you can and should evaluate which encompass the time spent away from work. From the list rank the five most important non-job factors.

1. Climate
2. Proximity to family
3. Volunteer activities
4. Cultural activities
5. Spouse's desires
6. Recreational activities
7. Rural community
8. Suburban community
9. Metropolitan community
10. Commuting distance
11. Frequency of moves
12. Cost of living
13. Continuing or adult education
14. Public schools
15. Others—(list)

Non-job factors

1. _____

2. _____

3. _____

4. _____

5. _____

Considering the *non-job* factors you ranked above, describe the characteristics of an ideal non-job environment.

_____

_____

_____

_____

_____

_____

The ideal job and the ideal non-job environment you have described make up what might be called your desired life style.

There are long-range implications to the initial employment decision you will soon make. While many entry-level positions are similar, they may lead to entirely different positions when you have progressed two or three steps in a company's career path. Therefore, it is to your advantage to identify goals you hope to achieve. By establishing both short and long-range goals, you will have "benchmarks" to measure your career progress. Of course it will be necessary to review and perhaps modify these goals because of additional experiences, new information, or changed circumstances.

By stating your preferred or ideal life style, you have already set some general goals. The next section is designed to set specific career goals.

GOAL SETTING As a model for goal setting, complete the following items related to the job search process.

I plan to interview for jobs in the following type(s) of industries or organizations.

_____

_____

I plan to interview _____ organizations. I plan to accept a job
                          number
by _____.
      date

Similarly, you should state below some of your goals for the first
year of employment. For example, you may want a certain type of
training, or you may want an immediate project assignment. You
could want a job leading to a specialty field, or one that would allow
you to look at a number of career directions before committing yourself to one of them.

_____

_____

_____

_____

Now state below some of the goals you want to accomplish in five
years.

_____

_____

_____

_____

Finally, state below your long-range goals.

_____

_____

_____

_____

Having completed the exercises in this workbook, you should now
explore opportunities which will be compatible with your life style
and will also be in keeping with your skills, interests, goals and
your educational background. This will necessitate obtaining and
evaluating information on entry-level positions and organizational
career paths. To help you make these career decisions, you may
want to discuss them with your career planning and placement
office, faculty, other students as well as friends and relatives.

Appendix II

How to Stand Out in a Big Organization: Up-and-Coming BankAmericans Share Their Unwritten Techniques for Getting Ahead

by Harvey Radin, with Linda Roberts

You've aced it, right?

No sweat to getting ahead in your career, because you've planned your strategy by the numbers. Three nights a week absorbing that business curriculum at school was well worth the effort. You've got four of the bank's training courses under your belt and have mapped a career development plan with your boss. And the extra American Institute of Banking classes. Another gold star for sure.

It all looks fine on paper. So now you can afford to sit back, relax, and wait for something beautiful to happen. You're bound to be noticed. And when you are, you'll probably get a promotion or a raise . . . that is, if everything works out according to formula.

But in spite of these efforts, there's no guarantee supervisors will recognize your achievements. What then? Does your career languish on the back burner? Or is there something more you can do?

Yes, there is, according to 15 employees interviewed by Linda Roberts and me. All were BankAmericans you'd be likely to hear described as "getting ahead."

As one of them explained, "I rose from an entry level job to vice president. I worked and trained hard all down the line. But I also did something extra, something that shot me ahead of competition that frequently possessed just as much talent."

This employee built his entire career by taking advantage of adversity. "I'd been given a terrible assignment as acting supervisor of a totally screwed up department," he said. "Poorly organized and overstaffed, it was a disaster from top to bottom."

After careful evaluation, he attacked his problem head on. And in a matter of months he had turned everything around by motivating his staff, streamlining the work flow, and cutting wasted effort. With the former disaster running like a well-oiled machine, senior

Note: "How to Stand Out in a Big Organization" is reprinted by permission from *BankAmerican*, October 1976, Los Angeles, California.

281

management took note. In their eyes this employee was an instant hero.

"Didn't take long to dawn on me," he said. "Keep doing the spectacular, and everyone will keep noticing. Now that I've drawn that conclusion, I search for similar assignments. And now I've got a certain savvy about what it takes to stand out and get ahead."

Certainly preparation and training are essential for those seeking the attention of senior management. But that something extra—that certain savvy—is often gained through an understanding of those unwritten techniques, the kind you won't find in school textbooks. Your boss may not tell you about them. Or your best friends either. I'm talking about the know-how you absorb by being part of the corporation.

Profiting from eight years of business experience, another officer attributes her success to doing extra assignments above and beyond the call of duty. "But be careful," she warned. "Make it something worthwhile. Don't create a lot of paperwork that'll only waste your supervisor's time."

Tracing her own experience, she described how she applied this strategy after stumbling on a series of pamphlets outlining information she thought her boss would want to know. But was he really interested? "I'm not clairvoyant," she said. "Guess you could say I was taking a calculated risk."

With that in mind, she sequestered herself at home for the better part of a weekend, reading the pamphlets and then summarizing their content on a couple of easy-to-read, typed pages.

"I found out later that I'd guessed right," she explained. "As it turned out, my brief report was both needed and appreciated."

Getting your name associated with something important and making sure senior management is aware of what you've done— two more rules of thumb practiced by employees who get ahead.

"I call it 'personal public relations,'" said another employee who keeps her eyes open for projects that will result in publication of special reports. When one comes up, she volunteers. While this employee enjoys being involved, she also knows it's important to be recognized.

Elaborating on her strategy, she said, "When I know reports will be read by senior people, I try to get assigned to write them. Sure, it means hard work because I'm volunteering for extra assignments or generating them on my own. But it pays off. The way I see it, I'm the one in charge of my career. And I help establish a direction through concrete accomplishments that, I trust, will be recognized by those who count."

Many employees nudge their career along by using some of the techniques just described. They develop plans, gear themselves to progress at a prescribed pace, and keep plugging despite unexpected delays. Others, taking a cue from the lyrics of an old Beatles song, "get by with a little help from their friends."

In the business world a friend is often a mentor, someone to turn to for both guidance and opportunity. The opportunity for developmental assignments, for example, and exposure to new situations and people. Impressed by your performance, the mentor develops an interest in your career. He or she shares valuable experience that can add to your job expertise. And with luck, the mentor becomes your booster, telling others in the business about the good work you do.

Because a young employee has attracted the attention of several mentors—all supervisors in her department—she is now poised for promotion from a clerical job to an official position. Dazzled by her positive attitude and skills, the mentors are anxious to boost her career.

A supervisor summed it up: "She's so bright all the time, so willing. She's never turned off by assignments. Even if the sky is falling, I can depend on her to get things done and get them done well."

That kind of reputation is tough to overlook. Sooner or later in casual conversation, one supervisor becomes a mentor by telling another, "I've got someone special in my department who does one heck of a job."

Another mentor of this same employee said, "I'll do my best to see her get ahead. While I shudder at the thought of losing someone so good, I wouldn't think of standing in the way of her career."

It pays to show your zest for doing the job. And it's often wise to add an additional ingredient to the formula—knowledge of your boss's style.

One employee we interviewed stumbled on this technique the hard way. He used to overwhelm his boss with new ideas. "Great things were always popping into my head," he explained. "Bursting with enthusiasm, I'd run to my boss to reveal the latest brainstorm."

In return for his enthusiasm, the employee was met with an icy reception. "Couldn't figure it out until one day, by accident, I tried another approach. Instead of making an oral presentation, I outlined a new idea in a memo."

As it turned out, the boss was far more receptive. Explained the employee, "Everything earlier had been poorly received because I had failed to understand my boss's systematic and orderly style.

Tips for Getting Ahead

In confidential interviews BankAmericans revealed some techniques that have worked in their efforts to get ahead. Here are a baker's dozen tips based on their ideas. (The accompanying article has the details.)

• *Do something spectacular!* Take on a tough assignment or go where the record has been dismal. Make a name for yourself.

• *Pick your boss.* Her or his image will have a halo effect on you, and winners have winning techniques you can pick up.

• *Conduct personal P.R.* Make contacts, get your name on special projects and reports, volunteer for high-exposure assignments.

• *Get a "mentor"*—a supervisor who values your work and will help provide the assignments and exposure that will promote your professional growth.

• *Adopt the habits and image* of the "club" (grade, level, position) you aspire to.

• *Learn to look to the people above you* as resources—to smooth the way, to help in a crisis.

• *Bowl 'em over!* Impress supervisors with sheer energy and staying power. Get a "can-do" reputation—someone who can always be relied on to get the job done right.

• *Rely on your peers as resources,* for both present and future needs.

• *Never underestimate the power of your staff* to help or hinder you. Use your staff to make you look good.

• *Do a co-worker a favor.* You never know when you'll need one.

• *Identify your boss's style.* You'll find it easier to present and sell your ideas.

• *Develop the knack of handling a situation* when you're (1) not prepared; (2) lack knowledge; (3) going to miss a deadline, etc.

• *When you've made a mistake,* disarm them with candor. Gain good will by admitting your responsibility.

Put it in writing! That's what he preferred. To him, oral ramblings were sloppy and out of order. Deviate from his style, and he'd just turn you off.

"Now I analyze new supervisors to determine whether they're idea people, methodical organizers, or instant-action types. I then adjust my approach to more closely fit those styles."

Adjustments were equally important to another employee who had launched a rock 'em, sock 'em career. Recognized by supervisors right off the bat, he was considered a hard worker with a nose-to-the-grindstone image.

"That was fine at first," he conceded. "But after a while the serious image began working against me. I was so busy all the time that I forgot the importance of having friends. To co-workers, I was the office drudge—that guy who never joined anyone for coffee because he was always too busy. In a sense I was being excluded from a fellowship of co-workers that happened to include my boss."

How important is fellowship? To this employee it was very important. "Others resented me for excluding myself from the group," he explained. "So I loosened up. Without compromising work standards, I made time for others and was soon recognized as both hard worker and good friend. Being part of the team means a lot when you work closely with people on a day-to-day basis."

Carrying that idea a step farther is a young officer who in every new assignment gathers around him a group he calls his "network of competent people." Comparable to a buddy system in the military, this network is something like oil on the wheels of a machine. It makes everything run smoother.

"My competent people represent other departments that I work with each day," said the employee. "I call them on the spur of the moment when I'm researching important information. They help me cut through the red tape. Or they warn me of some new development that may affect one of my projects. Often they provide introductions to those I need to know. In return for these favors, I help members of the network whenever I can."

But another employee believes in going it alone. Rather than joining teams and competent groups, he prefers independence.

"When I'm sure that I'm right about the success of a project, I push hard to get it accepted by senior management. Sometimes that means sticking my neck out. But if I've done my homework, that isn't as dangerous as it sounds. To be noticed, you've got to make your own decisions. To make good decisions, you can't be scared of management or overly concerned about job security."

There was recently a question of purchasing expensive, new equipment that could revolutionize operations in his department. "After months of thorough research, I was convinced of the equipment's value," he explained. "But there was still the nagging question: 'Should I take full responsibility for spending a sizable chunk of the bank's money?' While I could have put the final decision in senior management's lap, I decided to make it my own show."

Had everything backfired, a specific portion of this employee's anatomy might have been relegated to a sling. But the story ends happily and the equipment is working fine. For his role in the drama, this employee has earned the reputation of being both tough and decisive.

"Much depends on how others perceive you," agreed a 30-year old attorney. "Appearance still counts for plenty." Cultivating a style she calls her "business look," this employee dresses business-like, acts businesslike, and speaks businesslike.

"I can be informal when I choose," she said, "but I know my appearance will influence how people react to me. Also my demeanor. In certain situations I take charge. Say I've called a meeting. I never let a peer—or a supervisor—take over, if I can help it. By exercising personal control over the meeting, I demonstrate my effectiveness."

Personal style and strategy vary from person to person. For Linda Roberts and me, there's one tactic that's just got to work when we turn in this story. No need to tell our editor how hard we slaved. We'll just attach the bill for candles. The ones we had to light when the single lightbulb in the loft burned out shortly after midnight. . . .